Dynamics of Law and Justice

NEERA BHARIHOKE

SERIALS PUBLICATIONS
NEW DELHI (INDIA)

First Published - 2010

ISBN: 978-81-8387-353-6

Published by

SERIALS PUBLICATIONS
4830/24, Prahlad Street, Ansari Road
Darya Ganj, New Delhi-110002 (India)
Phone : 23245225 Fax : 91-11-23272135
E-mail: serials@sify.com

Contents

Preface

The concept of law and justice is as dynamic as the concept of society. As the societal values undergo a change so does the meaning and content of law and justice. There are multiple theories of law as well as justice. Some consider law to be a reflection of morals and values of a society while other perceive of it as a vehicle for bringing the change in society. Similarly justice is perceived differently by different schools of justice. Most of the theories proceed on the assumption that whatever be the content of law, be it the command of the sovereign or be it the expression of ideals and aspirations of people forming the nation, once defined, the law becomes rigid and looses its flexibility. Flexibility is brought in the concepts of law at the stage of delivery of justice by courts of law. Law is given its substance, content and meaning by interpreting the law for attaining justice.

Contents of justice give the laws a new meaning and content. When a hungry boy steals bread, the law is that he has committed theft but whether the boy needs to be punished and if yes what should be the quantum or kind of punishment can probably be decided on the basis of theory of justice applied to the facts of the case. Such are the dimensions and sweep of the concept of law and justice that there cannot be a universal definition of the two concepts. The present volume of this book reflects that dynamism in these concepts by way of presentation of varied papers in context of different countries and cultures.

The attempt in this scholarly work is to bring to the light issues, factors and at times to find solutions to the various problems which make these concepts change their meaning in different backgrounds. The articles incorporated here also reflect upon how the change in policies or polity of a nation brings about the change in the notions of law and concept of justice. The wide range of topics covered in the present volume has made the contents richer and presents a panoramic picture of the various facets of law and justice.

One can conclude by the philosophical dichotomy illustrated by Amartya Sen when he makes the distinction between *Neeti* (Law) and *Nyaya* (Justice). He states *Neeti* is about arrangements and rules about the right thing to do and *Nyaya* is about what is happening in the real world.

Neera Bharihoke

International Journal of Jurisprudence and Philosophy of Law
|| Vol. 2 ✦ No. (1-2) ✦ 2008 ✦ 1-15 ||

A New Paradigm for Law and Justice

J. P. MISHRA*

INTRODUCTION

Strange is the world we live in. The more we try to make it better, the worse it becomes, or so it appears at least. The law, which was once the means to add value to our lives, has become a means to protect (commercial value of) things rather than man. The emergence of intellectual property rights presents a glaring example where the man stands next in importance to the things he creates. Examples are many. The justice, on the other hand, has become a thing desired by all but gettable by a chosen few. After a considerable run from pillar to post, either the quality of justice is robbed off by delay it permits or the justice is awarded in a way that leaves the awardees even more aggrieved.

It is ironical but true that we have become more educated (if one goes by literacy rates), rich (going by per capita income or by the increasing number of rich persons in our country), armed (taking into account the weapons of mass destruction that we have to our credit) and what not; but at the same time we are more ignorant (the way we fight for ourselves only, forgetting for the woes of our brethren), poor (going by the burgeoning number of the poverty and hunger stricken mass of humanity) and unsafe (as is evident by unnatural deaths owing to accidents, natural phenomena, or acts of aggression, insurgency or terrorism etc). When we see the rich get richer with each passing day, and the

* *Faculty of Law, University of Allahabad (India)*

poor more so; the words and phrases, used incessantly by the scholars of the times or the admirers of the system, in praise of law and justice simply become too hard to digest.

There is a manifold increase in corruption and terrorism, and decrease in human values. The world looks to have a great appetite for the rights which it wants to realize through any which means, paying scant care for the duties or, equivalently, the rights of others[1]. The systems of law and justice appear to have been missing some cardinal principles governing the life of man and his innate relations with the nature that precedes and pervades him.

Perhaps we need to change our vision of man and nature entirely, and adopt a universal and holistic view of things vital for our existence. In other words, we need look at things differently. The sections that follow touch these points only tangentially in an effort to hint at those values which may prove to be guiding forces in our quest for a new set of paradigms designed to make better the world we live in.

LAW AND JUSTICE

Law has been variously defined but still defies a complete definition. Having been viewed through spectacles of different ideologies it has got itself defined in as many ways. Accordingly, a sovereign[2], a society[3], common consciousness[4], norms[5], rules[6], nature[7] etc have been brought to the aid of jurists in order that a complete definition may be woven. However, the fact remains that the concept of law pervades all these concepts but is enveloped by none. It is thus that the law has to take care of not only the changes in the various fields but also prepare itself to face the impact of these changes on the world we live in.

Justice, broadly speaking, is the balancing of interests either equally or equitably. This is done in the light of the law in force for the time being. This implies that there is a change in the facets of justice corresponding to changes in law with respect to a given field. However, the fact remains that the judiciary does more than merely applying the law to a case at hand; it also has to see whether law is worth its name, or whether the law is pertinent to the point under consideration, or whether the law sufficiently covers the matter under dispute, or finally, whether there is a gap in law that needs be filled for the administration of justice.

There have taken place tremendous changes during the past few centuries, particularly the 20th century, providing new frontiers of law-making[8] and broadening the canvas of justice[9]. As the law embraced human rights[10], environment[11], industrial property[12], intellectual property[13], cyber space [14]and biotechnology[15] etc; the new fora for administration of justice emerged. The latter half of the last century witnessed the growing trend of globalisation which, in turn, offered certain new platforms[16] not only to mobilise international support required for smooth functioning of law but also to ensure uniformity in the administration of justice, as far as practicable, at the domestic and international levels.

It may not be out of place to recall that even before globalisation became a reality for us, the legal and judicial changes in one nation kept on having their influence on other nations. India, whose constitution had been drafted in a way to have the best of several working constitutions of the world at that time, could not remain uninfluenced by several such changes taking place in Britain[17] and America[18]; but sometimes chose her own path[19]. The growing number of global agencies addressing various walks of life has created an atmosphere where every nation sees no option but to fall in line with latest developments in the field of law and justice characterised by these agencies.

Novel manifestations of our ever-changing perceptions of law and justice are marked by increasing number of independent nations who at the same time feel more and more dependent on others in their march towards development. On the other hand globalisation has landed all nations in a state where problem of one spreads like contagious disease to others very soon and what would otherwise have been confined to a specific region has become a global phenomenon. This spread of negative elements seems to have outsmarted the benefit that we once dreamt of deriving out of a state of globalisation.

The fear of nuclear catastrophe, the issue of terrorism, the dangers of biotechnological inventions, the increasing erosion of values in our life, the pollution of earth and the environment, the increasing gap between the poor and the powerful and the like are the problems the gravity whereof has increased exponentially even as the law and justice make their best endeavour to curb and remedy these for the welfare of mankind.

PARADIGM SHIFT

The march of mankind towards the future is always guided by the way it looks at the world. This world view has its base in certain patterns of thoughts and concepts that run through it. These patterns or standards or models are called paradigms. Viewed thus a vision of the world is woven around a set of such paradigms. Therefore when our world-view undergoes a drastic change, the underlying patterns of thoughts, concepts etc also change i.e. we adopt a new set of paradigms that replaces the existing one. This replacement of one set of paradigms by the other is called a paradigm shift. In this regard two things are noteworthy: first, that such a shift is an essential feature of man's progress towards fulfilment; and second, that such revolutionary changes as require a paradigm shift altogether do not occur every day.

The term 'paradigm shift' was first used by famous scholar Thomas Kuhn in 1962[20] in order to explain the scientific advancement and, according to him, it reflected that stage of transformation where 'one conceptual world-view is replaced by another'. However, the term is no more confined to the discipline of science alone; and is now frequently used for any set of thoughts and concepts that help us view the world in a more meaningful way than hitherto fore. For example, the view that sun revolves the earth gave way to the view that the earth revolves the sun; the view that the Universe had been created by the Almighty was dominated by the view that the world actually evolved; and the view that God is true was eclipsed by the view that science alone is true etc. We can say that such revolutionary changes mark the paradigm shift from geo-centrism to heliocentrism, creation to evolution, and faith in God to faith in Science respectively.

Why is it Needed Right Now?

We have a plethora of laws trying–or so they claim- to give us better rights/avenues for our development. Yet we are not a happy people. The hunger stricken population runs in to hundreds of millions in India alone; supposing that we do not look at the world map and count countries like Somalia. And, things become unbelievably unpleasant once we think globally on a point. Our road accident deaths, for example, surpass the total death toll of any of the world wars[21].

The man for whom all this hullabaloo had been made seems to have been lost in the haze that the modern efforts have created. His aspirations lie buried under the carpet of the rich. The change of the world has meant for him almost the replacement of one system of oppression by the other with no respite in deed.

While there is no denying the fact that tremendous improvements have taken place for betterment of our life solely due to the application of sci-tech, advances in science and technology have given a new face to terrorism which has grown much more strong and ugly than what it was earlier. Law and justice both are trying desperately to overcome these ugly aspects of human action but their success is dismal. Also, there is the rising level of mass discontent reflected in the mass movements and social action litigations to fight the policies of the government[22].

On the premise that a certain section of our society remained downtrodden for long started the efforts of what is called protective discrimination theory; taking in its sway the scheduled castes, scheduled tribes and, finally, the other backward classes. But the result is that the poorest of the poor do not have any caretakers and the lion's share of the state bounty given in the name of OBCs and the like is being swallowed by those who hardly need it, but thanks to the system, which showers all the abuses to a caste-based society but at the same time makes the caste the sole criterion for bracketing people for beneficial treatment. The ruling party breathlessly advertises its secular credentials but announces in the same vein to award reservations to the poor on purely communal grounds. Since no party wants to lose even one vote no party musters enough courage to oppose such unequal and discriminatory measures of the ruling class. The same politicians, however, look sideways on the issue of 30 per cent reservation to women in the Legislature.

Genetic engineering has emboldened the man to do things that disturb the state of nature. Japan's invention of genetically modified mouse that is able to see cat eye to eye is a harbinger of things to come[23]. In our enthusiasm to always do new things, we have tried to clone Einstein etc forgetting rudimentary rules of probability that out of innumerable co-ordinates of space and time that go in to making a person, the change of even a few of these may produce altogether a different person. But the most unfortunate point is that all over the world such efforts are flourishing-publically or privately-and so are the laws to prevent it. It is like what the phrase 'to create a ghost and fight with it' would have ever suggested.

India has adopted most of the British model minus, of course, the Crown. While India is trying to overcome the negativities of the system so adopted, UK looks all set to adopt a similar one. The Constitutional Reform Act, 2005 in Britain is a pointer to this direction. The UK will now have an Upper House (largely elected/ partly nominated), a system of courts headed by the Supreme Court, and, a set of human rights enforceable through these courts much like India; not to talk of the European Charter of Fundamental Rights which, as is the case with our Directive Principles of State Policy, is agreed in principle by all the members but is not binding on them. However, the matter of copying is only on the surface of our talk. What runs deeper than this is the meaninglessness of the system we adopt and discard and readopt and discard.

It seems the model of development or the idea of man, law and justice that we entertain at present have something patently basic (or, natural) lacking in them. If so, then, it is pertinent to ponder whether we have come to the last point on the path of that development which we had somehow modelled for us; and whether this pattern of things that we have developed is not going to deliver goods in anyway better than what it already has? We stand in the need of altogether a new set of paradigms for our further journey towards fulfilment because, as Thomas Aquinas assured us long ago, we are but a means in the scheme of some super-human legislator who wants to achieve certain ends through us like, say, survival, continuity, perfection etc[24].

VALUES THAT WE NEED

Let us begin with an analogy. A tree is as strong as its roots. If the roots are hollow or rotten or without substance; the tree can not withstand winds, let alone the storms. But the most important factor is the ground on which the tree stands: from which its roots, trunk, branches and leaves get the food. A system of law and justice, likewise, is as good as the set of values it is supported by; and, of course, the philosophical foundation it has.

Our present system of law and justice is mostly based on materialistic values that focus on the physical comfort and encourage a cut-throat competition with pure and ultimate motive of becoming financially more well off than others. Since this does not ensure peace of mind and purity of thought as it obviously can not, the man becomes desperate to accelerate his efforts little knowing that the model he is a slave to is inherently incompetent to provide him with the kind of pleasure and peace he is longing for. There are a few cardinal values a healthy system can not afford to ignore but which unfortunately our present system does not possess in their true spirit.

Ever since the emergence of positivist and other schools that sprang up in reaction to the natural law philosophy, the law stands divorced from *morality*. Minus its moral content, law becomes merely a collection of rules that govern our external conduct; because it is morality alone that disciplines us internally. Living in such a system which is devoid of morality, a man tries to ensure that he acts in such a way that lets him go scot free[25]. Seldom does he pause to think whether he ought to do what he is going to. The litmus test to check the validity of his actions, truly speaking, is whether it benefits him. And, the same criterion is there for a nation *vis-à-vis* other nations. The twentieth century witnessed a great debate known as the naturalist-positivist debate[26] but the fact remains that morality is more or less a forgotten value in the modern system of law and justice.

All are equal in the eyes of law. So goes the rhetoric, but the fact that law has often been used to serve the interests of few even at the cost of the interests of others shows that rhetoric is not always the reality. Sometimes the law is used to protect discriminatory actions of state on the ground that *equality* allows reasonable classification of persons[27], at other times it is used to protect a caste as a class[28], and at still other times to treat even one person as a class![29] Every system of law has a fairly good share of inequality; it is the quantum that differs. If the ancient system favoured one class, the modern system is favouring some other. Thus, it is certain that both systems have the same ending i.e. one particular class empowered, and others impoverished. Unless we profess as also follow the equality in its true sense, we can not ensure the welfare of one and all. If we do not lose sight of the fact that equality is a relative concept rather than absolute, pragmatic rather than myopic, and inclusive rather than exclusive; law and equality can go hand in hand.

Closely related to equality is the value of *universality*. Presently, law of one country (or, region for that matter) hardly takes note of the law of other countries so long as her interests are protected. This has robbed the law of its universality. In this context it may be noted that Zeno (350-260 B. C.) and his followers believed that entire universe was made up of just one element, that is, reason[30]. Reason is the spark of divine in man and hence all men of the world are equal. Arguing thus they inferred that since reason was an element universally present in every man, it was possible to make law universally applicable to all. However, Zeno's philosophy, which later provided ground for natural law theory that flourished in Rome and elsewhere for quite a long time, had echoed much earlier in Indian philosophy. Geeta informs us:

The present system of law and justice dwells primarily on the specifications of punishments that are to be awarded to the law-breakers, and pays almost no care to give incentives to those who have acted to uphold the law. As a result one comes to feel the presence of law and justice often through the medium of punishments only. Such things only arouse hatred between the man punished and the rest of the society. The promotion of *love for all* i.e. man and nature both does not form the subject-matter of law today. Forgetting this reality we ceaselessly try to find solutions to new challenges in new legislations.

Modern law and justice seldom encourage *a sense of duty*[31]. Our belief that legislation is the panacea of all ills manifests itself in the creation of newer rights like, say, human rights, intellectual property rights, property rights, fundamental rights and a host of other rights. This, at best, may and actually does result in creation of new fora for enforcement and adjudication of these rights. The state of affairs, however, remains almost the same if not worsens; because, as the sense of possessiveness of man increases, so does his greed for more and more rights.

CONCLUSION/SUGGESTION

The law of modern times is always seen under heavy influence of some particular field which appears to be in fashion in the global market. This is why there is a phase when the thrust is entirely on environment, at other times the human rights, and at yet another time the intellectual property; often without having a look at our own system. For example, the human rights was an essential feature to be added to those nations of the world where either due to non-democratic systems or owing to some historical or conventional reasons the basic rights of man found no place in their law. But under the said impression of global fashionableness India too made law on human rights almost forgetting that there already existed fundamental rights under the Constitution which were capable of supporting every human interest. Now, India feels perturbed when the international organizations want her to support gay's rights etc. under the garb of human rights[32].

Ulterior motives of politicians behind issues otherwise uncontroversial have created problems the nation finds hard to solve. The way the issue of social justice is being handled serves as an example. The reservation which once proved to be a powerful electoral weapon seems to have boom-ranged in the face of the politician who finds it difficult to solve the riddle why the castes or classes that were not backward etc in 1950 have become so after tasting the fruits of development for more than 50 years!

The justice delivery system of the modern times too is quite vulnerable in that it is not capable of focusing on more than one element at a time. This is why sometimes there is much hue and cry over the prisoner's rights; at other times the judiciary seems all out to punish the offender in the strictest possible terms. There was a phase when the judiciary was in a mood to break all the conventional rules of procedure which it felt were the barriers on the path of justice. At other times, the judiciary riding high on the bandwagon of judicial activism would not hesitate a bit in usurping the powers of the other two wings of the government.

The burgeoning cases of corruption, the rising crime graph, newer ways of committing crime, demands to protect immoral ways of life under the pretext of personal freedom, and the experiments in science and technology to play God and disturb the order of nature are all offshoots of the model of law and justice that we follow: a system which is based on and influenced by the Western model of the world view which is predominantly materialistic.

However, it is equally true that materialism can not be written off from any model of world view one can think of because it is one of the four elements that according to Indian philosophy give meaning to ones being[33] that is purushartha.

Therefore, it is suggested that the paradigm shift has to be from individuality to universality, from discrimination to equality, from ostensibly immoral demands to a sense of morality, and from a clamour for right to a sense of duty to name just a few. To say this is not to suggest to undo whatever has been or being done but to advocate for a change of point of thrust in our scheme of things rather than to reject the scheme altogether. That is to say, this paradigm shift is meant to ensure that fruits of development are tasted equally meaningfully by one and all rather than a chosen few-whether men or nations.

And this shift in paradigms must embrace law and justice first.

NOTES

1. As Kant says: "Act in such a way that the maxim of your action may be made the maxim of universal action; or, your action is right if it can co-exist with equal freedom of others."
2. Austin, for example, defines law as 'the command of the sovereign, backed by sanctions'.
3. See, the views of scholars of the sociological school like Ehrlich, who says that the living law is that which the people obey in practice as against the law in the statute-books; Ihering, who feels that a law without purpose is no law; and Duguit, who asserts that law is good only if it promotes what he terms the 'social solidarity' *et al.*
4. The German scholar Savigny says that law is the product of the common consciousness (volkgeist) of the people; Gierke tries to understand law in terms of the associations which, according to him, are based either on the theory of collaboration or domination; and Hegel is of the opinion that law is evolved out of the interaction between the opposites for example, the thesis and anti-thesis etc.
5. Hans Kelsen says that law has a normative structure, and a norm is an ought-proposition; for example, if A commits theft, A ought to be punished. A norm derives its validity from a higher norm, which again derives its validity from still higher norm, and so on. The norm which gives validity to all the norms is called the grund norm. The grund norm validates all other norms but does not stand in the need of validation itself; because, as Kelsen said, the grundnorm is an ex-hypothesis. The grund norm of a country may be a constitution, a dictator's will or, simply, the socio-political reality.

6. HLA Hart presents a legal system as a system of rules: the primary rules creating rights and duties, and the secondary rules. The secondary rules are of three types, one for the identification, the other for the modification, and still other for the adjudication of the primary rules. Thus a legal system, says Hart, is the union of primary rules with the secondary rules of modification, identification and adjudication.
7. The naturalists see nature as the source of all law, and claim that since natural phenomena are the same everywhere, it is possible to derive natural norms of conduct that are universally applicable to man regardless of the co-ordinates of space and time. The theory was propounded by Zeno and his disciples who said that the entire universe is composed of but one element, that is, reason. The reason is the spark of divine in man, and since it is present in every man, all men are equal. Arguing thus, they presented cosmopolitan concept of law, which blossomed in the theories of St Augustine and others and reached its perfection in the theory presented by Thomas Aquinas who declared; "Law is an ordinance of reason, made by one who has the care for the community, and promulgated."
8. The Human Rights Act, 1998; the House of Lords Act, 1999; Terrorism Acts of 2005 and 2006; Equality Act, 2006 and the Constitutional Reform Act, 2005, to name but a few, has introduced far-reaching changes in the UK law. The signing by Britain of the European Charter of Fundamental Rights on December 13, 2007 has further enriched the legal fabric there. The American Constitution, originally having only seven Articles, has been amended 27 times so far (the last one in 1992 related to pay revision of the legislators). The Constitution of India is flexible enough to absorb the emerging demands of the changing times and has been amended 94 times (till June 12, 2006) including the amendments of far-reaching consequences, like, the abolition of right to property as a fundamental right, the introduction of fundamental duties, the anti-defection provisions, the reservation in jobs etc for the other backward classes, placement of environment in concurrent list as also in the Directive Principles, making right to education a fundamental right etc.
9. In *Marbury b. Madison,* Justice Marshall established the efficacy of judicial review for all times to come; even though it had, literally speaking, not been provided in the Constitution. American judiciary also evolved the concept of Social Action Litigation (SAL) to ensure that procedural technicalities of law might not come in the way of administering justice to people who really deserved it. In the U K, enactments like Human Rights Act, 1998 and the Constitutional

Reform Act, 2005 give a new face to the system of justice in UK because the latter provides for replacement of the House of Lords by the Supreme Court of Justiciary as the highest court of UK w. e. f. 2008 itself after the Act becomes effective.

The judicial innovation of American courts galvanized the Indian courts and thus proved to be a precursor to judicial activism in India. Similarly, the policy of protective discrimination promoted by American judiciary in case of Blacks somehow helped the Indian judiciary uphold the policy of reservation to the other backward classes in order to achieve social justice. Justice Marshall's path-breaking judgment in *Marbury v. Madison* on judicial review echoed in the Supreme Court's decisions in *Keshavanand Bharati v. State of Kerala (1973,* the 'basic structure theory'), *Indira Nehru Gandhi v. Rajnarain* (1978, the judicial review is a part of the basic structure) and, recently, in *IR Coelho (Dead) by LRs v. State of Tamil Nadu* (2007, even the legislations placed in the IX Schedule of the Constitution are judicially reviewable).

10. Long after trying to replace the natural law theory with other theories the thinkers and politicians alike were convinced that rights of an individual as a human being, irrespective of his religion, nationality etc should be protected. This global consciousness symbolized in the Universal Declaration of Human Rights (1948) soon got acceptance at the regional and national levels. The human rights jurisprudence so developed has become a part of modern jurisprudence.

11. It appeared almost paradoxical that the industries which aimed at betterment of our life were eating upon the environment so essential for our life. Stockholm Conference saw the issue blossom in to international environmental law while the concept of sustainable development became driving force for the Earth Summit. The green house effect, global warming, ozone layer depletion and climate change-the offshoots of pollution-have dominated the international debates ever since .The United Nations Conference on Climate Change in Bali-which concluded on December 14, 2007-is the latest such attempt which aims to prepare a roadmap for reduction of emission of green house gases, thus attempting to update Kyoto Protocol that expires in 2012.

12. The industrialization brought with it the prospects of huge production coupled with equally potential apprehension of misuse and malpractices in the creation, consumption, trade and commerce of the same. These prepared a ground for germination of industrial property rights.

13. The intellectual property laws, which are designed to protect the ideas with commercial value, quickly became the catch-word of modern legal system.

14. The world of machines-the cyber space- is where most of us today want to live in. Electronic laws, as cyber laws are often referred to, have made their presence felt in various walks of life, for example, e-governance, e-banking, e-commerce etc; and have induced changes in other branches of law also.
15. While some of the biotechnological inventions do seem to augur well with the increasing pressure of population and incidental needs of food, shelter etc; the efforts for cloning man to create a cloned race altogether are worrying. The law on the point remained in a state of flux until TRIPs tried to evolve certain parameters for patenting etc of biotechnological inventions.
16. The United Nations and its various organisations in general and International Court of Justice in particular, the Universal Declaration on Human Rights, the Trade Related Aspects of Intellectual Property Rights, the World Trade Organisation and its Dispute Resolution System are some of the prominent examples.
17. Justice in India got a fillip when the Supreme Court followed the Ridge v. Baldwin to invite the rules of fair hearing in to Maneka Gandhi v. Union of India interpreting the Article 21 (the right to life and personal liberty) which on the one hand marked a shift in the approach adopted by the Court in the previous cases but also metamorphosed the "procedure established by law" in to the "due process of law".
18. The impact of Justice Marshall's path-breaking judgment in Marbury v. Madison echoed in the judgment of Indian apex court when it ruled in Indira Nehru Gandhi v. Rajnarain that the Legislature can not take away the power of judicial review by inserting in to a piece of legislation phrases like "this shall not be called in to question in any court of law".
19. The Indian Supreme Court ventured to modify the rule of strict liability (laid down in Rylands v. Fletcher in 1868) in to one of absolute liability holding that the owner of the premises where handling of hazardous substances was being done owed an absolute and non-delegable duty towards anybody who got adversely affected due to such handling.
20. See, Thomas Kuhn's book "The Structure of Scientific Revolution", p. 10.
21. According to data released on the World Day of Remembrance for Traffic Victims, 1260000 people lost their life and 5000000 got injured while there was financial loss of about 1000 billion dollars during 2005-06. In India 100000 people lost their lives during this period. For further details, see Amar Ujala Allahabad Edition dated 18.11.2007.

22. For example, Janadesh March 2007 which prompted about 27000 landless people coming from 18 different states of India to walk on foot for several hundred kilometers and hold a rally in New Delhi on October 28,2007 to arouse the government about their plight. Seeing that leaders of Congress, Left and other parties lost no time in sharing the platform with the activists, the Government sprang in to action with the Prime Minister announcing the setting up of two high-power committees- one of these headed by himself- to look in to their demands.

23. See, The Hindustan Times, Lucknow Edition, dated 14.12.2007. In the same paper there is a news item showing the cats cloned by South Korean scientists. These cloned cats glow in the dark when exposed to ultra violet beams.

24. See, his book Summa Theologia.

25. See, the Bad man's theory suggested by famous realist Justice Holmes.

26. See, in particular, the debate between HLA Hart who admits that law should have a shared morality; and Leo Lon Fuller who strongly feels that law should not only have external morality (like patriotism and other lofty ideals) but also the internal morality (like reasonableness, intelligibility etc). Also see, The Concept of Law by Hart, and The Morality of Law by Fuller.

27. For example, see the judicial approach in pre-Maneka Gandhi phase.

28. Such was the approach in Indra Sawhney case.

29. For Example, see the Court's approach in Chiranjit Lal Chaowdhury v. Union of India: AIR 1951 SC 41.

30. See: Jurisprudence–The Philosophy and Method of the Law by Edgar Bodenheimer, Third Indian Reprint 2001, at p. 13.

31. It took India almost three decades before she could write fundamental duties in her Constitution.

32. When some gay persons were arrested on January 03, 2006, by Lucknow police, it was condemned by a non governmental organization 'Human Rights Watch which wrote to the Prime Minister about what it termed as "shameful" harassment of gay men. The United Nations agency on AIDS, UNAids also condemned the arrests. For more details, see BBC News UK version at *http://news.bbc.co.uk/1/hi/world/south_asia/4602068.stm*.

33. All the four purusharthas, namely, dharma, artha, kama and moksha are collectively known as purushartha chatushtaya. The first three are collectively known as trivarga, and scholars like Manu and Vyas

feel that the true observance of these relative values leads to the fourth, that is, moksha which is an absolute value. Of the three, says Manu, kama and artha must be rejected if contrary to dharma" (*Manusmriti* IV/176).

State Responsibility and Ecosystem Degradation: Will the Ramsar Convention on Wetlands Suffice?

—a sense of wonder—

R. P. GUNPUTH*

"The destruction and loss of habitats and species bring with it known and unknown ecological consequences: what is ultimately threatened is the ability of ecosystems to purity water, regenerate soil, protect watersheds, regulate temperature, recycle nutrients and waste, and maintain the atmosphere"[P. Sands (1994): International Law in the field of Sustainable Development, British Yearbook of International Law].

INTRODUCTION

Devices to forecast cyclones, earthquakes and tsunamis are insufficient unless States are invited to play a more important role through dialogue and communication, which in turn are capable of reflecting a real sense of wonder.

Climate change and global warming are dangerous both to humanity and the environment. The ecosystem is so fragile, and nature nurtures disasters, which remain uncontrollable. Human intervention has something to do with nature's wrath since long but nature has never been in good harmony with mankind. Today, there are more victims from nature's havocs, environment destruction or modification compared to civil and world wars. It is

* *Senior Lecturer of Law-University of Mauritius, Faculty of Law and Management.*

time therefore to react promptly for securing a better international environment for the future generation.

Though there have been a network of multilateral treaties, which aim to halt environment degradation, attacks on the ecosystem, protection of endangered species of the wild flora and fauna[1], prevent the loss of biological diversity[2] (deforestation[3], the destruction of temperate forests, wetlands[4] and coral reefs) and to prevent air pollution[5]; to favour the Human Environment[6], the environment and development[7]; protection of the sea[8], conservation of marine living resources[9], the depletion of the ozone layer[10], the reduction of greenhouse gases (GHG) and carbon dioxide (CO_2) according to the Kyoto Protocol to the United Nations Framework Convention on Climate Change (UNFCCC) none of them is capable, however, of explaining clearly State responsibility in the event of ecosystem degradation. This aspect, as sensible as it seems to be, is often overlooked or ignored.

But why is it so difficult to bring a State before an Arbitration Tribunal or an international court for reparation and to grant compensation[11] in case of liability? State responsibility to reparation caused to environment and ecosystem degradation is an obstacle by itself because the achievement of an international co-operation[12] to ecosystem is, nonetheless, a myth (-I-) but disasters cause havoc to the environment which in turn nurtures poverty, which is a reality (-II-).

I

THE REPARATION: A MYTH OF INTERNATIONAL CO-OPERATION TO ECOSYSTEM

There are globally more then 50,000 treaties but international instruments seem useless if there is no proper discussion around a table to settle State responsibility for injuries committed by a State to the environment and ecosystem.

Through international response, government implications, reactions from donors there is time for a public sense and sensibility. Implementation is one of them: The Republic of Mauritius is a model when this question is in issue: it has diligently implemented international instruments[13] both derived and inspired from existing treaties, conventions and international customary rules into its statutory books[14] and this initiative may save the national environment, the wetlands, the fauna and flora, the ecosystem and endangered species. The Fisheries and Marine Resources Act (1998), the Wildlife and National Parks Act (1993) and the Wetlands Bill are based on this model.

Is the *'Mauritian Model'* applicable at international level? If not, what are the obstacles for an international co-operation and for how long they are going to last? However, at international level, before a State responsibility may comply with reparation to ecosystem it is inevitable that it has to overcome some weaknesses as regards to ecosystem degradation (-A-) but there is a glimpse of hope with the response of the United Nations' International Law Commission (-B-).

Ecosystem Degradation: Weaknesses for Reparation at International Level

International co-operation is a myth but ecosystem destruction is a reality. Therefore, to what extent are conventions, such as the Ramsar Convention, binding upon other member States? What happens to States for their international wrongful acts and how far are they liable for their *'injurious consequences'*? Answers have been, up to now, very evasive when these questions are in issue.

Firstly, it is important to remember that the drafting of conventions and establishment of new ones by international organisations will not be efficient if there is no friendly co-operation between States. Long time existing instruments have supported this co-operation but at international level soft law[15], in contrast with hard law which is found largely in most international customary law rules, such as declarations and resolutions issued from diplomatic and international organisations are not binding at all and there is still no *"attempt to employ the language of obligations found in treaties and they are not enforceable*[16]*"*.

Secondly, conventions related to the amelioration have a better effect if they are permanently implemented into domestic legislations in the form of statutes. Perpetrators to the environment and the ecosystem are punished by local penal sanctions or by the *'polluter pays principle'*: the establishment of an Environment Appeal Tribunal (E.A.T) in the Republic of Mauritius demonstrates to what extent the legislature is concerned about environmental degradation.

The sanctions are not very persuasive indeed: it takes the form of a fine whereas at international level may the International Court of Justice (ICJ), an international organ for the settlement of international disputes, impose a State responsibility to reparation since the famous case of *Nicaragua v. United States*[17]? Recently, however, there have been some judgments, which show that some declarations provide prohibitions, which *"has become part of customary international law*[18]*"*

Nevertheless, many States have refused to consent to the jurisdiction of the ICJ and in the absence of an international judicature or a central authority both *stare decisis* and *opinio juris*[19] of the Court have no binding character though it may have *"normative value"*[20]

Ecosystem Amelioration: The International Response to Reparation

To fill the gaps the International Law Commission of the United Nations has tried to respond positively by preparing some draft articles but in vain: at international level it is relatively more difficult[21] to accuse a State's liability, to prove the extent of its consequences and eventually, to ask damages though very often in practice States which are liable for damages come up before the International Court of Justice or a competent court to settle agreement amicably[22].

The most important Draft Articles submitted by the International Law Commission in the past ten years are the Draft Articles on "State Responsibility". It is customary rule that States have to prove liability for damage caused to its territory by another State(s) for internationally wrongful acts.

In order to obtain reparation a State must be responsible for committing a wrongful act, which constitutes a breach of an international obligation of the State. It is using its territory to cause harm or injury to another State including its citizens and property. The injured State is entitled to full reparation in kind, compensation, satisfaction, assurances and guarantees of non-repetition.

The injured State may ask for reparation before the International Court of Justice or before an Arbitration Tribunal to settle dispute provided there are clear and convincing evidence. In the *Trail*

Smelter Arbitration[23] sulphur dioxide from a smelter in Canada damaged crops found in the United States and the Arbitration Tribunal stated that *"no State has the right to use or permit the use of its territory in such a manner as to cause injury by fumes in or to the territory of another or persons or properties therein"*.

But how will the Arbitration Tribunal or an international jurisdiction deal with States, which are liable for acts, which, this time, are not prohibited by international law? The International Law Commission has made an attempt to punish States, which cause injurious consequences of acts, which are not prohibited under international law and the draft articles include a risk of causing significant transboundary harm but the Draft Articles were suspended by the International Law Commission since they were highly controversial.

II

THE PREVENTION: A REALITY OF INTERNATIONAL CO-OPERATION TO ECOSYSTEM

Most conventions, including the Ramsar Convention, provide for protection of the environment but they fail to address the most important issue: prevention. In fact, State responsibility to the environment and ecosystem can be solved by prevention and constant international alertness. It includes information, support from the medias, technological improvement, devices to forecast tsunamis and public awareness to response rapidly.

How to prevent the prevention? In order to prevent a State's liability there is need for an international disarmament coupled with efforts to fight against terror (-A-) and the prevention of climate change and global warming (-B-) to preserve the environment.

The Terror of International Armament and its Impact on the Environment

After World War II most States were committed to reduce their arsenal. Most agreements were reached before the General Assembly of the United Nations during its Conference on Disarmament. Weapons are more and more destructive and since they cause irreparable damage to the environment it is time to ban atomic and nuclear tests. Both the United Nations and the

International Committee of the Red Cross have united to prohibit the use of nuclear tests in the atmosphere, in the outer space and under water[24] and to encourage States not to use the environment as a means of warfare[25].

Environment modification and manipulation of natural processes for hostile purposes may cause uncontrollable phenomena such as tsunamis, hurricanes, floods, droughts, tidal waves and earthquakes. The effects may eventually be long lasting with serious impacts on wild life and human life. The Protocol[26] I (1977) of the Geneva Conventions (1949) strictly forbids attacks on the environment or by way of reprisals.

Conscious that terrorists, lord warriors or freedom fighters may use chemical and bacteriological weapons[27] to cause destruction, damage and injury to another State party. The United Nations have established the Rome Statute (1998). Its article 8[28] enacts that the International Criminal Court will have jurisdiction in respect of war crimes that consist in: *'intentionally launching an attack in the knowledge that such attack will cause incidental widespread, long-term and severe damage to the natural environment which would be clearly excessive in relation to the concrete and direct overall military advantage anticipated''*.

Climate Change and Global Warming and its Impact on the Environment

Climate change and global warming may destroy wetlands. In fact, State liability to climate change and global change is more than a challenge. Sea level is rising continuously causing the disappearance of wetlands, the fauna and the flora. With global warming either there are too much water or not at all. This explains why most wetlands in Bangladesh and in the Netherlands have disappeared under sea level. In Mauritius, wetlands around Terre-Rouge near the capital, which welcomed most migratory birds, and Baie-du-Cap, a zone to encourage reproduction of crabs, are also in danger. Some areas like Pointe d'Esny, near Mahebourg, and the Blue Bay Marine Park have been identified and are today zones of preservation of the fauna and the flora.

Most industrialised countries of the world are accountable for the rapid increase in temperature and are liable for the emission of greenhouse gases and carbon dioxide in the atmosphere. As explained, there is no proper sanction at international level to punish State responsibility. The Kyoto Protocol only commits States members to the protocol to reduce their emission of carbon dioxide whilst the United Nations Framework Convention on Climate Change (1992) sets out a forum for discussion. One of the outcome, optimistic in the true sense, of the Kyoto conference reveals that most State members are prepared to help developing countries and to protect natural resources for the benefit of future generations.

CONCLUDING REMARKS

For State responsibility to perform with efficiency there is a real need of communication both locally and internationally, to manage wetlands so as to enable preservation and tourism opportunities, to develop zones, which may encourage eco-tourism with financial support from the government for sustainable development and donors are encourage to finance projects related to wetlands development.

Sense and sensitisation are both important: education and curriculum development, population awareness, media presentation and communication concerning issues of environment protection are important to enhance community participation. The law must be stricter to polluters by imposing penalties, which are even more severe.

Wetlands cannot survive without water and the ecosystems need hydrological cycles to maintain this tempo. Today, water is scarcer than before and tomorrow it may become a luxurious product. It is vital to understand the importance of biological diversity, human activities that provoke nature's wrath, human intervention to modify the environment and that development of hotels on the coasts of the island are restricted where it may set hurdles to wetlands and development of wetland ecosystems.

Unlike many countries, in Mauritius there are natural reservoirs (Mare aux Vacoas, Mare-Longue, La Nicolière), natural indigenous forests (Macabé, Black River Gorges, Nature Park, Pétrin) and mountains (Moka Range, Piton du Milieu, Montagne Lion, Trois Mamelles), coastal reefs, unspoiled lagoons, dormant volcanoes (Trou aux Cerfs, Trou Kanaka) and unlimited beaches which are overcrowded with tourists and roamers on week-ends, and which have the merit to be protected. Rainfall is abundant and the sun shines all the year round.

But above all the best recommendation is still 'human consciousness'!

NOTES

1. The Convention on International Trade in endangered Species of Wild Fauna and Flora (CITES) of 1973 controls international trade of endangered species (wild animal and plants) through quotas and outright bans to ensure their survival. There is also the Bonn Convention on the Conservation of Migratory Species of Wild Animals (1979), which aim to conserve terrestrial, marine and avian migratory species and their habitats. There is also the Convention of migratory species of wild animals (CMS), the African Eurasian Migratory Waterbird Agreement (AEWA) and the Ramsar Convention.
2. Convention on Biological Diversity (1992).
3. United Nations Convention to Combat Desertification.
4. Ramsar Convention (1971), which came into force in 1975.
5. The United Nations Economic Commission for Europe (ECE) has negotiated the Convention on Long-range Transboundary Air Pollution (Acid Rain Convention) 1979 to control the reduction of air pollution in Europe and North America.
6. Stockholm Declaration (1972).
7. The Rio Declaration (1992)
8. Law of the Sea Convention (1982). This convention, inter alia, provides for the protection of coasts and the marine environment, marine scientific research and rights to living and non-living resources.
9. The International Convention for the Regulation of Whaling (1946).
10. The Vienna Convention for the Protection of the Ozone Layer (1985) followed by the Montreal Protocol (1987). Greenhouse gases and carbon dioxide deplete the ozone layer (O3), which is responsible to shield the fauna and flora from the sun's harmful ultraviolet radiations.
11. The Basel Convention on the Control of Transboundary Movement of Hazardous Wastes and their Disposal (1989) obligates States parties to reduce shipping and dumping of dangerous wastes across borders. A protocol was adopted in 1999 on liability and compensation resulting from cross-border movement of hazardous wastes.
12. Cold war, tensions between States, terrorism, conflicts between countries of the Middle-East, disputes for the Cachemire territory,

the death of S. Hussein, the supremacy of the USA in international political and economical relations, are some of the main obstacles which explain why it is so difficult to establish a friendly relations among States.

13. The Wetland Bill (200700), another blended project from the Ramsar Convention and international instruments, is before the Parliament and is another piece of legislation useful to improve the ecosystem once it is assented by the President of the Rep. of Mauritius.

14. The Environment Protection Act (2002), The Geneva Convention Act (1982), The Radiation Protection Act (2003), The Biological And Toxin Weapons Act (2004).

15. The Stockholm Declaration of the United Nations Conference on the Human Environment (1972) and the Rio Declaration on the Environment and Development (1992), for examples, are based on this model.

16. According to Pr. Dugard J. (2000), *International Law: A South African Perspective,* Juta & Co, Ltd., 475 p., p. 316.

17. Nicaragua v. USA 1987 81 AJIL 77-183. Nicaragua brought a case before the ICJ claiming that the United States had mined its harbours and intervened militarily in Nicaragua. The USA refused to appear before the I.C.J and it repudiated the findings of the Court!

18. In Filartiga v. Pena-Irala 630 F 2d 876 (1980) concerning the prohibition of torture: is it part of international customary law?

19. In the *Nicaragua Case 1986 ICJ Reports 14* the Court held that it "has however to be satisfied that there exists in customary international law an *opinio juris* as to the binding character of such abstention from the use of force. This *opinio juris* may, though with all due caution, be deduced from, inter alia, the attitude of States towards certain General Assembly resolutions. The effect of consent to the text of such resolutions may be understood as an acceptance of the validity of the rule or set of rules declared by the resolution".

20. According to the Advisory Opinion concerning the *Legality of the Threat or Use of Nuclear Weapons* 1996 ICJ Reports 226.

21. As far as the emission of gases in the atmosphere is concerned it is difficult to know with precision which countries are not respecting the Kyoto Protocol, the amount of GHG emitted and the depletion of the ozone layer clearly explain how difficult it is to pinpoint a particular State.

22. The Lockerbie Affair, concerning a crash of a Pan American flight 103 in 1988, where Libya brought two cases before the ICJ but the cases

were removed from the Court's docket in September 2003, as part of a larger agreement was reached between the parties.

23. Trail Smelter Arbitration 1938-1941.
24. Treaty Banning Nuclear Weapon Tests in the Atmosphere, in Outer Space, and Under Water (1967).
25. The ENMOD Convention (1976).
26. Article 35, paragraph 3 of Add. Protocol I.
27. The 1925 Protocol. Convention on the prohibition of the Development, Production and Stockpiling of Bacteriological (Biological) and Toxin Weapons and on their Destruction (1972). The chemical Weapons Convention (1993).
28. Article 8, par. 2 (b, iv).

REFERENCES

Dugard, J. (2000), *International Law: a South African Perspective*, Juta & Co. Ltd., 475 p., pp. 315-327.

Gunputh, R. P. (2007), *Alarm Bell Around the Cat's Neck*, p. 9.

Gunputh, R. P. (2007), *Vers une meilleure Planification de l'eau douce dans un Etat de droit-un cadre légal dans un cadre mauricien*, p. 13.

Gunputh, R. P. (2007), *Unveiling a Disaster Law in a Climate of Poverty-nature's Wrath Nurtures Poverty.*

Sahni P., Dhameja A. & Medury U. (2001), *Disaster Mitigation: Experiences and Reflections*, Prentice-Hall of India (New Delhi), p. 214.

Deconstruction: A Play of Signifiers

Arti Nirmal* & Nalini Shyam Kamil**

INTRODUCTION

Born in 1930 in Algeria, the French philosopher, scholar, teacher and critic, Jacques Derrida is one of the most widely acclaimed and debated critic of late twentieth century. He enjoys an emphatic influence upon the critics, theorist and scholars of his time in U.S.A. and worldwide. In 1960s he came up with publications namely *De la grammatologie* (Of Grammatology) and *L' Ecriture et la difference* (Writing and Difference) in order to acquaint readers with the playful relationship between language and meaning. He further wrote *Dissemination* (1972) *Glas* (1976), *The Post Card* (1980) to strengthen his point of view but his paper *"Structure, Sign and Play in the Discourse of the Human Sciences"* presented at a symposium at John Hopkins University in 1966 set a critical upheaval by introducing his 'theory of deconstruction'. Deconstruction basically is *"an approach to the reading of literary and philosophical texts that casts doubt upon the possibility of finding in them a definitive meaning, and that traces instead the multiplication (or dissemination) of possible meanings"*[1].

DECONSTRUCTION: A PLAY OF SIGNIFIERS

Derrida's deconstruction is basically a skeptical theory which involves the practice of textual interpretation. In his own words,

---

* *Lecturer in English, Dr. Shyama Prasad Mukherjee Govt. Degree College, Sant Ravidas Nagar., Bhadohi, U.P.*

** *Lecturer in English, Jagatpur Post Graduate College, Jagatpur, Varanasi, U.P.*

"Deconstructive readings and writings are...not simply analyses of discourse....They are also effective or active...interventions, in particular political and institutional interventions that transforms contexts without limiting themselves to theoretical or constative utterances even though they must also produce such utterances"[2]. His ideas were primarily inspired by F. Nietzsche's 'idea of questioning of truth and knowledge', Martin Heidegger's 'subversive phenomenological study' and Sigmund Freud's 'Psychoanalytic theories'. Besides this, he also derived several of his key concepts for deconstruction from Ferdinand de Saussure's structuralism based on linguistic design. Contrary to the traditional method of literary analysis which focused mainly on the historical background of a text known as diachronic study, Saussure proposes a synchronic mode of text analysis that reflects solely on the literariness of the given text at a particular time. He challenges the need of any fixed reference point to determine the meaning of a language and considers every work as mere text constituted of several signs. Thus for Saussure, any work or literature becomes a text which implies a system of signs (= signifier + signified) and promotes that the sign is never constant and therefore its meaning is always in flux. Derrida, though picks up some of these structuralist views but takes a clean turn to develop his own novel theory of deconstruction. In other words, we may say that deconstruction is an evaluation and development of structuralism. It is *"an interpretative strategy of post structuralism"*[3] which employs procedures of analysis different from all the previous critical practices.

Derrida himself refuses to give any pat definition to his own coinage due to its indeterminate nature, however, it can be defined in general as 'an operation to take an idea, a set of values or an institution to understand its mechanism by removing the cement that constitutes it'. According to deconstruction theory a given text *"resists any process of interpretation that would fix their meaning, appearing to 'undo' themselves as we try to tie them up"*[4]. He accepts Saussure's idea that language is self competent and that meaning is evolved out of the differences between different linguistic units and thus, develops his deconstruction theory to bring into book the entire philosophical and metaphysical study since Plato that presumes that the text has a stable meaning. He adopts a subversive manner of reading a text and provides his axial preposition in *Of*

Grammatology (1976) that there is nothing beyond the text: *'it n'y a rien hors du texts'*.

Considering text as an independent autonomous entity he contents that the traditional mode of reading a text makes several false assumptions such as:

(a) language is capable of expressing constant and unchanging meaning,

(b) the author of a given text is the sole determiner of its meaning; and

(c) in the hierarchy of language, writing is secondary to speech.

Saussure, in his *"Course in General Linguistics"* (1916) says that the *"concepts are purely differential, not positively defined by their content but negatively defined by their relation with the other system"*[5] He converted language units into linguistic signs which include the signifier and the signified where the signifier is the sign or the sound that we produce and signified is the concept. For structuralist the nature of the bond between the signifier and the signified is arbitrary. Taking these ideas as basis Derrida posits that it is the play of language that should guide in the process of interpreting a text. Therefore, for the proper analysis of a text it is required to understand the free play of the linguistic signs within the text where by 'free play' Derrida means "the disruption of presence" which may be seen as an ongoing interplay of absence and presence.

Unlike Saussure's structuralism which believes that *"language does have an oral tradition that is independent of writing"* and also that *"the spoken word alone constitutes the object"*[6]. Derrida questions the established belief of 'logocentrism'. It was believed earlier that *'logos'* i.e. *'words'* are supreme because in biblical age God delivered himself through *'words'* (in phonic or sound form) and these words had fixed and permanent character. This logocentric approach was mainly phonocentric which means spoken sounds or words. Derrida discovered 'logocentrism' and advocated that sound or words spoken by the source evaporates or vanishes without leaving behind any concrete trace and its conversion into writing is never pure because of contamination and interpolation. Hence, he rejects the philosophical and metaphysical belief in logocentrism because there is no centre that may control the play of meanings and thereby suggest the indeterminate nature of 'logos' often interpreted as words, God, being and ideal world. He estimated *'logo centrism'* as a fallacy, an illusionary one and thus reverses the hierarchal order to reinforce that *'Writing is prior to Speech'*. A text because of this virtue lacks any station which can authorize, guide or control the play of signifiers.

Logocentrism and phonocentrism thus are co-related because in logocentrism it is believed that a speaker speaks whatever he wants and the concept that the speaker's intention determines the meaning is the chief ground of logocetric theory in western philosophy of language. Hence, Derrida further elucidates in his *Of Grammatology* that it is fallacious to think that writing is secondary to speech because "speech is a species of writing"[7]. About Derrida's perception of logocentrism Christopher Norris opines: *"He sets his deconstructive sights against the ruling metaphysics which subjugates language to thought, rhetoric to logic and style to the notion of a plentitude of meaning"*[8].

> Deconstruction, basically is not destruction or decomposition, rather it is a way of 'reconstruction' as Barbara Johnson succinctly remarks in *The Critical Difference*:
>
> *Deconstruction is not synonymous with destruction... the deconstruction of a text does not proceed by random doubt or arbitrary subversion, but by the careful teasing out of warring forces of signification within the text itself*[9].
>
> In the similar vein, J. M. Balkin also observes:
>
> *Deconstruction is not a denial of the legitimacy of rules and principles; instead, it is an affirmation of human possibilities that have been over looked or forgotten in the privileging of particular legal ideas.... By recalling the elements of human life relegated to the margin in a given social theory, deconstructive readings challenge us to remarks the dominant conceptions of our society*[10].

This statement can be analyzed by taking an illustration of peeling off of an onion. Just as in order to view the inner bulb of an onion we need to peal off the covering layers one by one, similarly, to understand and analyze a given text which is actually a constellation of signifiers we should attempt to tear away the various layers preserving the meaning inside. Deconstruction theory is somewhat analogous to the *'intentional fallacy'* proposed by New Critics–Wimsatt and Beardsley who discard the notion of author's role in providing meaning to the text. For them the author is not the only source of its meaning and the words do not refer to any external source except its own literary structure for the meaning.

The French critic Roland Barthes' slogan *'Death of the Author'* in 1968 ushered new avenues for thinking and text analysis by establishing reader at the centre of all. Thus, reader becomes the sole determiner of a text's meaning. Barthes emphasizes however, that, to achieve this goal it is very necessary that the text should have self-generating linguistic codes and patterns. These ideas set the background for Derrida to formulate one of the typical analytical procedures, a deconstructive reading that focuses on binary oppositions within the text.

The deconstructive method proceeds by means of slow and ingeniously detailed reading which H.P. Grice termed as 'implicature'. It avoids the misunderstanding that meaning is created straightway from words to things rather than from words to words. Deconstruction, has *"subsequently become synonymous with a particular method of textual analysis and philosophical argument involving the close reading of works of literature, philosophy, psychoanalysis, linguistics and anthropology to reveal logical or rhetorical incompatibilities between the explicit and implicit planes of discourse in a text and to demonstrate by means of a range of critical techniques how these incompatibilities are disguised and assimilated by the text"*[11].

Now the question arises: 'how the play of signifiers leads to meaning?' Here comes Derrida's 'concept of undecidability of text' which affirms that we cannot fix the meaning of the signifiers. The multiplicity of meaning emerges by virtue of this changing nature. To draw from Saussure's structuralist theory we may say that there is '"no intrinsic, organic or "motivated" reason for signifying a particular concept by means of a particular word; the meaning of a word is arbitrary agreed upon by a set of social convention. Hence words acquire value or identity between signifier and signified but through each word's opposition to every other words within a system of interdependence in which both signifiers and signified are defined in terms of what they are not, that is, in terms of a simultaneous linguistic presence and absence," or what Saussure calls "difference"[12]. Thus, for Saussure, language is a play of 'erasures' and there is no positive element in it. Derrida picks his idea of "difference" and employs it to "deconstruct" western philosophy where metaphysical ideologies such as truth, God, reason, absolute, being and reality are decided with respect to some fixed point of reference i.e. an ontological axis or origin or an end that subsides absences in favour of metaphysical stability. Derrida elaborates structuralist differential view and suggests that in every signifier we have a multiple absences. For example 'Rat' is a possibility of absence in 'Cat'.

He further explains that the meaning of any 'signifier (written or spoken) is the sum of the signifier and all the absences. As per Derrida's theory when we search for any signified (i.e. the meaning or concept) of the signifier, we arrive at another signified and in this way the meaning is chased like a mirage every time. This renders an open ended quality to the text and enables it free for any number of interpretation. This open-endedness becomes an important characteristic of postmodern writing and discourse and thus paves way for various reader centered theories, namely Reader Response theory by Wolfgang Isher & Stanley Fish and Speech Act theory by John Austin and so on. In order to deconstruct the hierarchal sense of presence, Derrida formulates the 'portmanteau' term 'differance'. He uses the spelling–"ance" instead of "ence" to indicate a 'fusion of two senses'. Hence, the meaning of a signifier is a product of difference or what we call the probable meaning.

This brings us to Derrida's concept of 'discrimination of meaning' which says that presuming every signifier if we approach forward, it decomposes further into various meanings and emerges as new signifiers. Hence, there is no unit, no decidability of meaning in any text whether literary or philosophic, or legal or scientific. In this manner, deconstruction demonstrates "the necessary instability of meaning and the necessary fluidity of identities, as well as the necessary incoherence of correspondence theories of truth"[13]. He also clears the distinction between a literary and non-literary text and thereby dilutes the distinction or classification of genres by converting it into a set of linguistic sign.

Derrida suggests several deconstructive procedures out of which two significant operations have been discussed below:

(1) *First Operation* suggests the identification of those junctures in a text where a binary oppositions (eg. Speech/writing,

male/female, presence/absence, and outside/inside) or even a single word fragments down to show radical incongruities in the logic or rhetoric. Thus by deconstructing such numerous dipoles which are essential structural units in logocentric language, it can be revealed that there lies a difference in the apparent unity.

(2) *Second Operation* asks to deconstruct or dismantle any venture to establish a fixed limit to a text with an objective to differentiate inside from the outside. It also allows applying deconstructive method for the analysis of a law, principle or ideology pertaining to any literary or non-literary subject.

The above mentioned operations in this way open up new perspectives to text reading and encourage readers to analyze them from their own point of view. It renders multiplicity to meaning and open for interpretation. The aim of deconstruction, then, is not to destroy but to dismantle some illusionary setups, often by revealing how their traditional nomenclature is unstable and contaminated by their supposed opposites. Deconstruction and Criticism, Geoffery Hartman says:

> *[...] deconstruction... refuses to identify the force to literature with any concept of embodied meaning and shows how deeply such logocentric or incarnationist perspectives have influenced the way we think about art.*[14]

Successors of Derrida like Paul de Man (*Allegories of Reading* 1979) and J. Hillis Miller (*Fiction and Repetition* 1982) took the theory of deconstruction with their own constructions. De Man's approach to textual analysis has close affinity with Derrida himself in terms of uncovering hierarchal opposition within the texts, on the other hand, Miller is unique for suggesting the possibility of *ad infinitum* and the advocacy of a "tradition" of presence. Deconstruction for De Man is not something to be superimposed by the critic; instead it goes into the very formation of literature. Like I.A.Richards he focuses on rhetoric and studies metaphors as the chief attribute of literatures and however, varies from Derrida in his view that different forms of literary discourse differ in thought though not in species. In the similar manner, J. Hillis Miller too, believes in the figural nature of language but denies the complete absence of referentiality. Defining the self annihilating nature of deconstruction, Miller writes:

> *The deconstruction, rather, annihilates the ground on which the building stands by showing that the text has already annihilated that ground, knowingly or unknowingly. Deconstruction is not a dismantling of the structure of a text but a deconstruction that it has already dismantled itself*[15].

CONCLUSION

Thus, we see how Jacques Derrida the 'father of deconstruction' has shown that the philosophical texts often strive to repress and undermine their own essential character as written discourse. His deconstruction theory basically is a reading of text that pursues the hidden metaphors and random nature of signifiers where this covertness is simultaneously concealed as well as revealed. Jacques Derrida who was one of the most celebrated and notoriously different philosophers of his time, failed to precisely define his code of intellectual discourse, yet it has been endlessly interpreted in several ways. Owing to this quality he has been declared as "The exponent of enigmatic theory"

NOTES

1. Drabble, Margaret (ed.) (2005), *The Oxford Companion to English Literature*. Sixth Edition. New Delhi , OUP. 2005, 265.
2. Derrida (a), Jacques (1986), "Critical Response", trans. Peggy Kamuf, *Critical Inquiry*, 13, August 1986, 168.
3. Pattanayak, B. K. (2003), *Aspects of post structuralism, Derrida's Theory of Deconstruction and Feminist Criticism. Bareilly*. Prakash Book Depot. 2003, 11.
4. Drabble, Margaret (ed.) (2005), *The Oxford Companion to English Literature*. Sixth Edition, New Delhi, OUP. 2005, 266.
5. Saussure, Ferdinand de (1966), "Course in General Linguistics", Baskin, Wade (trans.) New York, McGraw-Hill, 1966, 111-22.
6. Derrida (b), Jacques (1976), *Of Grammatology*. Spivak, G.C (trans.) Baltimore: The Johns Hopkins University Press, 1976, 30.
7. Selden, Raman (1989), *A Reader's Guide to Contemporary Literary Theory*. Second Edition. Harvester : Harvester Wheatsheaf, 1989, 89.
8. Norris, Christopher (1985), "Deconstruction and "Ordinary Language": Speech vs Writing in the Text of Philosophy", *Style, Structure and Criticism* David Birch (ed.). New Delhi: Bahri Publications Pvt. Ltd. 1985, 107-124 at 110.

9. Johnson, Barbara (1985), *The Critical Difference:Essays in the Contemporary Rhetoric of Reading*, JHU Press, 1985, 5.
10. Balkin, J. M. 'Deconstructive Practice and Legal theory' (1987) *96 Yale Law Journal* 743 p. 763.
11. Kneale, J. Douglas, *<http://www.press.jhu.edu/books/Hopkins-guide-to-literacy-theory/deconstruction, html> 8/11/04 p.1*
12. Saussure, Ferdinand de (1966), "Course in General Linguistics", Baskin, Wade (trans.) New York, McGraw-Hill, 1966, 111-22.
13. Barnett, Clive (1999), "Deconstructing Context: Exposing Derrida", *Transactions of the Institute of British Geographers, New Series*, Vol. 24, No. 3, 1999, 277-293. *http://www.jstor.org/stable/623128 acc. 01/09/2008*
14. Hartman, Geoffery (1979), 'Preface'. *Deconstruction and Criticism*. New York, Continuums, 1979, VII.
15. Miller, J. Hillis (1979), "On Edge: The Crossways of Contemporary Criticism", *Bulletin of the American Academy of Arts and Sciences*, Jan 1979, 18-19.

The Iraqi Special Tribunal Under the International Humanitarian Law

ALI ADNAN ALFEEL*

INTRODUCTION

The people of Iraq have a legal and moral right to build a structure for the prosecution of the leading figures in the Ba'athist regime. More to the point, the judges who have risked their lives to build the rule of law in Iraq should rightfully expect the support and encouragement of the world rather than a cautious and lukewarm assurance that the civilized peoples of the world wish them the best. I was involved in the conceptual development and drafting of the Statute for the Iraqi Special Tribunal (IST), and have subsequently spent many hours with the judges and investigators of the court as they prepare to undertake their important work. I have gained a deep respect for the legal ethos and professional courage of the members of the Iraqi bar who have risked their lives and those of their families to serve the Iraqi people. My experience has convinced me that the creation of the IST is not only warranted under the existing structure of international law, but accords with the highest aspirations of those who purport to believe in the rule of law.

The creation of the IST was borne of necessity after the fall of Saddam Hussein's regime. The exercise of punitive criminal accountability pursuant to domestic laws is at the heart of our

* *Criminal Law Assistant Lecturer, Public Law Department, College of Law / University of Mosul.*

understanding of what it means to have a society built on the rule of law, which in turn makes it the *sine qua non* of true sovereignty. This principle is so essential that the pursuit of justice often becomes a focal point for the military forces deployed to a society where the legislative and judicial systems have become corrupted, replaced, or have simply collapsed under the weight of tyranny(1). Assuming its proper role on behalf of the Iraqi people, the Interim Iraqi Governing Council made the creation of an accountability mechanism for punishing those responsible for the atrocities of the Ba'athist regime one of its earliest priorities(2). After an extensive and genuine partnership that entailed months of debate, drafting, and consideration of expert advice solicited from the Coalition Provisional Authority (CPA), the Iraqi Governing Council issued the IST Statute on December 10, 2003(3). The announcement of the Statute culminated a developmental process carried out under the auspices of the Legal Affairs subcommittee of the Iraqi Governing Council led by Judge Dara, and by sheer coincidence preceded the capture of Saddam Hussein by only four days.

Ancillary to the announcement of the Statute, the Iraqi Governing Council and CPA requested that the Defense Institute of International Legal Studies (DIILS)(4) present a seminar on investigating and prosecuting international crimes in accordance with international norms. The diverse group of 96 Iraqi judges, prosecutors, and lawyers who gathered in Baghdad were among the first Iraqis outside the Governing Council to review the Statute. Members of this group repeatedly and enthusiastically referred to Saddam's regime as the "entombed regime." The members of the Iraqi legal community that we were teaching later formed the pool of Iraqis who were initially considered for various positions inside the Iraqi Special Tribunal. I was in the room with those Iraqi judges and prosecutors in Baghdad when they learned of the successful capture of President Hussein. In the frenzy of joy and palpable relief that followed the electric news(5), one of the judges hugged me and exclaimed "Today is day one!" His spontaneous vision captured the sense of many Iraqis that the definitive end of the Hussein regime was a watershed event for those dedicated to leading Iraq towards stability and sovereignty founded on respect for human rights and the rule of law. In addition, judges have reiterated to me on a number of occasions that they view their important work as the doorway that will expand the influence and application of international humanitarian law across the Arab-speaking areas of the world.

The dedication of the Iraqi legal professionals to restore the rule of law reflects the broader societal thirst for accountability that is a foreseeable feature of a post-conflict civil society emerging from widespread and official governmental human rights abuses[(6)]. As a microcosm of Iraqi society, the overwhelming majority of that original group of 96 legal professionals had suffered the loss of immediate family members to the criminal acts of the regime. One judge was the only survivor of seven brothers. The elation of the Iraqi people mirrored that of other societies where the civilian population prized justice and an end to repression in the immediate aftermath of operations even in areas where the citizens suffer from extreme poverty and overwhelming material needs[(7)]. The demise of the regime fanned the long-subdued embers of hope that the citizenry had never quite forgotten; people began to openly discuss the dim but potent aspiration that they might be able to live in peace and stability secure in the knowledge that the rule of law would protect their home and family. The priority that the common people attach to the restoration of true justice perhaps reflected an inchoate realization that the freedom from oppression achieved by coalition forces could not be sustained without effective restoration of personal accountability based on law. The elation that Iraqi citizens expressed as the statues of Saddam Hussein fell in Baghdad testified to their deep desire for the restoration of a society built on the rule of law rather than one dominated by the whims of a dictator supported by the machinery of bureaucratic oppression.

The IST was created with the express goal of bringing personal accountability to those Ba'athists that were responsible for depriving Iraqis of their human rights, and of virtually extinguishing the real rule of law for over two decades[(8)]. It would be ironic indeed if the mechanism created by the Iraqis to address the human rights failings of the past in itself became the vehicle for denying and suppressing human rights into the future. The purpose of this paper is to assess the creation and implementation of the IST in light of relevant human rights norms. From my perspective, the men and women who have committed themselves to serve the IST are the ones who have shouldered the burden of replacing the osmosis of fear that pervaded Iraq under Saddam's rule with the peace and societal stability that flows from a solid rule of law.

It is false to presume that the Tribunal will be capable of achieving only the shadow of justice through the vehicle of undermining the core human rights of those who will face charges under its authority. Such an assumption is unwarranted as demonstrated by a closer examination of the structure of the Statute and its accompanying Rules of Evidence and Procedure. In particular, the interface of the IST Statute with the preexisting structure of the Iraqi Code of Criminal Procedure reveals a developed web of legal protections that fully accord with existing human rights principles. This paper will discuss the basis under international law that warranted the formation of the IST and describe the salient features of the Tribunal's structure. After noting some of the most important points of comparison between the IST and earlier accountability mechanisms, the paper will conclude with a detailed explication of the relationship between the Tribunal and the most important of the existing human rights norms related to the process of criminal accountability for crimes derived from international law.

LEGAL AUTHORITIES FOR THE CREATION OF THE IRAQI SPECIAL TRIBUNAL

The Law of Occupation

The relationship of a subjugated civilian population to the foreign power temporarily exercising *de facto* sovereignty is regulated by the extensive development of the law of occupation(9). As a matter of legal rights and duties, "[t]erritory is considered occupied when it is actually placed under the authority of the hostile army."(10) This legal test is met when the following circumstances prevail on the ground: first, that the existing governmental structures have been rendered incapable of exercising their normal authority; and second, that the occupying power is in a position to carry out the normal functions of government over the affected area(11). For the purposes of United States policy, occupation is the legal state occasioned by "invasion plus taking firm possession of enemy territory for the purpose of holding it."(12)

Although a state of occupation does not "affect the legal status of the territory in question,"[13] the assumption of authority over the occupied territory implicitly means that the existing institutions of society have been swept aside. Because the foreign power has displaced the normal domestic offices, the cornerstone of the law of occupation is the broad obligation that the foreign power "take *all* the measures in his power to restore, and ensure, as far as possible, public order and safety . . ." (emphasis added)[14].

In the authoritative French, the occupier must preserve "l'ordre et la vie publics" (*i.e.* "public order and life")[15]. On that legal reasoning alone, the establishment of the IST could have been warranted under the inherent occupation authority of the Coalition as an integral part of the strategic plan for restoring public calm and peaceful stability to the civilian population across Iraq. From that perspective, the IST is the intellectual twin to the International Criminal Tribunal for the Former Yugoslavia (ICTY) because the United Nations Security Council established the ICTY with a groundbreaking 1993 Resolution[16] that was premised on the legal obligation of the Security Council to "maintain or restore international peace and security."[17]

The IST and ICTY[18] are both founded on the assessment by the officials charged with preserving stability and the rule of law that prosecution of selected persons responsible for serious violations of international humanitarian law will facilitate the restoration of societal peace and stability ("l'ordre et la vie publics" in the language of the Hague Regulations). After the first defendant, a Serb named Dusko Tadic, challenged the legality of the ICTY, the Trial Chamber ruled that the authority of the Security Council to create the tribunal was dispositive[19]. Just as the Security Council has the "primary responsibility" for maintaining international peace and security under the United Nations Charter[20], the law of occupation imposed a concrete legal duty on the CPA to facilitate the return of stability and order to Iraq after the fall of the regime. As criminal forums conceived and created pursuant to the broader responsibility of empowered authorities to maintain or restore peace and security, both the ICTY and IST were appropriate non-military mechanisms (though each was creative in its own time and in different ways)[21].

In the context of Iraq, of course, the legal framework of occupation rests on a delicate balance. On the one hand, the civilian population has no legal right to conduct activities that are harmful to persons or property of the occupying force, and may be convicted or interned based on such unlawful activities[22]. Article 42 of the 1949 Geneva Convention Relative to the Protection of Civilian Persons in Time of War (hereinafter referred to by its more common appellation the IVth Geneva Convention) specifically permits the deprivation of liberty for civilians if "the security of the Detaining Power makes it absolutely necessary."[23] Even large-scale internment may be permissible in situations where there are "serious and legitimate reasons" to believe that the detained persons threaten the safety and security of the occupying [24] power. At the same time, the coercive authority of the occupying power is limited by a specific prohibition against making any changes to the governmental structure or institutions that would undermine the benefits guaranteed to civilians under the Geneva Conventions[25]. Thus, the baseline principle of occupation law is that the civilian population should continue to live their lives as normally as possible.

This baseline principle rests on the reality that mere occupation does not effect a transfer of sovereignty; hence, the occupying power must protect the lives and property of the civilian population from the uncertainties inherent in the transfer of political authority to the maximum practicable extent. This concept may be termed the minimalist principle, though some observers have termed it the principle of normality[26]. As a policy priority flowing from the mandates of the IVth Geneva Convention, domestic law should be enforced by domestic officials insofar as possible, and crimes not of a military nature that do not affect the occupant's security will normally be delegated to the jurisdiction of local courts[27]. The IST fits this legal/policy model precisely as it was created and subsequently ratified by Iraqi authorities as an Iraqi domestic statute.

However, the international legal regime does not doggedly elevate the provisions of domestic law and the structure of domestic institutions above the pursuit of justice. Despite the minimalist principle, international law allows reasonable latitude for an occupying power to modify, suspend, or replace the existing penal structure in the interests of ensuring justice and the restoration of the rule of law. In its temporary exercise of functional sovereignty over the occupied territory, and as a pragmatic necessity, the occupation authority must ensure the proper functioning, *inter alia,* of domestic criminal processes and cannot abdicate that responsibility to domestic officials of the civilian population who may or may not be willing or able to carry out their normal functions in pursuit of public order(28). Pursuant to the baseline principle of normality, Article 43 of the 1907 Hague Regulations mandates that the occupying power must respect, "unless absolutely prevented, the laws in force in the country."(29)

The duty found in Article 43 of the Hague Regulations to respect local laws unless "absolutely prevented" (in French "*empêchement absolu*") imposes a seemingly categorical imperative(30). However, rather than being understood literally, *empêchement absolu* has been interpreted as the equivalent of "*nécessite.*"(31) In the post World War II context, this meant that the Allies could set the feet of the defeated Axis powers "on a more wholesome path"(32) rather than blindly enforcing the institutional and legal constraints that had been the main bulwarks of tyranny(33).

Article 64 of the IVth Geneva Convention explained the implications of older 1907 Hague Article 43 language by explaining the exception to the minimalist principle in more concrete terms. In ascertaining the implications of the 1949 Article 64 language with regard to the 2003 occupation in Iraq, it is important to realize its drafters did not extend the "traditional scope of occupation legislation."(34) Hence, the law of the Geneva Convention amplified the concept of necessity understood at the time to be embedded in the old Hague Article 43. Article 64 incorporates the preexisting baseline of normality within the confines of protecting the legal rights of the civilian population. Article 64 accordingly reads as follows:

The penal laws of the occupied territory shall remain in force, with the exception that they may be repealed or suspended by the Occupying Power in cases where they constitute a threat to its security or an obstacle to the application of the present Convention. Subject to the latter consideration and to the necessity for ensuring the effective administration of justice, the tribunals of the occupied territory shall continue to function in respect of all offences covered by the said laws.

The Occupying Power may, however, subject the population of the occupied territory to provisions which are essential to enable the Occupying Power to fulfill its obligations under the present Convention, to maintain the orderly government of the territory, and to ensure the security of the Occupying Power, of the members and property of the occupying forces or administration, and likewise of the establishments and lines of communication used by them[35].The plain language of Article 64 must be interpreted in good faith in light of the object and purpose of the Fourth Convention[36], which seeks to alleviate the suffering of the civilian population and ameliorate the potentially adverse consequences of occupation subsequent to military defeat. The first paragraph balances both the minimalist intent of the framers with the overriding purpose of balancing the concurrent rights of both the civilian population and the right of the occupier to maintain the security of its forces and property. The second paragraph of Article 64 morphed the implicit meaning of "necessary" drawn from the old Hague Article 43 into an explicit authority to amend the domestic laws to achieve the core purposes of the Convention. Article 64 has thus been accepted and implemented by states in light of the common sense reading and the underlying legal duties of the occupier to permit modification of domestic law under limited circumstances[37].

Legal Authority for the Promulgation of the IST

The touchstone of analysis for the promulgation of the IST is to recognize that the CPA mission statement gave it affirmative authority as the "temporary governing body designated by the United Nations as the lawful government of Iraq until such time as Iraq is politically and socially stable enough to assume its sovereignty."[38] On one level, the revalidation by Iraqi authorities of the IST after the return of full Iraqi sovereignty makes an analysis of IST formation under the umbrella authority of the CPA a moot point. At the same time, the IST as it exists today is cloaked in a seamless garment of legality both in terms of its origination and in its ongoing existence as a distinct branch of Iraqi bureaucracy. The CPA posited its power as the occupation authority in Iraq in declarative terms: "The CPA is vested with all executive, legislative, and judicial authority necessary to achieve its objectives, to be exercised under relevant U.N. Security Council resolutions, including Resolution 1483 (2003), and the laws and usages of war."[39] The appellation "Coalition Provisional Authority" was a literal title in every aspect: (1) It represented the members of the coalition ultimately composed of over twenty nations, (2) it was intended to be a temporary power to bridge the gap to a full restoration of Iraqi sovereign authority, and (3) (perhaps most importantly) it exercised the obligations incumbent on those states occupying Iraq in the legal sense, and conversely enjoyed the legal authority flowing from the laws and customs of war.

This understanding of CPA status comports with the diplomatic representations made at the time of its formation[40]. The United Nations Security Council unanimously recognized "the specific authorities, responsibilities, and obligations under applicable international law of these states (the members of the coalition) as occupying powers under unified command (the "Authority)."[41] The CPA was therefore recognized as the entity legally responsible for implementing the obligations imposed by the law of occupation.

Security Council Resolution 1483 passed unanimously on May 22, 2003, and called upon the members of the CPA to "comply fully with their obligations under international law including in particular the Geneva Conventions of 1949 and the Hague Regulations of 1907."[42] Resolution 1483 is particularly noteworthy for the formation of the IST because the Security Council specifically highlighted the need for an accountability mechanism "for crimes and atrocities committed by the previous Iraqi regime."[43] The Security Council further required the CPA to exercise its temporary power over Iraq in a manner "consistent with the Charter of the United Nations and other relevant international law, to promote the welfare of the Iraqi people through the effective administration of the territory."[44] Though strikingly similar to the declaration of allied power in occupied Germany after World War II[45], CPA Regulation 1 was therefore founded on bedrock legal authority flowing from the Chapter VII power of the Security Council as supplemented by the preexisting power granted to the occupier by the laws and customs of war[46]. Resolution 1483 operated in conjunction with the residual laws and customs of war to establish positive legal authority for the formation of the IST by the CPA and Governing Council. The subtle linkage between Article 43 of the Hague Regulations and Article 64 gave the CPA broad discretion to delegate the authority for promulgation of the IST to the Governing Council as a matter of necessity. At its core, Article

64 protects the rights of citizens in the occupied territory to a fair and effective system of justice. As a first step, and citing its obligation to ensure the "effective administration of justice," the CPA issued an order suspending the imposition of capital punishment in the criminal courts of Iraq and prohibiting torture as well as cruel, inhumane, and degrading treatment in occupied Iraq[47]. The declaration of a duty to ensure the "effective administration of justice" in CPA Order Number 7 was an inarguable derivative of the duty imposed by the Security Council Resolution 1483 to work towards the "effective administration of the territory" of Iraq. Exercising his power as the temporary occupation authority, Ambassador Bremer signed CPA Order Number 7, which suspended some aspects of domestic law and amended the Iraqi Criminal Code in other important ways seeking to suspend or modify laws that "the former regime used ... as a tool of repression in violation of internationally recognized human rights."[48]

Furthermore, the subsequent promulgation of CPA Policy Memorandum Number 3 on June 18, 2003 was based on the treaty obligation to eliminate obstacles to the application of the Geneva Conventions because it amended key provisions of the Iraqi Criminal Code in order to protect the rights of the civilians in Iraq[49]. The IVth Geneva Convention prescribed a range of procedural due process rights for the civilian population in occupied territories that presaged the evolution of human rights norms following World War II[50]. The implementation of these goals in Iraq accorded with the established body of occupation law and simultaneously fulfilled the requirements of Security Council Resolution 1483 pursuant to the duty of all states to "accept and carry out the decisions of the Security Council."[51] Though Policy Memorandum Number 3 effectively aligned Iraqi domestic procedure and law with the requirements of international law, it was at best a stopgap measure that was neither designed nor intended to bear the full weight of prosecuting the range of crimes committed by the regime. Indeed, Section 1 of the original June 18, 2003 Policy Memorandum Number 3 expressly focused on the "need to transition" to an effective administration of domestic justice weaned from a "dependency on military support."[52]

The second paragraph of Article 64 of the IVth Convention is the key to understanding the promulgation of the IST. Juxtaposed against the Article 64 authority to "subject the population of the occupied territory to provisions which are essential to enable the Occupying Power to fulfill its obligation under the present Convention,"[53] Article 47 of the Fourth Convention makes clear that such "provisions" may include sweeping changes to the domestic legal and governmental structures. Article 47 implicitly concedes power to the occupying force to "change . . . the institutions or government" of the occupied territory, so long as those changes do not deprive the population of the benefits of the Civilians Convention[54]. Of particular note to the IST process, Article 47 also prevented the CPA from effectuating changes that would undermine the rights enjoyed by the civilian population "by any agreement concluded between the authorities of the occupied territories and the Occupying Power."[55] Thus, the CPA could not hide behind the fig leaf of domestic decision-making to simply stand by as domestic authorities in occupied Iraq created a process that would have undermined the human rights of those Iraqi citizens accused of even the most severe human rights abuses during the period of the "entombed regime." United States Army doctrine reflects this understanding of the normative relationship with the reminder that "restrictions placed upon the authority of a belligerent government cannot be avoided by a system of using a puppet government, central or local, to carry out acts which would have been unlawful if performed directly by the occupant."[56]

The Commentary to the IVth Geneva Convention also makes clear that the occupying power may modify domestic institutions (which would include the judicial system and the laws applicable thereto) when the existing institutions or government of the occupied territory operate to deprive human beings of "the rights and safeguards provided for them" under the Fourth Geneva Convention[57]. These provisions of occupation law are consistent with the allied experiences during the post-World War II occupations, and were intended to permit future occupation forces to achieve the salutary effects inherent in rebuilding or restructuring domestic legal systems when the demands of justice require such reconstruction. Against that legal backdrop, direct CPA promulgation of the IST Statute and the accompanying reforms to the existing Iraqi court system could have been justified based on any of the three permissible purposes specified in Article 64 of the

IVth Geneva Convention (*i.e.* fulfilling its treaty obligation to protect civilians, maintaining orderly government over a restless population demanding accountability for the crimes suffered under Saddam, or enhancing the security of coalition forces).

In other words, both Articles 47 and 64 provided a positive right to the CPA to impose a structure on the Iraqis for the prosecution of the gravest crimes of the Ba'athist regime. Given the state of occupation law, the reality of the matter is that the delegation of authority to the Governing Council to establish the IST meant that it was grounded in the soil of sovereignty rather than being susceptible to a portrayal of the Tribunal as a vehicle for foreign domination. If the CPA had the power to unilaterally create a structure for the prosecution of leading Ba'athists, the decision to delegate responsibility for developing and promulgating the IST to the Iraqi officials follows as a logical extension. Closer examination shows that the formation of the IST under the authority of the Iraqi Governing Council actually mirrored the practice in World War II occupations in which the British and Americans created guidelines to direct Germany towards democracy, but ultimately gave the Germans great latitude in rebuilding their country(58). At the same time, the affirmative obligations of Article 47 required a CPA role to ensure that the judicial structure that emerged as a function of Iraqi domestic politics and was promulgated as a domestic statute fully complied with relevant human rights obligations(59) as well as the specific treaty obligations that inhere to the people of Iraq as "protected persons" within the meaning of the Geneva Conventions. The development of the IST Statute was an authentic partnership between Iraqi officials and coalition officials who had the legal duty to protect the rights of all Iraqis. Nevertheless, the process of developing the statute was opaque to the outside world, which at the time allowed some observers to criticize the IST because of the perception (and assumption) that it would function in fact as a "puppet court of the occupying power."(60) Lawyers hired by Saddam Hussein's wife rapidly played the legitimacy card by claiming that the IST could not impose any punishments lawfully because it lacked legitimacy, or lawful creation(61).

Despite these early and unfounded criticisms, the delegation of authority to the Governing Council to develop and implement the IST did serve to increase the legitimacy of the institution and enhance the long range utility of the IST as a vehicle for restoring respect for the rule of law to the citizenry of Iraq. The people of Iraq demanded justice, and the eventual imposition of individual criminal responsibility on regime elites is likely to be far more beneficial to the ultimate restoration of respect for the rule of law when its genesis and execution are the responsibility of Iraqi officials whose interests are directly linked to the long term welfare of the Iraqi people.

THE STRUCTURE OF THE IRAQI SPECIAL TRIBUNAL

Organs of the Tribunal

The Iraqi jurists who gathered in Baghdad in December 2003 were anxious to learn about the best practices for ensuring a neutral and effective judicial system free to function beyond the reach of political control. The Statute echoes this concern by mandating in its very first provision that the IST "shall be an independent entity and not associated with any Iraqi government departments."(62) Because the Iraqi domestic system is built on a civil law model, the IST is the most modern effort to meld common and civil law principles into a consolidated system that comports with accepted standards of justice. The Tribunal is structured similarly to the existing *ad hoc* international tribunals in that it contains one or more Trial Chambers(63), and an Appeals Chamber(64) that is chaired by the President of the Tribunal who is responsible for exercising oversight of the "administrative and financial aspects of the Tribunal."(65)

Additionally, the Tribunal contains a Prosecutions Department of up to twenty prosecutors(66). Reflecting the concern of Iraqi jurists who watched the Ba'athist machinery corrode the rule of law, the Statute makes clear that "[e]ach Prosecutor shall act independently. He or she shall not seek or receive instructions from any Governmental Department or from any other source, including the Governing Council or the Successor Government."(67)

Lastly, up to twenty Tribunal Investigative Judges will be responsible for gathering evidence of crimes within the jurisdiction of the IST "from whatever source" considered "suitable."(68) As they investigate individuals for the commission of crimes proscribed under the Statute, the Investigative Judges will serve for a term of three years under terms and conditions as set out in the preexisting Iraqi Judicial Organization Law. As a critical aspect of their mandate, the Investigative Judges "shall act independently as a separate organ of the Tribunal"and "shall not seek or receive instructions from any Governmental Department, or from any other source, including the Governing Council or the Successor Government."[(69)]

Jurisdictional Reach of the IST

The principle that states are obligated to use domestic forums to punish violations of international law has roots that run back to the ideas of Hugo Grotius[(70)]. The United States Constitution incorporated this idea as an expression of congressional power in Article 1, § 8[(71)]. As early as 1842, American Secretary of State Daniel Webster articulated the idea that a nation's sovereignty also entails "the strict and faithful observance of all those principles, laws, and usages which have obtained currency among civilized states, and which have for their object the mitigation of the miseries of war."[(72)] Though internationalized judicial mechanisms have permanently altered the face of international law[(73)], the domestic courts of sovereign states are the courts of first resort while international mechanisms provide a useful but not essential backdrop in circumstances where the domestic courts are unable or unwilling to enforce individual accountability for serious violations of international norms[(74)]. The Iraqi Special Tribunal is built on the truism that sovereign states retain primary responsibility for adjudicating violations of crimes defined and promulgated under international law[(75)].

Grounded as it is in the right of a sovereign state to punish its nationals for violations of international norms, the temporal jurisdiction of the IST covers any Iraqi national or resident of Iraq charged with crimes listed in the Statute that were committed between July 17, 1968 and May 1, 2003 inclusive[(76)]. In addition, its geographic jurisdiction extends to acts committed on the sovereign soil of the Republic of Iraq, as well as those committed in other nations, including crimes committed in connection with Iraq's wars against the Islamic Republic of Iran and the State of Kuwait[(77)].

Articles 11-13 of the Statute establish the competence of the Tribunal to prosecute genocide (Article 11), crimes against humanity (Article 12), and war crimes committed during both international and non-international armed conflicts (Article 13)[(78)]. These substantive provisions are perhaps the most significant aspects of the Statute because they accurately incorporate the most current norms under international humanitarian law into the fabric of Iraqi domestic law for the first time. In addition, Article 14 conveys jurisdiction over a core group of crimes defined in the Iraqi criminal code[(79)]. Article 14 of the IST Statute is one of the strongest pieces of evidence that the drafting of the Statute was a genuine collaborative process in which the Governing Council spoke strongly on behalf of the citizens it represented.

The Iraqi lawyers involved in drafting the Statute educated the American lawyers about the contents of the Iraqi Criminal Code and demanded inclusion of a select list of domestic crimes because the proscribed acts were so corrosive to the rule of law inside Saddam's Iraq.

Article 14 accordingly reads as follows: The Tribunal shall have the power to prosecute persons who have committed the following crimes under Iraqi law:

(a) For those outside the judiciary, the attempt to manipulate the judiciary or involvement in the functions of the judiciary, in violation, *inter alia*, of the Iraqi interim constitution of 1970, as amended;

(b) The wastage of national resources and the squandering of public assets and funds, pursuant to, *inter alia*, Article 2(g) of Law Number 7 of 1958, as amended; and

(c) The abuse of position and the pursuit of policies that may lead to the threat of war or the use of the armed forces of Iraq against an Arab country, in accordance with Article 1 of Law Number 7 of 1958, as amended[(80)].

For armchair lawyers tempted to dismiss the Tribunal as a bald assertion of coalition power, Article 14 is a window into the soul of the Iraqi bar because it reveals the offenses deemed most egregious by peace-loving Iraqis seeking to rebuild an Iraq based on freedom. The officials who committed the acts included in Article 14 in essence waged war on the Iraqi people and society; the prosecution of those acts was seen *by the Iraqis* as a prerequisite for restoring the rule of law inside Iraq. From the Iraqi perspective, the crimes listed in Article 14 are of comparable severity to the grave violations of international norms found in Articles 11-13. Therefore, the Iraqis felt that prosecution of the domestic crimes described in Article 14 would be a necessary component of the broader IST objective of helping to heal the wounds inflicted on Iraqi society by the Ba'athists.

Furthermore, Article 14(a) is especially notable. Inclusion of the domestic offense of involvement in the functions of the judiciary implicitly signifies the urgent priority that the Iraqis attach to judicial independence. The International Covenant on Civil and Political Rights requires a "fair and public hearing by a competent, independent, and impartial tribunal established by law."(81) As a matter of historical record, the mechanics of establishing a judiciary free of political control was the very first question asked as the DIILS team began to teach the jurists assembled in Baghdad in December 2003(82) Ba'athist deprivation of trial rights and the subsequent imposition of punishment as an extension of Ba'athist political power unrelated to evidence had a traumatizing effect on Iraqi society. The search for truth based on evidence rather than raw power is the essence of a legitimate trial process. The perversion of legitimate judicial functions under the farce of politically motivated playacting was an especially galling aspect of Saddam's rule for those trained jurists whose proper judicial functions were bypassed and undermined by the regime.

Given this history, the provision of fair trials in the IST will be an important aspect of its legitimacy and serve as an important contrast to the fraudulent processes under the regime. The right to a fair and public hearing before an independent and impartial tribunal established by law is a basic right derived from both human rights norms(83) and the law of occupation (as a subset of the laws and customs of war)(84). While the Statute itself mandates the independent functioning of both the Investigative Judges and the Prosecution, there is no such correlative provision regarding the judges serving in either the Trial or Appeals Chambers. This gap led Human Rights Watch to recommend that the judges be required in writing to act independently and receive no instructions from any external source(85). Despite the picayune textual crease pointed out by Human Rights Watch, the very fact that the Iraqis demanded the inclusion of Article 14(a) strongly compels the conclusion that they will be keenly sensitive to any attempts to exert political control over the conduct of trials and fiercely resistant to external attempts to manipulate the IST.

The early experience of the IST also demonstrates that it is a robust institution that has to date been able to withstand pressures on its independent operation[86]. Awareness of Saddam's successful efforts to undermine the real rule of law through the façade of justice also explains one unusual but little noticed linguistic quirk found in the English translation of the IST Name. The jurists who gathered in Baghdad in December 2003 expressed a great deal of outrage at the manner in which the Hussein regime imposed its will on the Iraqi people through the use of Special or "Revolutionary" courts conducted by untrained minions[87]. As a group, they were pleased to see the inclusion of Article 14(a). Despite the fact that the Statute plainly covers the full range of crimes recognized under current international law (genocide, crimes against humanity, and violations of the laws and customs of war during both international and non-international armed conflicts), the Iraqi officials who drafted the Tribunal Statute were determined to demonstrate the contrast between the IST and the corrupt judicial farces ordered by the regime. As a deliberate amendment at the very last editing session, the authoritative Arabic text used a different term to make a clear distinction from the "Special" or "Revolutionary" courts run under Ba'athist authority, which resulted in a slightly off kilter English translation. Article 1 of the IST Statute accordingly states "[a] Tribunal is hereby established and shall be known as the "Iraqi Special Tribunal for Crimes Against Humanity."[88] This subtle, but powerful reminder shows the keen judicial awareness of the Iraqi lawyers responsible for the IST statute as well as their commitment to the long-term restoration of the rule of law within Iraq.

Procedural Rights for the Accused [89]

The provisions governing the right of the accused are among the most highly scrutinized and vital provisions of the IST Statute. The Coalition Provisional Authority Order that delegated authority to the Iraqi leaders to promulgate the Statute required that the IST meet "international standards of justice."[90] Under the terms of the

Statute, the Trial Chambers must "ensure that a trial is fair and expeditious and that proceedings are conducted in accordance with this Statute and the rules of procedure and evidence, with full respect for the rights of the accused and due regard for the protection of victims and witnesses."(91) To illustrate the transformation of justice in a free Iraq, the Statute specifies that "[n]o officer, prosecutor, investigative judge, judge or other personnel of the Tribunal shall have been a member of the Ba'ath Party."(92)

In its core operative provision, the Statute incorporates a full range of trial rights that, in the aggregate, are fully compatible with applicable human rights norms. Echoing the fundamental guarantees of the International Covenant on Civil and Political Rights(93) and other human rights instruments(94), Article 20 of the Statute states:

(a) All persons shall be equal before the Tribunal. (b) Everyone shall be presumed innocent until proven guilty before the Tribunal in accordance with the law. (c) In the determination of any charge, the accused shall be entitled to a public hearing, having regard to the provisions of the Statute and the rules of procedure made hereunder. (d) In the determination of any charge against the accused pursuant to the present Statute, the accused shall be entitled to a fair hearing conducted impartially and to the following minimum guarantees:

1. to be informed promptly and in detail of the nature, cause and content of the charge against him;
2. to have adequate time and facilities for the preparation of his defense and to communicate freely with counsel of his own choosing in confidence. The accused is entitled to have non-Iraqi legal representation, so long as the principal lawyer of such accused is Iraqi;
3. to be tried without undue delay;
4. to be tried in his presence, and to defend himself in person or through legal assistance of his own choosing; to be informed, if he does not have legal assistance, of this right; and to have legal assistance assigned to him, in any case where the interests of justice so require, and without payment by him in any such case if he does not have sufficient means to pay for it;

5. to examine, or have examined, the witnesses against him and to obtain the attendance and examination of witnesses on his behalf under the same conditions as witnesses against him. The accused shall also be entitled to raise defenses and to present other evidence admissible under this Statute and Iraqi law; and
6. not to be compelled to testify against himself or to confess guilt, and to remain silent, without such silence being a consideration in the determination of guilt or innocence.[95]

Article 20 of the IST Statute provides the range of personal rights to breathe life into the esoteric obligation found in Article 20 of the 1970 Interim Constitution of Iraq, which provides that an accused is "innocent, until proved guilty at a legal trial."[96] The constitution also proclaims in evocative terms that "the right of defence (sic) is sacred in all stages of investigation and trial in accordance with the provisions of the Law."[97] The parallelism between Article 20 of the Constitution and Article 20 of the IST Statute is pure coincidence, but illustrates a judicial integrity and awareness of individual rights that is ingrained in the Iraqi legal consciousness. During his first appearance before an IST investigative judge, Saddam Hussein challenged the legal authority of the IST and demanded to know "how can you charge me with anything without protecting my rights under the constitution."[98] At the time of this writing, Saddam remains in custody on the authority of the investigative judge who decided at that July 2004 hearing that there was probable cause to believe that he had committed one or more offenses within the jurisdiction of the IST; along with the other leading Ba'athists, he is not currently facing any definite criminal charges, but will eventually benefit from the procedural and personal rights embodied in the IST process.

THE HUMAN RIGHTS INFRASTRUCTURE OF THE IST

The Synthesis of Civil and Common Law in the IST

International tribunals and the more recent phenomenon of internationalized domestic tribunals require a complex intermingling of procedural approaches derived from both civil and common law. Modern accountability mechanisms permit a range of hearsay evidence that would never be admitted for trial purposes in common law courtrooms[99] while often providing provisions for plea agreements designed to enhance the efficiency of adjudication in a manner seldom seen in civil law systems[100]. Civil law systems driven by investigative judges provide for more expeditious trial proceedings which minimize discrimination between rich and poor perpetrators because the investigative judge is charged with collecting evidence to support all sides of the case (the defense team is therefore not required to spend its own resources in gathering exculpatory evidence)[101]. On the other hand, the adversarial system may be more suited to a full airing of the available evidence in court and may be best suited for the purpose of compiling an accurate and comprehensive record of the history associated with the crimes in question, which after all is one of the vital purposes of individual accountability mechanisms[102]. Paraphrasing Justice Jackson's assessment of the International Military Tribunal at Nuremberg, "no history" of the era of Iraq under Ba'athist rule will be "entitled to authority" if it ignores the factual and legal conclusions that will be presented in open court in the IST[103].

The procedures for the introduction of evidence are perhaps the most notable aspect of the commingling of common and civil law traditions. The International Military Tribunal at Nuremberg set the precedent for simplifying evidentiary requirements in favor of a full airing of available facts before a panel of judges. Justice Jackson noted "peculiar and technical rules of evidence developed under the common-law system of jury trials to prevent the jury from being influenced by improper evidence constitute a complex and artificial science," and accordingly accepted that rules of evidence at Nuremberg should put the premium on the probative value of the evidence[104]. Justice Jackson also commented on the reality that, while dispensing with rigid rules of evidence gave the International Military Tribunal "a large and somewhat unpredictable discretion," it also permitted both the prosecution and defense to select "evidence on the basis of what it was worth as proof rather than whether it complied with some technical requirement."[105]

Since 1945, rather than operating under restrictive rules of evidence, all of the tribunals applying international humanitarian law have permitted evidence so long as it is relevant and "necessary for the determination of the truth."[106] This standard (drawn from the International Criminal Court Statute) compares favorably to the IST Rule of Procedure that permits the Trial Chamber to admit "any relevant evidence which it deems to have probative value."[107] Rather than developing a straitjacket set of rules related to the introduction of evidence, the IST Trial Chamber has the broader mandate to "apply rules of evidence which will best favour (sic) a fair determination of the matter before it and [which] are consonant with the spirit of the Statute and general principles of law."[108] Of course, these evidentiary provisions operate against the backdrop of Iraqi procedural law that requires the prosecutor to produce a quantum of evidence sufficient to satisfy the court of the guilt of the defendant[109].

Regardless of the procedural forms adopted, international law is clear that no accused should face punishment unless convicted pursuant to a fair trial affording all of the essential guarantees embodied in widespread state practice[110]. Common Article 3 (meaning that it is repeated as article 3 in each of the four Geneva Conventions of 1949) states this principle with particularity by requiring that only a "regularly constituted court" may pass judgment on an accused person[111]. Interpreting this provision in light of state practice, the International Committee of the Red Cross (ICRC) concluded that a judicial forum is "regularly constituted if it has been established and organized in accordance with the laws and procedures already in force in a country."[112] Accepting the ICRC benchmark of legitimacy, the IST meets the criteria derived from the law of war better than any of the other tribunals established to adjudicate violations of humanitarian law because it is designed to apply the general principles of criminal law drawn from existing Iraqi criminal law rather than simply supplanting those norms with externally mandated principles. The IST Statute provides that the President of the Tribunal "shall be guided by the Iraqi Criminal Procedure Law" in the drafting of the rules of procedure and evidence for the admission of evidence as well as the other features of trial[113]. Furthermore, the Statute specifically lists the provisions of Iraqi law that contain the general principles of criminal law to be applied "in connection with the prosecution and trial of *any* accused person" (emphasis added)[114].

The structure of the IST and its accompanying procedures are similarly valid when measured against applicable human rights principles. The International Covenant on Civil and Political Rights (ICCPR) phrases the concept noted above as requiring that a tribunal be "established by law."[115] The United N tions Human Rights Commission adopted a functional test that the tribunal should "genuinely afford the accused the full guarantees" in its procedural protections[116]. Litigating its first case, the International Criminal Tribunal for the Former Yugoslavia (ICTY) was forced to determine whether this human right is violated *per se* by the prosecution of an accused before a post hoc tribunal created after the commission of the crimes[117]. Noting that the ICCPR drafters rejected language specifying that only "pre-established" forums would provide sufficient human rights protections, the ICTY Appeals Chamber concluded:

The important consideration in determining whether a tribunal has been "established by law" is not whether it was pre-established or established for a specific purpose or situation; what is important is that it be set up by a competent organ in keeping with the relevant legal procedures, and should that it observes the requirements of procedural fairness[118]. For the purposes of human rights law, the IST is "established by law" because it is established by the authorities empowered under both international law and the authority of the United Nations Security Council and because it is explicitly designed to provide the full range of human rights to the accused. The IST Statute establishes a firm duty on the court to "ensure that a trial is fair and expeditious and that proceedings are conducted in accordance with this Statute and the rules of procedure and evidence, with *full respect for the rights of the accused* and due regard for the protection of victims and witnesses" (emphasis added)[119]. Similarly, the Trial Chamber must "satisfy itself that the rights of the accused are respected"[120] and publicly support its decisions with "a reasoned opinion in writing, to which separate or dissenting opinions may be appended."[121] The Iraqi Judicial Law specifies that the judge shall be bound to "preserve the dignity of the judicature and to avoid any thing that arouses suspicion on his honesty."[122] An *a priori* conclusion that the IST judges will ignore their professional ethos by willfully undermining the rights of the accused would betray an unseemly smugness and paternalism on the part of the international community.

The fact of the matter is that the IST Statute and Rules of Procedure and Evidence are far from unique in their civil law foundations. Each conflict environment and accountability mechanism has required a slightly different set of blended procedures. For example, in the domestic prosecutions in Argentina, the trials were conducted using special procedures necessitated by the volume of information and the number of victims in comparison to normal crimes[(123)]. In the case of the IST, the civil law foundations of the Iraqi Criminal Code provided the baseline, which was then modified where appropriate to comply with relevant human rights norms and occupation law. Unlike the International Criminal Tribunal for the Former Yugoslavia[(124)] and the Special Court in Sierra Leone[(125)], the punitive authority of the IST derives from the sovereign authority of the Iraqi people rather than the derivative authority of the United Nations Security Council. The analytical start point for the IST is therefore found in the existing body of Iraqi laws and procedures, even though the eventual destination is on the same intellectual block as the other tribunals. Comparison of the *ad hoc* tribunals with the treaty based forums such as the International Criminal Court and the Special Court for Sierra Leone reveals that these tribunals borrow the "best" elements of both adversarial and inquisitorial trials. Where there are lacunae that remain in the IST Rules and Procedures, they are automatically filled by resort to the underlying principles of Iraqi domestic law, even as the judges are charged to interpret the substantive international crimes by "resort to the relevant decisions of international courts or tribunals as persuasive authority. . . ."[(126)]

Finally, the set of principles and rules emplaced at the formation of the IST will likely not solidify as rigid sets of static constraints. If the IST Rules and Procedures prove inadequate to ensure full respect for the rights of the accused as required by the Statute, then the judges may amend the rules accordingly[(127)]. The President of the International Criminal Tribunal for the Former Yugoslavia has said that the frequent amendments to the tribunal rules are necessary because the judges are "pragmatic people" grappling with the balance between truth and justice[(128)]. The ICTY Rules of Evidence and Procedure have thus been modified more than thirty times. In order to facilitate case management and improve the pace of trials, the ICTY judges have moved away from the common law moorings prevalent at formation of the ICTY and clearly evolved a more civil law centric set of rules and procedures[129].The conclusion is clear that the IST Rules and Statute are validly promulgated and legally sufficient to protect the fundamental rights of the accused, but may be amended if needed due to the emerging exigencies that may arise in the pragmatic application of the rules as they appear on paper.

Cornerstone Procedural Protections for the Accused

No legal issue related to the IST can be definitively determined by reference to a single source. Article 17(a) of the Statute sets out a hierarchy of sources that will guide the judges: (1) the Statute itself; (2) the Rules of Procedure and Evidence; and (3) the existing body of Iraqi Criminal Procedure and substantive laws[130]. In addition, the IST Statute makes clear that the judges "may resort to the relevant decisions of international courts or tribunals as persuasive authority for their decisions."[131] The IST Statute is linked to the underlying provisions of Iraqi domestic law and the Rules of Procedure and Evidence to form a tightly woven fabric of legal protections. Accordingly, any conclusions derived about the core principles and protections of the IST can be drawn only after ALL of the relevant sources are considered. In a sense, the IST is similar to the ICTY•in that the judges will rely to some extent on analogy to the national laws of the territory where the conflict occurred or to what they perceive to be the practices of other states or tribunals in applying the sophisticated set of principles found in international humanitarian law. This is identical to the repeated methodology of the ICTY judges[132]. The difference for the IST judges is that the Iraqi process is explicitly built on the preexisting foundation of domestic law familiar to the judges; hence, the IST Rules of Procedure and the Statute are often silent or incomplete on a given subject precisely because the issue is definitively addressed in the underlying domestic Code. This article will conclude by pointing out some of the most notable areas where a casual reading of the IST Statute alone would lead to shallow or incomplete conclusions about the extent of IST protection of the defendant's human rights.

Provision of Counsel

Article 20 of the IST Statute provides for the fundamental right "to have adequate time and facilities for the preparation of [the] defense and to communicate freely with counsel . . . in confidence."[133] Such counsel may include non-Iraqi lawyers, so long as the "principal lawyer" is an Iraqi[134]. The IST Statute further provides that the Tribunal will pay for the costs of counsel "in any such case if he or she does not have sufficient means to pay for it."[135] The experience of the ICTY indicates that this will be a major expense associated with the IST, as the provision of gratis counsel consumed ten per cent of the ICTY budget, to the tune of some $10-13 million per [136] year.

The counsel retained by a suspect or accused is then required to "file his power of attorney with the Judge concerned at the earliest opportunity."[137] The Judge, in turn, shall consider the counsel to be qualified "in accordance with the *Iraqi law of lawyers*" (emphasis added)[138]. This small phrase constitutes an important safeguard in the IST process because it means that the counsel who will practice in the IST chambers remain bound by the codes of practice and ethics governing their profession and are qualified in accordance with the rigorous standards found in Iraqi law[139]. In light of the serious allegations of misconduct of counsel in other tribunals[140], the IST Rules provide that a judge or chamber may impose sanctions against counsel whose "conduct remains offensive or abusive, demeans the dignity of the Special Tribunal, [or] obstructs the proceedings."[141]

Furthermore, the fact that the principal attorney remains bound by the Iraqi code of professional conduct gives some force to the underlying right of the court to "prevent the parties and their representatives from speaking at undue length or speaking outside the subject of the case, repeating statements, violating guidelines or making accusations against another party or a person outside the case who is unable to put forward a defense (sic)."[142]

Apart from providing for the appointment of counsel, the IST gives counsel a robust and visible role. The IST Rules stipulate that the investigating judge must notify all suspects of the following rights "in a language he speaks and understands" during their first appearance for questioning:

(i) The right to legal assistance of his own choosing, including the right to have legal assistance provided by the Defense Office if he does not have sufficient means to pay for it;

(ii) The right to have the free assistance of an interpreter if he cannot understand or speak the language to be used for questioning;

(iii) The right to remain silent. In this regard, the suspect or accused shall be cautioned that any statement he makes may be recorded and may be used in evidence[143].

In accordance with Iraqi procedural law, any statement of the accused to the investigating judge is recorded in the written record and "signed by the accused and the magistrate or investigator."[144] Thus, every suspect (to include Saddam Hussein) who has appeared before the IST investigative judges to date has been notified of their rights to counsel and has acknowledged their comprehension of those rights in writing. Those who assume that the IST will ignore and subvert the rights of defendants in the future must also assume that the investigative judges will abandon this established practice, but in doing so they would depart from a foundational aspect of criminal practice in Iraq which by an measure meets human rights standards.

Of course, as would be expected, an accused may voluntarily waive his right to have legal assistance during questioning, but only if the Investigative Judge determines that the waiver is voluntarily and intelligently made[145]. The Investigative Judge "shall not proceed without the presence of counsel" when questioning a suspect who has invoked the right to assistance[146]. Furthermore, if a suspect has waived his right to counsel but then invokes that right, "the questioning should be stopped and never resume again until the defence (sic) be present."[147] These provisions comport fully with the relevant human rights provisions and are in complete accordance with the practices of other international tribunals[148].

Conduct of the Defense

The primary gap on the face of the IST Statute is that it is silent on the actual provisions for the defense of an accused. Of course, Article 20 protects the right to present a full defense, but the Statute itself does not reveal the manner in which those protections can be achieved. Rule 49 of the IST Rules of Evidence and Procedure outlines the functions of the Defense Office as a separate organ inside the IST, beginning with the requirement that the IST Director "shall establish a Defense Office for the purpose of ensuring the rights of accused."[149] From that premise, the defense team operates against the mesh of practice built into the IST framework.

The entire Iraqi criminal justice system is grounded on the role of the investigative judge as an impartial authority whose mandate is to objectively search for all available evidence, both incriminating and exculpatory[150]. Indeed, under Iraqi law, investigating officers "are required to use all available means to preserve evidence of an offense,"[151] and must prepare the written report collating the evidence for the subsequent use of trial judges in the event that charges are documented to warrant a trial[152]. The IST Rules build on this practice by requiring the prosecutor to provide all exculpatory evidence to the defense, as well as any evidence which "may be relevant to issues raised in the Defense Case Statement."[153] Under the normal principles of Iraqi law, the trial courts rely on the findings of investigative judges and the written report as being dispositive on factual matters; hence the additional overlay of an IST trial process flavored with the adversarial model could logically lead to longer trials which may or may not serve the true interests of justice from the societal and personal perspectives[154].

On the other hand, in preparing for a full trial of the issues, the defense team benefits from the underlying provisions of Iraqi criminal procedure law in two major ways. First, the defense team may leverage the power of the investigative process to generate information or perspective relevant to the conduct of the defense. The Iraqi criminal procedure code permits the investigator to appoint, at government expense, one or more experts on matters "connected to the offense being investigated."[155] The investigative judge may retain an expert "of his own accord or based on the request of the parties."[156]

Secondly, in the preliminary investigation stage of any criminal proceeding under the Iraqi civil law system, the investigating judge has full *subpoena* power to compel the production of relevant evidence. The investigative judge may "issue an order for the arrest of any witness who fails to attend in due time for him to be compelled to attend in order to give evidence."[157] Similarly, the investigating judge has authority to order physical searches of places or persons[158]. The IST Rules embody this practice in that "either party" may request that the investigative judge "make such orders, summonses, subpoenas and warrants as may be necessary in the interests of justice."[159]

Prevention of Coercion

Perhaps the most misunderstood and most vital aspect of the IST structure is the mechanism to prevent the use of any evidence adduced by torture or other improper techniques. Just as in other war crimes trials, cases before the IST may rely in part on evidence obtained prior to the time the defendant or other persons enjoyed a binding right to counsel[160]. Nevertheless, the Trial Chambers of the IST hold the penultimate power to protect the basic human rights of the accused. Though empowered to admit relevant evidence based on its probative value alone, the Trial Chamber should consider "[t]he voluntariness of any statement and any circumstances that might verify or impugn the statement."[161] In particular, the IST Rules come closer to a full blown exclusionary rule than almost any foreign jurisdiction by requiring the Trial Chamber to consider whether "the means by which evidence was obtained casts substantial doubt on its reliability."[162]

Apart from the specific admonition noted above to the suspect or accused that any statement may be recorded and used as evidence (which is acknowledged and signed by both the accused and the investigative judge), the IST requirements exceed even United States domestic law by requiring:

Whenever an Investigative Judge questions an accused, the questioning shall be recorded by audio, video, court reporter or by other means. The accused shall be informed that the questioning is being recorded. At the conclusion of the questioning the accused shall be offered the opportunity to clarify anything he has said, and to add anything he may wish, and the time of conclusion shall be recorded. The content of the recording shall then be transcribed (if done by audio or video) as soon as practicable after the conclusion of questioning and a copy of the transcript supplied to the suspect[163].

In practice, these recordings and the subsequent transcriptions should more than suffice to persuade fair-minded observers that the IST Trial Processes and ultimate judgments do not derive from coercive techniques.

These IST procedures are also built on a deeper tradition of respect that is ingrained in Iraqi criminal procedure (though it is fair to assume that the perception of the world is colored by the willful abuses of these basic human rights under the Ba'athist regime). For example, at the investigative stage, a witness "may not be addressed in a declaratory or insinuating manner and no sign or gesture may be directed at him that would tend to intimidate, confuse or distress him."(164) Any public official or agent who uses torture to extract evidence from "an accused, witness, or informant" also commits a crime under the Iraqi criminal code(165). As a logical extension of this criminal prohibition, Iraqi procedural law prohibits the "use of any illegal method to influence the accused and extract a confession."(166) Finally, the IST incorporates the underlying norm of Iraqi criminal procedure in that the court can accept a confession only if it has been corroborated and when "it is satisfied with it."(167) Similarly, Iraqi law requires that "it is a condition of the acceptance of the confession that it is not given as a result of coercion."(168) Those who ignore these established jurisprudential roots to believe that the IST process will ignore and undermine core human rights protections betray an unseemly smugness that is unwarranted by the actual provisions of law and the IST guarantees as they will be implemented in practice.

CONCLUSION

The Iraqi people almost universally support the concept of prosecuting Saddam and other Ba'athist officials inside Iraq rather than simply allowing an external tribunal to exercise punitive power(169). They suffered the injustices and indignities of the Ba'athist regime and have the strongest stake in the restoration of authentic justice. For the ancient Greeks, the pursuit of justice symbolized a quest for order and harmony(170). Plato conceived of justice as "the highest order of things" on both the personal and societal level(171). The aspiration for justice embodies the proper balance of power, wisdom, and temperance which in turn generate societal stability. In any case, it seems clear that the choice of punishments should be reserved for sovereign governments answerable to a society in which they live and work rather than the mandarins who minister to the machinery of international politics(172). The Iraqis deserve the frontline role in serving the needs of their own nation, and their families and their culture. They are best placed to make the difficult decisions over how many of the millions of possible charges should be investigated and where the proper balance between justice and vengeance should be struck[(173)]. The lawyers and investigators who have risked their lives and endangered their families by agreeing to serve their nation on the IST are patriots worthy of our respect and our assistance.

The formation of the IST as a domestic mechanism created under the authority of a sovereign Iraqi government culminates the developmental arc of recent efforts to implement accountability[(174)] for violations of international humanitarian law. The IST is closer to the conflict in temporal terms as well as the available evidence and the victims of the crimes[(175)] The Iraqi people will determine the legitimacy and ultimate effectiveness of the trials, and they will reap the benefits derived from restoring the rule of law, just as at the time of this writing they are currently paying a disproportionate share of the costs for the insurgents who continue to murder civilians. The IST also represents a return to the first principles of international criminal law because it is grounded in the fertile soil of state sovereignty. In light of the inspiring growth of the field of international criminal law since World War II, it is often forgotten that the Moscow Declaration specifically favored punishment through the national courts in the countries where the crimes were committed "according to the laws of these liberated countries and of the free governments which will be erected therein."[(176)] The military commissions established in the Far East similarly incorporated the principle that the international forum did not supplant domestic mechanisms[(177)]. Even the Secretary-General of the United Nations Security Council is persuaded that "no rule of law reform, justice reconstruction, or transitional justice initiative imposed from the outside can hope to be successful or sustainable."[(178)]

Truth-based trials that conform to the principles of fundamental fairness will be a tangible demonstration that Iraqi society is on the road to a future built on the values of justice and personal liberty. The IST may not be a perfect creation, and it will certainly suffer growing pains as it grapples with the incredibly complex and emotionally charged cases that lie down the road to justice. "Justice" is an intellectual abstraction achieved only through emotional investment and intellectual struggle. The drafters of the IST and those patriots who will implement its provisions are all too aware that willful failure to protect basic human rights could corrode the very core of the society that they have risked their lives to build. If those who claim to support the principles of justice and of the rule of law refuse to help in the name of human rights, they can only do so by turning a blind eye to the rich jurisprudential roots of the IST. As the Iraqis build a rule of law for themselves, those who advocate the rule of law should extend their solidarity rather than seeking to elbow the Iraqis aside and substitute an artificial view of what they deem best for Iraq.

NOTES

1. See Michael A. Newton, Harmony or Hegemony? The American Military Role in the Pursuit of Justice, 19 *CONN J. INT'L L.*, 231 (2004).
2. Interview with David Hodgkinson, Office of Human Rights and Transitional Justice, Coalition Provisional Authority, Baghdad (Dec. 11, 2003).
3. Statute of the Iraqi Special Tribunal, Dec. 10, 2003, Art. 38, 43 I.L.M. 231, *available at http://iraq-ist.org/en/about/statute.htm, (last visited June 4, 2005) [hereinafter IST Statute].*
4. *See* Defense Institute of International Legal Studies Mission, *at http://www.dsca.mil/diils/* (last revised May 5, 2005). The Defense Institute of International Legal Studies (DIILS) provides education teams to address over 330 legal topics, with a focus on Justice Systems, the Rule of Law, and the execution of disciplined military operations. Since its inception in 1992, DIILS officers have presented programs tailored to the needs of the host country to over 23,000 senior military and civilian government officials in 95 nations around the world. Seminars are designed for audiences of 40 to 60 military and civilian executive personnel from the host country, and take place both in the host nation and in the United States.
5. The members of the joint team of military lawyers knew of the apprehension just prior to the receipt of the news by the judges. A cell phone rang, and one of the judges sprang to his feet and interrupted the ongoing class. He shouted the news, and the entire class disintegrated for the day. The celebratory fire of AK-47s punctuated the Iraqi afternoon and lasted most of the night. The classroom celebration was long and joyous as normally reserved older gentlemen danced and hugged and cried with relief at the news. For a description of the broader mood of the Iraqi people, see Anne

Barnard & Michael Kranish, *Baghdad Falls: Euphoric Iraqis Topple Symbols; US Warns That War Not Over*, BOSTON GLOBE, Apr. 10, 2003, at A1.

6. Non-governmental Organizations and the U.S. Department of State have catalogued a panoply of human rights abuses under Saddam's rule in Iraq, inter alia, the deaths of 50,000 to 100,000, Kurds; the destruction of 2,000 Kurdish villages; the internal displacement of 900,000 Iraqi civilians; summary executions of over 10,000 political opponents; beheadings; prostitution; and the intentional deprivation of food to the civilian population. OFFICE OF THE PRESS SECRETARY, THE WHITE HOUSE, PAST REPRESSION AND ATROCITIES BY SADDAM HUSSEIN'S REGIME, (Apr. 4, 2003), *available at http://www.state.gov/s/wci/fs/19352.htm (last visited* June 4, 2005).

7. *See, e.g.*, Georges Anglade, *Rules, Risks, and Rifts in the Transition to Democracy in Haiti*, 20 FORDHAM INT'L L.J. 1176, 1190 (1997) ("In the presence of an inhuman spectacle of misery and its urgent material needs, one tends to forget that the primary needs of people are liberty, justice, and security. Because a pauper also needs justice, the object of a transition to democracy becomes the modern organization of justice in a State of law. This demands destruction of the old military-police apparatus in order to give birth to another organization in charge of public order. It also requires that the institutions of justice and the body of functionaries that make them work be reconsidered so as to produce a 'just justice' and in order to guarantee a 'free freedom.' Haiti must reconstruct judicial power separate from the executive power, which too often has controlled judicial power. Justice by law is thus the initial goal in the transition to democracy as well as the object of the transition itself. It is essentially through the achievement of this goal that Haiti can unite a country broken in two, and create a single people from two profoundly antagonistic factions. Economic analysis also poses justice as a preliminary condition necessary to development.").

8. *See* IST Statute, art. 1, Dec. 10, 2003, art. 38, 43 I.L.M. 231, *available at http://iraq-ist.org/en/about/statute.htm* (last visited June 4, 2005).

9. *See generally* Annex to Hague Convention IV Regulations Respecting the Laws and Customs of War on Land, Oct. 18, 1907, Arts. 42-56, (entered into force Jan. 26, 1910), *reprinted in* Documentation on the Laws of War 73 (3d ed., Adam Roberts & Richard Guelff eds., 2000) [*hereinafter* 1907 Hague Regulations]; Geneva Convention Relative to the Protection of Civilian Persons in Time of War, Aug. 12, 1949, arts. 47-78, 6 U.S.T. 3516, 75 U.N.T.S. 287 [hereinafter Civilians Convention].

10. 1907 Hague Regulations, Oct. 18, 1907, art. 42, *reprinted in* Documentation on the Laws of War 73 (3d ed., Adam Roberts & Richard Guelff eds., 2000). *See also* DEPARTMENT OF THE ARMY, FIELD MANUAL 27-10: THE LAW OF LAND WARFARE, 351 (1956) [hereinafter FM 27-10] (devoting the whole of Chapter 6 of the United States Army Field Manual related to the law of armed conflict to explicating the text of the law related to occupation as well as the United States policy related to occupation), *available at http://www.globalsecurity.org/military/library/policy/army/fm/27-10/* (last visited Jul. 25, 2005).

11. UK Ministry of Defence, the Manual of the Law of Armed Conflict 275, 11.3 (2004).

12. FM 27-10, *supra* note 12, 352.

13. Protocol I Additional to the Geneva Conventions of 12 August 1949 and Relating to the Protection of Victims Of International Armed Conflicts, Annex I, art. 4, U.N. Doc. A/32/144 (1977), 16 I.L.M. 1391 (1977), 1125 U.N.T.S 3, (entered into force Dec. 7, 1978) [hereinafter Protocol I]. The United States policy in this regard is clear that occupation confers only the "means of exercising control for the period of occupation. It does not transfer the sovereignty to the occupant, but simply the authority or power to exercise some of the rights of sovereignty." FM 27-10, *supra* note 12, 358.

14. 1907 Hague Regulations, Oct. 18, 1907, art. 42, *reprinted in* Documentation on the Laws of War 73 (3d ed., Adam Roberts & Richard Guelff eds., 2000).

15. *Id.* The conceptual limitations of foreign occupation also warranted a temporal limitation built into the 1949 Geneva Conventions that the general "application of the present Convention [law of occupation] shall cease one year after the general close of military operations . . . " *Id.* at art. 6. Based on pure pragmatism, Article 6 of the th Geneva Convention does permit the application of a broader range of specific treaty provisions "for the duration of the occupation, to the extent that such Power exercises the functions of government in such territory . . . ." *Id.* The 1977 Protocols eliminated the patchwork approach to treaty protections with the simple declarative that "the application of the Conventions and of this Protocol shall cease, in the territory of the Parties to the conflict, on the general close of military operations and, in the case of occupied territories, on the termination of the occupation . . . ." Protocol I, art. 3(b), U.N. Doc. A/32/144 (1977), 16 I.L.M. 1391 (1977), 1125 U.N.T.S 3.

16. *See* S.C. Res. 827, U.N. SCOR, 3217th mtg., U.N. Doc. S/RES/827 (1993).

17. U.N. CHARTER art. 39 (giving the Security Council the power to "determine the existence of any threat to peace, breach of the peace, or act of aggression" and it "shall make recommendations, or decide what measures shall be taken in accordance with Article[] 41 . . . to maintain or restore international peace and security").
18. *See also infra* note 114 and accompanying text for a similar conclusion in relation to the creation of the Special Court for Sierra Leone on the basis of an agreement between the Security Council and the government of Sierra Leone.
19. *Prosecutor v. Tadic*, Case No.: IT-94-1, Decision on the Defence Motion on Jurisdiction, Aug. 10, 1995, *available at http://www.un.org/icty/tadic/trialc2/decision-e/100895.htm* (last visited June 26, 2005) ("[T]his International Tribunal is not a constitutional court set up to scrutinise the actions of organs of the United Nations. It is, on the contrary, a criminal tribunal with clearly defined powers, involving a quite specific and limited criminal jurisdiction. If it is to confine its adjudications to those specific limits, it will have no authority to investigate the legality of its creation by the Security Council.").
20. U.N. CHARTER art. 24(1).
21. *Supra* note 16 and accompanying text.
22. Civilians Convention, Aug. 12, 1949, arts. 68, 78, 6 U.S.T. 3516, 75 U.N.T.S. 287 (permitting detention of civilians for "imperative reasons of security").
23. Civilians Convention, Aug. 12, 1949, art. 42, 6 U.S.T. 3516, 75 U.N.T.S. 287.
24. *See Prosecutor v. Delalic*, Case No. IT-96-21-A, Judgment (Feb. 20, 2001), *available at http://www.un.org/icty/celebici/appeal/judgement/cel-aj010220.pdf* (last visited June 26, 2005).
25. Civilians Convention, Aug. 12, 1949, art. 47, 6 U.S.T. 3516, 75 U.N.T.S. 287.
26. *See* Jean S. Pictet, Principles Du Droit International Humanitaire, CICR, Genève, at 50 (1966).
27. FM 27-10, *supra note* 12, 370.
28. Civilians Convention, Aug. 12, 1949, art. 54, 6 U.S.T. 3516, 75 U.N.T.S. 287 ("[T]he Occupying Power may not alter the status of public officials or judges, or in any way apply sanctions to or take measures of coercion or discrimination against them should they abstain from fulfilling their functions for reasons of conscience.").
29. 1907 Hague Regulations, Oct. 18, 1907, art. 43, *reprinted in* Documentation on the Laws of War 73 (3d ed., Adam Roberts & Richard Guelff eds., 2000).

30. *Id.*

31. Yoram Dinstein, *Legislation Under Article 43 of the Hague Regulations: Belligerent Occupation and Peacebuilding, in* 1 Program on Humanitarian Policy and Conflict Research Harvard University Occasional Paper Series 8 (Fall 2004). *See also* E.H. Schwenk, *Legislative Powers of the Military Occupant Under Article 43, Hague Regulations* 54 YALE L.J. 393 (1945).

32. Morris Greenspan, The Modern Law of Land Warfare 223-27 (1959).

33. For example, German forces were able to commit almost unthinkable brutalities under the shield of Nazi sovereignty based on the *Fuehrerprinzip* (leadership principle) imposed by Hitler to exercise his will as supreme through the police, the courts, the military, and all the other institutions of organized German society. The oath of the Nazi party stated: "I owe inviolable fidelity to Adolf Hitler; I vow absolute obedience to him and to the leaders he designates for me." Drexel A. Sprecher, Inside the Nuremberg Trial: A Prosecutor's Comprehensive Account 1037-38 (1999). Accordingly, power resided in Hitler, from whom subordinates derived absolute authority in hierarchical order. This absolute and unconditional obedience to the superior in all areas of public and private life led, in Justice Jackson's famous words, to "a National Socialist despotism equalled [sic] only by the dynasties of the ancient East." Opening Statement to the International Military Tribunal at Nuremberg, II Trial of the Major War Criminals before the International Military Tribunal 99-100 (1947).

34. G. Schwarzenberger, the Law of Armed Conflict 194 (1968).

35. Civilians Convention, Aug. 12, 1949, Art. 64, 6 U.S.T. 3516, 75 U.N.T.S. 287.

36. Vienna Convention on the Law of Treaties, art. 31(1), 1155 U.N.T.S. 331, 8 I.L.M. (1969) (entered into force Jan. 27, 1980).

37. UK Ministry of Defense, The Manual of the Law of Armed Conflict 293, 11.56 (2004). *See also* FM 27-10, *supra* note 12, 371 ("Nature of Laws Suspended or Repealed. The occupant may alter, repeal, or suspend laws of the following types:

    a. Legislation constituting a threat to its security, such as laws relating to recruitment and the bearing of arms.

    b. Legislation dealing with political process, such as laws regarding the rights of suffrage and of assembly.

    c. Legislation the enforcement of which would be inconsistent with the duties of the occupant, such as laws establishing racial discrimination.)

38. The Mission Statement read in full as follows: "The Coalition Provisional Authority (CPA) is the name of the temporary governing body which has been designated by the United Nations as the lawful government of Iraq until such time as Iraq is politically and socially stable enough to assume its sovereignty. The CPA has been the government of Iraq since the overthrow of the brutal dictatorship of Saddam Hussein and his deeply corrupt Ba'ath Regime in April of 2003." Coalition Provisional Authority, Overview, *available at http://www.iraqcoalition.org/bremerbio.html* (last visited June 4, 2005).

39. Coalition Provisional Authority Regulation Number 1 (May 16, 2003), *available at http://www.cpa-iraq.org/regulations/20030516_CPAREG_1_The_Coalition_Provisional_Authority_.pdf.* (last visited June 4, 2005). The CPA website is the only existing public record of actions taken by the Coalition Provisional Authority.

40. *See* Letter from the Permanent Representatives of the UK and the US to the UN Addressed to the President of the Security Council, May 8, 2003, UN Doc. S/2003/538, *available at http://www.globalpolicy.org/security/issues/iraq/document/2003/0608usukletter.htm (last* visited June 26, 2005).

41. S.C. Res. 1483, U.N. SCOR, 58th Sess., 4761st mtg. 4, U.N. Doc. S/RES/1483 (2003).

42. S.C. Res. 1483, *supra* note 43, at 5.

43. *Id.*

44. *Id.* at ¶ 4.

45. General Eisenhower's Proclamation said, "Supreme legislative, judicial, and executive authority and powers within the occupied territory are vested in me as Supreme Commander of the Allied Forces and as Military Governor, and the Military Government is established to exercise these powers . . . ." *Reprinted in* Office of Military Government for Germany (U.S), Military Government Gazette, Issue A, Page 1 (June 1, 1946) (copy on file with author).

46. The IVth Geneva Convention recognized the importance of individual rights enjoyed by the civilian population and the correlative duties of the occupier to that population. The structure of the IVth Convention rejected the concept of *debellatio* by focusing on the duties that an Occupying Power has towards the individual civilians and the overall societal structure rather than focusing on the relations between the victorious sovereign and the defeated government. Under the rejected concept of *debellatio,* the enemy was utterly defeated and accordingly the defeated state forfeited its legal personality and was absorbed into the sovereignty of the occupier. GREENSPAN, *supra* note 34, at

600-01. The successful negotiation of the Geneva Conventions in the aftermath of World War II marked the definitive rejection of the concept of *debellatio,* under which the occupier assumed full sovereignty over the civilians in the occupied territory. Eyal Benvenisti, The International Law of Occupation 95 (1993). *Debellatio* "refers to a situation in which a party to a conflict has been totally defeated in war, its national institutions have disintegrated, and none of its allies continue militarily to challenge the enemy on its behalf." *Id.* at 92.

47. Coalition Provisional Authority Order Number 7: Penal Code, June 9, 2003, Doc. No. CPA/ORD/9 June 2003/07, *available at* http:// *www.cpa-iraq.org/regulations/index.html#Orders (last visited June* 4, 2005) (copy on file with author).

48. *Id.*

49. Coalition Provisional Authority Memorandum Number 3: Criminal Procedures was revised on June 27, 2004. It is available at *http:// www.iraqcoalition.org/regulations/index.html#Memoranda (last* visited June 4, 2005).

50. Articles 64-78 of the IVth Convention detail a range of specific rights belonging to the civilian population of the occupied territory that correspond to those generally accepted as core human rights provisions, *inter alia,* the right to a fair trial with the accompanying due process, credit for pretrial confinement, etc. Civilians Convention, Aug. 12, 1949, arts. 64-78, 6 U.S.T. 3516, 75 U.N.T.S. 287. *Cf.* International Covenant on Civil and Political Rights, G.A. Res. 2200 (XXI), U.N. GAOR, 21st Sess., Supp. No. 16, at 52, art. 14, U.N. Doc. A/6316 (1966), 999 U.N.T.S. 171, 6 I.L.M. 368 (1967), (entered into force Mar. 23, 1976) (describing analogous provisions derived from international human rights law) [hereinafter ICCPR].

51. U.N. CHARTER art. 25.

52. Copy on file with author.

53. Civilians Convention, Aug. 12, 1949, art. 64(2), 6 U.S.T. 3516, 75 U.N.T.S. 287.

54. Civilians Convention, Aug. 12, 1949, art. 47, 6 U.S.T. 3516, 75 U.N.T.S. 287. *See also* FM 27-10, *supra* note 12, 365.

55. Civilians Convention, Aug. 12, 1949, art. 47, 6 U.S.T. 3516, 75 U.N.T.S. 287.

56. FM 27-10, *supra* note 12, 366 (further specifying that "Acts induced or compelled by the occupant are nonetheless its acts).

57. *See* IV Commentary on the Geneva Convention Relative to the Protection of Civilian Persons in Time of War 274 (O.M. Uhler & H.

Coursier eds. 1960) (explaining the intended implementation of the language of Article 47, Civilians Convention, Aug. 12, 1949, art. 47, 6 U.S.T. 3516, 75 U.N.T.S. 287: "any change introduced" to domestic institutions by the occupying power must protect the rights of the civilian population).

58. See Walter M. Hudson, The U.S. Military Government and the Establishment of Democratic Reform, Federalism, and Constitutionalism During the Occupation of Bavaria, 1945-47, 180 MIL. L. REV. 115, 123 (2004).

59. A full discussion of the extent to which human rights law applies in an occupation environment is beyond the scope of this paper. There is a growing awareness that some aspects of human rights may apply extraterritorially alongside the conventional obligations found in occupation law. The precise interrelationship between occupation law and human rights norms is debatable and ill-defined at present. See, e.g., European Court of Human Rights, Bankovic a.o. v. Belgium and 16 Other Contracting States, 12 Dec. 2001, Application No. 52207/99, para. 71 admissibility decision (rejected on jurisdictional grounds) (declaring in dicta on the one hand that the European Convention may impose obligations on states parties anywhere they exercise "effective control" while in another paragraph, para. 80, limiting that gratuitous language to territory that "for the specific circumstances, would normally be covered by the Convention" which means those state parties signatory). Contra European Court of Human Rights, Issa a.o. v. Turkey, 30 May 2000, Application No. 31821/96. (prove & edit) Obliquely referring to the connection between the two distinct bodies of law, the Inter-American Commission on Human Rights noted in dicta that While the extraterritorial application of the American Declaration has not been placed at issue by the parties, the Commission finds it pertinent to note that, under certain circumstances, the exercise of its jurisdiction over acts with an extraterritorial locus will not only be consistent with but required by the norms which pertain. The fundamental rights of the individual are proclaimed in the Americas on the basis of the principles of equality and non-discrimination—"without distinction as to race, nationality, creed or sex." Given that individual rights inhere simply by virtue of a person's humanity, each American State is obliged to uphold the protected rights of any person subject to its jurisdiction. While this most commonly refers to persons within a state's territory, it may, under given circumstances, refer to conduct with an extraterritorial locus where the person concerned is present in the territory of one state, but subject to the control of another state--usually through the acts of the latter's agents abroad. In principle, the inquiry

turns not on the presumed victim's nationality or presence within a particular geographic area, but on whether, under the specific circumstances, the State observed the rights of a person subject to its authority and control.

Inter-American Commission on Human Rights, *Coard v. United States*, 29 Sept. 29, 1999, Case 10.951, Report No. 109/00, 37, *available at http://www.oas.org* (last visited June 26, 2005).

60. Michael P. Scharf, *Is It International Enough? A Critique of the Iraqi Special Tribunal in Light of the Goals of International Justice*, 2 J. OF INT'L. CRIM. JUST. 330, 331 (2004) (the gravamen of the criticism was focused on the truisms that the IST statute had been drafted during the occupation by the United States, its funding was coming from the United States, its judges were selected by the U.S.-appointed provisional government, and the judges and prosecutors were to be assisted by U.S. advisors).

61. *See* Rory McCarthy & Jonathan Steele, *Legitimacy and Neutrality of Court Will Be Challenged*, THE GUARDIAN (London), July 2, 2004, *available at http://www.guardian.co.uk/Iraq/Story/0,2763,1252096,00.html* (last visited June 26, 2005).

62. IST Statute, art. 1(a), Dec. 10, 2003, art. 38, 43 I.L.M. 231, *available at http://iraq-ist.org/en/about/statute.htm* (last visited June 4, 2005). On May 8, 2004, Ambassador Bremer issued Coalition Provisional Authority Memorandum Number 12: Administration of Independent Judiciary, which laid out the governmental structures and procedures needed to ensure a robust and independent judiciary, *available at* http:// *www.iraqcoalition.org/regulations/index.html#* Memoranda (last visited June 4, 2005).

63. Each of which, according to Article 4 of the Statute, will consist of five "permanent independent judges" and independent reserve judges. IST Statute, art. 4(a)-(b), Dec. 10, 2003, art. 38, 43 I.L.M. 231, *available at http://iraq-ist.org/en/about/statute.htm. htm* (last visited June 4, 2005).

64. The Appeals Chamber has "the power to review the decisions of the Trial Chambers." *Id.* at art. 3. The IST Appeals Chamber proceedings should be deemed sufficient to protect the basic human right to an appeal just as the ICTY, ICTR, and ICC appellate chambers have been accepted by states.

65. *Id.* at art. 4(c)(ii).

66. *Id.* at art. 8(c).

67. *Id.* at art. 8(b).

68. *Id.* at art. 7(c), (i).

69. *Id* at art. 7(j).

70. *See* Richard Tuck, The Rights of War and Peace: Political Thought and The International Order from Grotius to Kant 102-03(1999).

71. Empowering the Legislative Branch to "Define and Punish Piracies and Felonies Committed on the High Seas, and Offenses against the Law of Nations." U.S. CONST. Art I, § 8.

72. John Bassett Moore, 1 A Digest of International Law 5-6 (1906).

73. *See generally* Paul R. Williams & Michael P. Scharf, Peace with Justice? War Crimes and Accountability in the Former Yugoslavia (2002).

74. *See* Michael A. Newton, *Comparative Complementarity: Domestic Jurisdiction Consistent with the Rome Statute of the International Criminal Court*, 167 MIL. L. REV. 20, 26-27 (Mar. 2001).

75. The necessity for domestic states to use domestic criminal forums and penal authority to enforce norms developed in binding international agreements is perhaps one of the most consistent features of the body of law known as international criminal law. *See, e.g.*, Convention on the Prevention and Punishment of the Crime of Genocide, G.A. Res. 2670, U.N. GAOR, 3rd Sess., pt. 1, at 174, U.N. Doc. A/810 (1948), 102 Stat. 3045, 78 U.N.T.S. 277, (entered into force Jan. 12, 1951) (Article V obligates Contracting Parties to enact the necessary domestic legislation to give effect to the criminal provisions of the Convention). Of particular note in the post 9/11 world, the imposition of criminal accountability for acts of terrorism is exclusively reserved to the courts of sovereign states through the welter of treaties created by sovereign states. *See* Michael Newton, *International Criminal Law Aspects of the War Against Terrorism, in* 79 International Law and the War on Terror 323 (Fred L. Borch & Paul S. Wilson, eds., 2003); *See also* M. Cherif Bassiouni, International Terrorism: Multilateral Conventions 1937-2001(2001).

76. IST Statute, art. 1(b), Dec. 10, 2003, art. 38, 43 I.L.M. 231, *available at http://iraq-ist.org/en/about/statute.htm* (last visited June 4, 2005).

77. *Id.*

78. *Id.* at arts. 11-13.

79. *Id.* at art. 14.

80. *Id.*

81. ICCPR, *supra* note 52, at 52.

82. *Supra* note 6 and accompanying text.

83. Protocol Additional to the Geneva Conventions of 12 August 1949, and Relating to the Protection of the Victims of Non-International

Armed Conflicts, Annex II, at art. 6(2), U.N. Doc. A/32/144 (1977), 26 L.M. 561 (1987)(entered into force Dec. 7, 1978) [hereinafter Protocol II]; ICCPR, *supra* note 52, para. 14(1); European Convention for the Protection of Human Rights and Fundamental Freedoms, at art. 6(1), 221 U.N.T.S. 221 (1953)[hereinafter ECHR], and the American Convention on Human Rights "Pact of San Jose, Costa Rica", Nov. 22, 1969, art. 8(1), OAS Treaty Series, No. 36, 9 I.L.M. 101 (1969) [hereinafter ACHR].

84. Civilians Convention, Aug. 12, 1949, art. 147, 6 U.S.T. 3516, 75 U.N.T.S. 287; Geneva Convention Relative to the Treatment of Prisoners of War, art. 130, 75 U.N.T.S. 287, 6 U.S.T. 3316, [hereinafter Convention on Prisoners of War]; Protocol I, art. 75(4), U.N. Doc. A/32/144 (1977), 16 I.L.M. 1391 (1977), 1125 U.N.T.S 3, (slightly changing the formulation to read as follows "impartial and regularly constituted court respecting the generally recognized principles of regular judicial procedure").

85. Human Rights Watch Memorandum to the Iraqi Governing Council on 'The Statute of the Iraqi Special Tribunal', para. A.1., (Dec. 2003), *available at http://www.hrw.org/backgrounder/mena/iraq121703.htm* (last visited June 26, 2005).

86. For example, when campaigning prior to the national elections held on January 30, 2005, interim Iraqi Prime Minister Ayad Allawi repeatedly sought to gain votes by frequently assuring both domestic and international audiences that the trials of leading Ba'athists (including Saddam Hussein and Chemical Ali) would begin imminently. The IST has thus far resisted exogenous pressures to rush the investigation and prosecution of cases, and has stated that trials would begin when judges are fully trained, and the development of cases is completed by the investigating judges and prosecutors.

87. Rajiv Chandrasekaran, *Tribunal Planners Hope to Start Trials by Spring*, WASH. POST, Dec. 16, 2003, at A1.

88. IST Statute, art. 1(a), Dec. 10, 2003, art. 38, 43 I.L.M. 231, *available at http://iraq-ist.org/en/about/statute.htm* (last visited June 4, 2005).

89. The Iraqi lawyers selected this term rather than "perpetrator" that was used in the International Criminal Court Elements of Crimes. There was extensive debate during the drafting of the Elements of Crimes for the International Criminal Court over the relative merits of the terms "perpetrator" or "accused." Though some delegations were concerned that the term perpetrator would undermine the presumption of innocence, the delegates to the Preparatory Commission (PrepCom) ultimately agreed to use the former in the Elements after including a comment in the introductory chapeau that

"the term "perpetrator" is neutral as to guilt or innocence. *See* KNÜT DORMANN, ELEMENTS OF WAR CRIMES UNDER THE ROME STATUTE OF THE INTERNATIONAL CRIMINAL COURT 9-16 (2002). prove.

90. *See* Coalition Provisional Authority Order Number 48: Delegation of Authority Regarding an Iraqi Special Tribunal at 2, (Dec. 10, 2003) *available at http://www.cpa-iraq.org/regulations/*20031210_ CPAORD_48_IST_and_ Appendix_A.pdf (last visited June 26, 2005).

91. IST Statute, art. 21(b), Dec. 10, 2003, art. 38, 43 I.L.M. 231, *available at http://iraq-ist.org/en/about/statute.htm* (last visited June 4, 2005).

92. *Id.* at art. 33.

93. *See supra* note 50 and accompanying text.

94. *See generally supra* note 78 and accompanying text.

95. IST Statute, art. 21(b), Dec. 10, 2003, art. 38, 43 I.L.M. 231, *available at http://iraq-ist.org/en/about/statute.htm* (last visited June 4, 2005). This provision of the IST Statute preventing any adverse inference from the silence of the accused is noteworthy because it is the first time that such a protection was specifically found in Iraqi law.

96. 1970 Interim Constitution of Iraq art. 20, *reprinted in* United States Institute of Peace, Iraqi Laws Referenced in the Statute of the Iraqi Special Tribunal (2004) (copy on file with author). The 1970 Interim Constitution is also available at *http://www.mallat.com* (last visited June 19, 2005). The Iraqi Law on Criminal Proceedings makes clear that the judge must release an accused if "there is insufficient evidence for conviction." Law on Criminal Proceedings with Amendments, Number 23 of 1971, Decree No. 230 Issued by the Revolutionary Command Council, Feb. 14, 1971, para. 203 [hereinafter Iraqi Law No. 23 on Criminal Proceedings], *available at https://www.jagcnet.army.mil/JAGCNETInternet/Homepages/AC/CLAMO-Public.nsf/* (follow "Iraq Criminal Prcedure Code" hyperlink) (last visited Jul. 25, 2005).

97. *Id.* All of the judges and investigators with whom I have dealt have been completely comfortable with the presumption of innocence and the duty of the prosecutor to produce evidence sufficient to warrant a guilty verdict.

98. Rupert Cornwell, *Saddam in the Dock: Listen to His Victims, Not Saddam, Says White House*, The Independent (London), July 2, 2004, at 6 (reporting that Hussein stated "[t]his is all theater" at his first pre-trial hearing). For those who have observed the Milosevic trial, Saddam's statements were eerily familiar. During his initial appearance before the ICTY on July 3, 2001, Milosevic challenged the

legality of the establishment of the ICTY. In a pre-trial motion, Milosevic stated "I challenge the very legality of this court because it is not established in the basis of law." *Milosevic Challenges Legality of U.N. Tribunal*, ONLINE NEWSHOUR, Feb. 13, 2002, *available at http://www.pbs.org/newshour/updates/february02/milosevic_2-13.html* (last visited June 19, 2005).

99. Geert-jan Alexander Knoops, An Introduction to the Law of International Criminal Tribunals: A Comparative Study 135-40 (2003).

100. *Id.* at 113-16. *See also* Revised Version of Iraqi Special Tribunal Rules of Procedure and Evidence, Rules 57 and 58, *available at http://www.law.case.edu/war-crimes-research-portal/pdf/IST_Rules_of_Procedure_and_Evidence. pdf* (last visited June 19, 2005) (detailing the procedures and substantive provisions for the entry of a guilty plea in the IST) [hereinafter Revised Version Iraqi Special Tribunal Rules of Procedure and Evidence].

101. United States Institute of Peace, Special Report 122, Building The Iraqi Special Tribunal: Lessons From Experiences In International Criminal Justice 6 (June 2004), *available at http://www.usip.org/pubs/specialreports/sr122.html* (last visited June 19, 2005).

102. *See* Michael P. Scharf & Paul R. Williams, *The Functions of Justice and Anti-Justice in the Peace-BuildingProcess*, 35 CASE. W. RES. J. INT'L L. 161, 175 (2003).

103. *Report to the President by Mr. Justice Jackson*, Oct. 7, 1946, *quoted in* 49 AM. J. INT'L L. 44, 49 (1955), *reprinted in* Report of Robert H. Jackson United States Representative to the International Conference on Military Trials 432, 438 (1945) (Justice Jackson also wrote: "[w]e have documented from German sources the Nazi aggressions, persecutions, and atrocities with such authenticity and in such detail that there can be no responsible denial of these crimes in the future and no tradition of martyrdom of the Nazi leaders can arise among informed people.").

104. *Id.* at xi. Interestingly, as a matter of historical record, the teams of international prosecutors at Nuremberg did not develop the detailed Elements of Crimes that have become an accepted feature of every subsequent international process.

105. *Id.*

106. *See* Rome Statute of the International Criminal Court, United Nations Diplomatic Conference of Plenipotentiaries on the Establishment of an International Criminal Court, July 17, 1998, U.N. Doc. A/CONF. 183/9 (1998), art. 69(3), 37 I.L.M. 999 (1998).

107. Revised Version Iraqi Special Tribunal Rules of Procedure and Evidence, *supra* note 102, Rule 79. This provision is adjacent to the

common sense caveat that the Trial Chamber should "exclude evidence if its probative value is substantially outweighed by the potential for unfair prejudice, considerations of undue delay, waste of time, or needless presentation of cumulative evidence." *Id.*

108. *Id.*

109. Iraqi Law No. 23 on Criminal Proceedings, *supra* note 92, para. 203.

110. For a summary of state practice and its implementation in treaty norms and military manuals around the world, see 1 Jean-marie Henckaerts & Louise Doswald-beck, Customary International Humanitarian Law, 352-75 (2005) [hereinafter ICRC Study].

111. *See, e.g.,* Civilians Convention, Aug. 12, 1949, art. 3, 6 U.S.T. 3516, 75 U.N.T.S. 287.

112. ICRC Study, *supra* note 106, at 355.

113. IST Statute, art. 16, Dec. 10, 2003, art. 38, 43 I.L.M. 231, *available at http://iraq-ist.org/en/about/statute.htm* (last visited June 4, 2005).

114. *Id.* at art. 17(a).

115. ICCPR, *supra* note 52, art. 14(1).

116. *See* General Comment on Article 14, H.R. Comm. 43rd Sess., Supp. No. 40, at para. 4, U.N. Doc. A/43/40 (1988); *Cariboni v. Uruguay,* H.R.Comm. 159/83. 39th Sess. Supp. No. 40 U.N. Doc. A/39/40. The Inter-American Commission has taken a similar approach. *See,* e.g., Inter-Am C.H.R., Annual Report 1972, OEA/Ser. P, AG/doc. 305/73 rev. 1, 14 March 1973, at 1; Inter-Am C.H.R., Annual Report 1973, OEA/Ser. P, AG/doc. 409/174, 5 March 1974, at 2-4.

117. *See* Michael P. Scharf, Balkan Justice: The Story Behind the First International War Crimes Trial Since Nuremberg 104-06 (1997).

118. Prosecutor v. Dusko Tadic a/k/a "Dule", Decision on the Defence Motion for Interlocutory Appeal on Jurisdiction, Oct. 2, 1995, para. 45, *available at http://www.un.org/icty/tadic/appeal/decision-e/51002.htm* (last visited June 19, 2005).

119. IST Statute, art. 21(b), Dec. 10, 2003, art. 38, 43 I.L.M. 231, *available at http://iraq-ist.org/en/about/statute.htm* (last visited June 4, 2005).

120. *Id.* at art. 21(c).

121. *Id.* at art. 23(b).

122. Law of Judicial Organization, Number 160 of 1979, Resolution No. 1724 Issued by the Revolutionary Command Council, Oct. 12, 1979, art. 7, Published by the Ministry of Justice, Official Gazette of the Republic of Iraq, Vol. 23, No. 27 at 2 (July 2, 1980), *reprinted in* United

States Institute of Peace, Iraqi Laws Referenced In the Statute of the Iraqi Special Tribunal (2004) (copy on file with author).

123. *See* Special Report No. 122, *supra* note 97, at 9-10.

124. *See* S.C. Res. 808, U.N. SCOR, 3175th mtg., U.N. Doc. S/RES/808 (1993).

125. The SCSL was established by a treaty between the Government of Sierra Leone and the United Nations to prosecute those with the "greatest responsibility" for violations of international humanitarian law. Agreement between the United Nations and the Government of Sierra Leone on the Establishment of a Special Court for Sierra Leone, Jan. 16, 2002, U.N.-Sierra Leone, *at http://www.sc-sl.org/scsl-agreement.html* (last visited June 19, 2005). The Appeals Chamber articulated the SCSL's legal basis in Prosecutor v. Charles Ghankay Taylor, Case No.: SCSL-2003-01-I, Decision on Immunity from Jurisdiction, May 31, 2004, *available at http://www.sc-sl.org/Documents/SCSL-03-01-I-059.pdf* (last visited June 19, 2005). The Appeals Chamber stated, "[I]t was clear that the power of the Security Counsel to enter into an agreement for the establishment of the court was derived from the Charter of the United Nations both in regard to the general purposes of the United Nations as expressed in Article 1 of the Charter and the specific powers of the Security Council in Articles 39 and 41. These powers are wide enough to empower the Security Council to initiate, as it did by Resolution 1315, the establishment of the Special Court by Agreement with Sierra Leone.") *Id.* at 13.

126. IST Statute, art. 17(b), Dec. 10, 2003, art. 38, 43 I.L.M. 231, *available at http://iraq-ist.org/en/about/statute.htm* (last visited June 4, 2005).

127. *Id.* at art. 16 ("The President of the Tribunal shall draft rules of procedure and evidence for the conduct of the pre-trial phase of the proceedings, trials and appeals, the admission of evidence, the protection of victims and witnesses and other appropriate matters (including regulations with respect to the disqualification of judges or prosecutors), where the applicable law, including this Statute does not, or does not adequately provide for a specific situation. ... Such rules shall be adopted by a majority of the permanent judges of the Tribunal.").

128. Interview by Ljubica Gojgic with Judge Theodor Meron, President of the International Criminal Tribunal for the Former Yugoslavia,in Belgrade (Sept. 18, 2003), *available at www.b92.net/intervju/eng/2003/meron.php* (last visited June 19, 2005). At the time of this writing, there have been thirty-six sets of amendments to the ICTY Rules of Procedure. *See http://www.un.org/icty/legaldoc/* (last visited June 19, 2005).

129. *See* KNOOPS, *supra* note 95, at 91-100 (listing a number of specific rules changes in the ICTY).

130. IST Statute, art. 17(a), Dec. 10, 2003, art. 38, 43 I.L.M. 231, *available at http://iraq-ist.org/en/about/statute.htm* (last visited June 4, 2005) ("Subject to the provisions of this Statute and the rules made thereunder, the general principles of criminal law applicable in connection with the prosecution and trial of any accused person shall be those contained: (i) in Iraqi criminal law as at July 17, 1968 (as embodied in The Baghdadi Criminal Code of 1919) for those offenses committed between July 17, 1968 and December 14, 1969; (ii) in Law Number 111 of 1969 (the Iraqi Criminal Code), as it was as of December 15, 1969, without regard to any amendments made thereafter, for those offenses committed between December 15, 1969 and May 1, 2003; and (iii) and in Law Number 23 of 1971 (the Iraqi Criminal Procedure Law)."

131. *Id.* at art. 17(b).

132. M. Cherif Bassiouni, Introduction to International Criminal Law 332 (2003) (referring to the Sentencing Judgements in *Prosecutor v. Erdemovic*, Case No. IT-96-22-T, para. 40 (Nov. 29, 1996) and *Prosecutor v. Stevan Todorovic*, Case No. IT-95-9/1-S, paras. 97-107 (July 31, 2001).

133. IST Statute, Dec. 10, 2003, art. 20(d)(2), 43 I.L.M. 231, *available at http://iraq-ist.org/en/about/statute.htm*, (last visited June 4, 2005).

134. *Id.* at art. 18(c).

135. *Id.*

136. Special Report No. 122, *supra* note 97, at 7.

137. Revised Version Iraqi Special Tribunal Rules of Procedure and Evidence, *supra* note 102, Rule 48(A).

138. *Id.*

139. *Id.* at Rule 48(C).

140. For example, repeated abuses by counsel were responsible for the ICTY shift from paying hourly defense fees to a flat fee system. Special Report No. 122, *supra* note 97, at 7.

141. Revised Version Iraqi Special Tribunal Rules of Procedure and Evidence, *supra* note 102, Rule 50.

142. Iraqi Law No. 23 on Criminal Proceedings, *supra* note 92, para. 154.

143. Revised Version Iraqi Special Tribunal Rules of Procedure and Evidence, *supra* note102, Rule 46(A).

144. Iraqi Law No. 23 on Criminal Proceedings, *supra* note 92, para. 128.

145. Revised Version Iraqi Special Tribunal Rules of Procedure and Evidence, *supra* note 102, Rule 46(B).

146. *Id.* at Rule 46(C).

147. *Id.*

148. *See, e.g.*, Rule 63 of the ICTY Rules of Evidence and Procedure, *available at http://www.un.org/icty/legaldoc/index.htm* (last visited June 19, 2005), reads as follows:

Questioning of Accused

(Adopted 11 Feb 1994, amended 3 Dec. 1996).

(A) Questioning by the Prosecutor of an accused, including after the initial appearance, shall not proceed without the presence of counsel unless the accused has voluntarily and expressly agreed to proceed without counsel present. If the accused subsequently expresses a desire to have counsel, questioning shall thereupon cease, and shall only resume when the accused's counsel is present.

(B) The questioning, including any waiver of the right to counsel, shall be audio-recorded or video-recorded in accordance with the procedure provided for in Rule 43. The Prosecutor shall at the beginning of the questioning caution the accused in accordance with Rule 42 (A)(iii).

149. Revised Version Iraqi Special Tribunal Rules of Procedure and Evidence, *supra* note 95, Rule 49(A).

150. *See generally* Salvatore Zappala, *The Iraqi Special Tribunal's Rules of Procedure and Evidence: Neither Fish nor Fowl?*, 2 J. CRIM. INT'L JUST. 855 (2004).

151. Iraqi Law No. 23 on Criminal Proceedings, *supra* note 91, para. 42.

152. *Id.* at para. 170. *See also id.* at para. 213(A) ("The court's its (sic) verdict in a case is based on the extent to which it is satisfied by the evidence presented during any stage of the inquiry or the hearing. Evidence includes reports, witness statements, written records of an interrogation, other official discoveries, reports of experts and technicians and other legally established evidence."??).

153. Revised Version Iraqi Special Tribunal Rules of Procedure and Evidence, *supra* note 102, Rule 62 (describing exculpatory evidence as "evidence known to the Prosecutor which in any way tends to suggest the innocence or mitigate the guilt of the accused or may affect the credibility of a prosecution witness or the authenticity of prosecution evidence.").

154. Zappala, *supra* note 152, at 861. For example, unlike the ICTY and ICTR rules, the IST Rules of Procedure explicitly build in a right of

cross-examination for the party who did not call a witness, even as they permit the judges to "put any question to the witness." Revised Version Iraqi Special Tribunal Rules of Procedure and Evidence, *supra* note 102, Rule 77.

155. Iraqi Law No. 23 on Criminal Proceedings, *supra* note 92, para. 69(A).

156. *Id.*

157. *Id.* at para. 59(C).

158. *Id.* at para. 74 ("If it appears to the examining magistrate that particular person is holding items or papers which would inform the investigation, he may issue a written order for the items to be submitted. If he believes that the order will not be obeyed or is worried that the items will be removed, he may conduct a search procedure in accordance with the paragraphs below.").

159. Revised Version Iraqi Special Tribunal Rules of Procedure and Evidence, *supra* note 102, Rule 53(A) (this authority also extends to the right of the Trial Judge or Trial Chamber to make such orders as "may be necessary for the purposes of the preparation or conduct of the trial.").

160. For example, in preparation for the Dachau trials, interrogation teams were sent to prisoner of war camps across the United States. One of the critical pieces of evidence against the camp commander of the Dachau camp came from a former German guard who had been captured in southern France in 1944 and was held at Camp Butler, North Carolina. Joshua M. Greene, Justice at Dachau: The Trials of An American Prosecutor 31 (2003).

161. Revised Version Iraqi Special Tribunal Rules of Procedure and Evidence, *supra* note 102, Rule 79(E)(ii).

162. *Contra* ICTY Rules of Procedure and Evidence, Rule 95, *available at http://www.un.org/icty/legaldoc/index.htm* (last visited June 19, 2005) ("No evidence shall be admissible if obtained by methods which cast substantial doubt on its reliability or if its admission is antithetical to, and would seriously damage, the integrity of the proceedings."). *See generally* Craig M. Bradley, Mapp *Goes Abroad*, 52 CASE W. RES. L. REV. 375, 394 (2001).

163. Revised Version Iraqi Special Tribunal Rules of Procedure and Evidence, *supra* note 102, Rule 47.

164. Iraqi Law No. 23 on Criminal Proceedings, *supra* note 91, para. 64.

165. Iraqi Penal Code No. 111 of 1969, para. 333, *reprinted in* United States Institute of Peace, Iraqi Laws Referenced in the Statute of the Iraqi Special Tribunal (2004) (copy on file with author) ("Any public official

or agent who tortures or orders the torture of an accused, witness or informant in order to compel him to confess to the commission of an offence or to make a statement or provide information about such offence or to withhold information or to give a particular opinion in respect of it is punishable by imprisonment or by detention. Torture shall include the use of force or menaces."??).

166. Iraqi Law No. 23 on Criminal Proceedings, *supra* note 91, para. 127 (Mistreatment, threats, injury, enticement, promises, psychological influence or use of drugs or intoxicants are considered illegal methods).

167. *Id.* at para. 213(C) (CPA Memorandum 3 deleted the additional language "and if there is no other evidence which proves it to be a lie").

168. *Id.* at para. 218 (CPA Memorandum 3 modified this provision by deleting the additional caveats that coercion could include both physical or moral components or even promises or threats).

169. Bathsheba Crocker, *Iraq: Going it Alone, Gone Wrong*, *in* Winning the Peace: An American Strategy for Post-conflict Reconstruction, 281 (Robert C. Orr ed., 2004).

170. Brian R. Nelson, Western Political Thought from Socrates to the Age of Ideology 31 (1982).

171. The Republic of Plato 52-53 (Francis MacDonald Cornford trans. & ed., 1945).

172. For a detailed account of the Cold War politics and unraveling of wartime unity that doomed the effort to convene a second International Military Tribunal after World War II to prosecute Major War Criminals, see Donald Bloxham, Genocide on Trial: War Crimes Trials and the Formation of Holocaust History and Memory, 28-37 (2001).

173. Allied prosecutors had to sift through the trial dossiers of more than 100,000 potential criminals in deciding who should be prosecuted and in what order. *See* Telford Taylor, The Anatomy of the Nuremberg Trials: A Personal Memoir 273 (1992). As another of the hundreds of examples, the victorious allies excluded the Krupps from the dock at Nuremberg for political and policy reasons rather than a sober assessment of how best to serve the needs of German society. BLOXHAM, *supra* note 168, at 22.

174. Some scholars have made a distinction between the *acknowledgement* of severe violations of international norms -- whether to remember or forget the abuses – and *accountability* for those crimes – or whether to impose sanctions on those who bear personal responsibility for the abuses. Simon Chesterman, You, The People: The United Nations, Transitional Administration, and State-building, 157 (2004).

175. Who, it should be remembered, also enjoyed basic human rights that were trampled by the regime.

176. IX Department of State Bulletin, No. 228, 310, *reprinted in* Report of Robert H. Jackson United States Representative To The International Conference on Military Tribunals 11 (1945) The Moscow Declaration was actually issued to the Press on November 1, 1943. For an account of the political and legal maneuvering behind the effort to bring this stated war aim into actuality, see Peter Maguire, Law and War: An American Story 86-110 (2001). The Declaration specifically stated that German criminals were to be "sent back to the countries in which their abominable deeds were done in order that they may be judged and punished according to the laws of these liberated countries and of the free governments which will be erected therein." The text of the Moscow Declaration is available at *http://www.yale.edu/lawweb/avalon/wwii/moscow.htm* (last visited June 19, 2005). The international forum was limited only to those offenses where a single country had no greater grounds for claiming jurisdiction than another country. Justice Jackson recognized this reality in his famous opening statement. He accepted the fact that the International Military Tribunal was merely a necessary alternative to domestic courts for prosecuting the "symbols of fierce nationalism and of militarism." Opening Statement to the International Military Tribunal at Nuremberg, II Trial of the Major War Criminals Before The International Military Tribunal 99 (1947). He further clarified that any defendants who succeeded in "escaping the condemnation of this Tribunal ... will be delivered up to our continental Allies." *Id.* at 100.

177. *See* Regulations Governing the Trial of War Criminals, General Headquarters, United States Army Pacific, AG 000.5, Sept. 24, 1945, para 5(b) ("Persons whose offenses have a particular geographical location outside Japan may be returned to the scene of their crimes for trial by competent military or civil tribunals of the local jurisdiction.") (copy on file with author).

178. Report of the Secretary-General, The Rule of Law and Transitional Justice in Conflict and Post-Conflict Societies, U.N. Doc. S/2004/616, para. 17 (Aug. 23, 2004), *available at http://documents-dds-ny.un.org/doc/UNDOC/GEN/N04/395/29/pdf/N0439529.pdf?OpenElement* (last visited June 19, 2005).

Domestic Violence Against Women–Etiology and Legal Regime

Pradeep Singh*

Domestic violence is the leading cause of injury to women. It is not a new emerging offence committed against women, for centuries there have been battered women and abused wives but only recently their battering have gained public attention as a socio-legal problem. Historically domestic violence has been considered as personal domestic problem particularly relating to adjustment, not as an act of violence and criminality, that's why very little attention has been paid to such activities therefore considered to be domestic affair and of little or no concern to the rest of the society. Domestic violence in comparison to the other offences is more heinous and ghastly as it is committed within the set up where a person seeks love, warmth and reinforcement, it is committed by that person to whom victim trust most for support and protection.

Term 'Violence against women' refers to Force, whether overt or covert used to wrest from a woman something that she does not want to give her -own free will, causes her either physical injury or emotional trauma or both. Domestic violence is most heinous crime in which victim has no willingness to file the complaint so the reported cases are very few on the basis of only decimal reported cases one cannot make generalization about criminal etiology and plight of women due to domestic violence. For the domestic violence usually a wider term Domestic abuse is used, which means

---

* *Reader, Law School, Banaras Hindu University, Varanasi.*

occurrence of one more of the following acts between family or household members:

(a) causing or attempting to cause serious physical harm or

(b) threatening another with imminent serious physical harm.

'Family or household members' means spouses, ex spouses, parents, children, persons otherwise related by blood or marriage or persons living in same household or who formerly living in same household. This definition incorporates all the victims of domestic violence viz. children, elderly parents, spouses, ex-spouses and people who live together but who may not necessarily related by blood or marriage. Domestic violence has been defined in Protection of Women from Violence Act, 2005:

"any act, omission or commission or conduct of the respondent shall constitute domestic violence in case it:

(a) harms or injures or endangers the health, safety, life limb or well being whether mental or

physical of the aggrieved person or tends to do so and includes causing physical abuse,

sexual abuse, verbal and emotional abuse and economic abuse;

or

(b) harasses, harms, injures or endangers the aggrieved person with a view to coerce her or any other person related to her to meet any unlawful demand for any dowry or other property or valuable security; or

(c) has the effect of threatening the aggrieved person or any person related to her by any conduct mentioned in clauses (a) or clause (b) or

(d) otherwise injures or causes harm whether physical or mental to the aggrieved person."[1]

The definition given in the Act of 2005 is very expansive which relates to physical or mental harm to women living in household setup and it is caused by someone related to her particularly husband. Act defines aggrieved person means any woman who is or has been in a domestic relationship with the respondent and who alleges to have been subjected to any act of domestic violence by the respondent.[2] Domestic violence may cause physical or mental injury and may be categorized as physical abuse, sexual abuse, verbal and emotional abuse and economic abuse. Act passed by Indian Parliament in 2005 attempts to protect weaker section of society from every probable category of violence. Violence committed by male members of the family against female members of the family endangers the family harmony, affects the socialization process of children by which thy may drift towards delinquency, societal fabrics may torn, affect the equality principle. In welfare state it is prime objective of state policy to protect every citizen particularly when he/she belongs to weaker section of society the state responsibility enhances greatly.

ETIOLOGY OF DOMESTIC VIOLENCE

For proper tackling any crime and criminality it is essential to know the causation of crime. Domestic violence is a social problem affecting the basic fabric of society needed to be tackled appropriately and in right manner therefore its causation should be gleaned out. What are the motivating factors in violence against women? This may be explained on the basis of three factors: (i) situations which bring about violent behaviour, (ii) characteristics of victims, and (iii) characteristics of victimizers. In this light Four causes may be identified in violence against women (a) Victims's provocation, (b) Intoxication, (c) Hostility towards women and (d) Situational urge.

Victim's Provocation

The male batterers often allege that it is the wife who creates the situation in which husband loses his self control and commits physical violence. Sometimes wife makes person–situation complex giving rise to violence against her. Victim provokes a person to use violence against her by her behaviour, which is often unconscious. The victim either triggers off or generates the violent behaviour of the offender. The wife generate or trigger off the violence by doing back-biting, talking to persons disliked by husband, ill treating in laws and husband, refusing to obey the dictates of husband, illicit relations, irritating the husband by her quarrelsome or nagging nature and interfering too much in affairs of husband. Schultz noted about stereotypes regarding battered women as:

(i) They are basically sadomasochistic. That is they enjoy being abused and have a need to be abused. Therefore the problem is difficult to eradicate since is roots lie deep in the victim's psych.

(ii) They actually instigate the assault through antagonistic verbal behaviour (for example nagging, insult and so on); if they would refrain from such verbal abuse, the battering would cease.

(iii) They are 'very masculine, outspoken, domineering women' (castrating by implication) who tend to exploit and profit from their husband's passiveness and dependency."[3]

In domestic violence cases making allegation on aggrieved person shows only that the problem has been analysed from male point of view, which resulted into making of victim's defenseless position as causes of violence and male batterer is defended and shown that legal discourse is not needed to cure this malady, if made, victim should be penalised or cured and her mental attitude should be tackled. These surmise of stereotypes of victim of domestic violence seems to be based on personal observations and have not been based on proper investigated empirical data in a systematic manner. Schultz, for instance based his observation on a sample of four persons, which should not be generalized for society at large. It is also important to note that the foregoing stereotypes clearly place the cause of violence within the victim, a phenomenon called *"blaming the victim"*. Such type of conclusion of study is only distorting the reality and victim should not be blamed as in dacoity one can not observe that the victim not taken proper steps of security so not the dacoit but the victim should be penalized and also taught for taking steps for avoiding situation of dacoity.

Intoxication

Another potent factor in domestic violence may be alcohol. Because of frequent association of alcohol with violence, it is believed that drinking causes the violence. Always it is found that there is a tendency of both the abuser and the abused to blame alcohol. The abuser uses it as an excuse for his behaviour and the wife assumes that if she can get her husband. To stop drinking, the physical abuse will end. Bonnie E. Carlson studied the domestic violence and found that there is a marked disparity between victims and assailants in noted with respect to alcohol and drug abuse. Only a small proportions of the victims admitted to being substance abusers (alcohol – 10 per cent, drug – 5 per cent), whereas the victims reported substance abuse to be much more prevalent among their assailants (alcohol – 60%, drug 21%).[4] Intoxication seems to be major factor in domestic violence. Intoxication leads violence i.e. some cases of violence occur when the aggressors are intoxicated and are in a widely excited and belligerent state of mind, scarcely comprehending the likely fall out of their actions. Alcohol acts primarily as a disinhibitor of pre-existing aggressive tendencies. Alcohol is not chief factor but only co-operative factor in domestic violence, violent, jealously and hatred attitudes are already lying within the batterer, intoxicating situation lifts the embargo and social checks loosened making consequence of wife battering. Due to intoxication monetary situation also disbalanced, he may be fired from his job or his earning capacity decreases at the same time he is in need of satisfying alcohol consumption urge for which he may asking money from his wife or may have unsettled mind set up. Due to alcoholism he may have personality problem and living aloof from the mainstream of society it also causes diminished control of societal norms resulting into violence.

The person using alcohol has some stressful situations and personality problem. Drinking is only symptom, not factor behind violence, it only lessens the social control in which situation the destructive energy accumulated due to stresses released resulting into wife battering. Bonnie E Carlson observed that–

> "Many victims incorrectly identify alcohol abuse itself as the major problem. Alcohol abuse is, infact, a symptom of structural stress and frustration, but it serves to exacebate rather than alleviate the problem. Many battered women state that when their husbands are not drinking, these men are able to function normally and fulfill their role responsibilities adequately. Many women have been beaten by their partners only when the men were inebriated. Thus, it would appear that alcohol use is not the cause of domestic violence, but rather that alcohol breaks down inhibitions, allowing many men to injure a woman who would not normally do so beause of strong normative inhibitions against such behaviour."[5]

Therefore, it is clear that alcohol is not the chief factor but only co-operative factor. The problem is already lying but only manifested and seen due to lessening of social control while the person is inebriated condition.

Situational Urge

There are some situations which create the opportunity and given situation provokes a person to use violence. In this category those cases may be included where violence is used neither because of victims behaviour nor because of the offender's psycho-pathological personality but rather because of the chance factors which create such situation which lead to violence. Offenders not plan the violent act but when they found the situation conducive or provocative, they use violence. Apart from these violent acts, these offenders had not been living a life of deviant behaviour. Situation arises such in which husband becomes unable to control himself from using violence e.g., in a wife battering case, it may be that conflict over money matters or on the ill treatment of husbands parents may provoke the husband to assault the wife. But this situation complex giving rise to wife battering only when husband has taken the element of using force against wife during socialization otherwise he cannot translate the situation in using the force.

Personality Traits

Every male is not wife batterer but there are only some persons who are indulging in wife battering. These persons have some personality problem which makes them prone for committing violence. Some identifying traits of the violence prone personality are: extremely suspicious, passionate, dominant, irrational, irritational, immoral, easily emotionally upset, jealous and possessive. Traits developed in early life affect the aggressive behaviour of a person in adulthood. According to Freudian concept every person has reservoir of natural drives of which aggressive element is major component which is suppressed or transformed by development of ego element, which is conscious part of personality, during the process of socialization and personality is directed in accordance with super go, which is actually social mores. If during socialisation process ego is not developed properly, the personality becomes faulty and natural drives manifested overtly in form of aggressive behaviour and victims is mostly wife, because socio-economically her position is weaker and husband is not fearing any reaction from her in same manner. This situation is substantiated by the fact that most of the batterer belong to lower strata of the society, unemployed and not properly educated. Sue Titus Reid observed that:

> "Despite the stereotype of the male batterer as a lower class, pathological male researchers have found that all races and social classes are involved. Statistically wife battering may occur more often in lower than the upper classes, but that may be due to variation in reporting. There appear to be three major variables associated with wife beating : Frustration or stress, sex roles or learned behaviour and alcohol. Stress in the male spouse may occur for many reasons. Frustration and stress may result from the man's deep sense of inadequacy as a male, as a provider and as a father or a husband. Insecurity in modern age may result from his extreme dependency on his wife, coupled with his fear of losing her."[6]

Bonnie E. Carlson found in his study that almost one third of assailants were unemployed. Out of employed only 12% were professional whereas 36% did unskilled work, 38% semiskilled or technical jobs and 14% were in business, sells and miscellaneous jobs.[7]

Aggression may be inflicted only on that person who is estimated that he will not react or question the authority. In wife battering this situation fact is applicable, only those wives are assaulted whose personality is submissive and socio-economic condition is not sound. Bonnie E. Carlson found that the employment data are equally revealing. 57% victims were unemployed, out of 43% victims employed outside the home, only three were employed in professional positions, the remainder worked in clerical, technical or unskilled jobs. In terms of socio-economic status are third victims had not finished high school, while another 25% were high school graduates but had no further formal education, 34% had some college or vocational training, only 7% had graduated from college.

In Indian context the situation is more vulnerable, here women are educated right from her birth to obey dictates and sustain suffering at the hand of husband. So their personality is submissive and receive the violence without any question as a fate. Here women are socio-economically dependent and not properly educated so not knowing about right, what they know is only duty and have no mental set up to question the authority of husband as inflictor of violence. Carlson observed that–

> "One trait that seemed to characterize all victims was their devastatingly low self concept. A factor contributing to this was that many had never worked outside the home. The second striking characteristics was the degree of isolation that most of these women experienced. Many had virtually no close friends or relatives with whom to share the pain and fear in their lives, others had depleted such resources and had found that sisters, mothers, friends and others no longer wanted to hear about their Plight."[8]

Socialisation

The personality and resultant behaviour pattern in human beings emerges due to socialization. Reacting violently in a given situation is learned in the process of socialization during formative age. Children who are reared in homes characterized by periodic violence between domestic partners usually have seen indulged in domestic violence in adulthood. Victims and assailants frequently grew up in homes in which they themselves were beaten severally or in which they saw violence between their parents. The modeling effects of aggression and violence have been well documented by social learning theorists and developmental psychologists. Simply observing aggressive behaviour occur without punishment is sufficient for learning such behaviour. This clearly suggests that children growing up in violent homes, especially boys, are far more likely to learn such patterns of behaviour and to use them when frustrated and circumscribed by stressful situations than the children who do not observe domestic violence in their homes. Keefe and Lebovics studied the socialization process of children and commission of domestic violence :

> "It is estimated that between 3.3 million and 10 million children in U.S. witness physical violence between their parents each year. This type of violence ranges from overhearing some form of violent behaviour from their bedroom to seeing severe acts of violence such as beatings or assaults with guns or knives. In many cases these youth observe repeated acts of violence..... The little that is known about the effects of interparental violence on adolescents

> indicates that when compared to youth from non-violent homes, adolescents witnesses of domestic violence have higher rates of aggression, more fantastic view of future and an increased risk for delinquency, school truancy and other risky behviour."[9]

Socialisation process triggers a violent reaction in the male if he comes from a home in which his mother was battered, a characteristic of many batterers, he may have accepted violence as an appropriate way to handle the problem between men and women and as a method of control. The girl child reared in the home where women are violently abused she will accept the situation of battering and will not oppose the situation of battering. Sue Titus Reid observed about battered women:

> ".....Battered women looks almost identical to that of her batterer, she of all ages, all ethnicity, from all socio-economic groups, has a low level of self esteem and for the most part has very traditional notion of male and female behaviour. She may feel that her husband is supposed to be in charge of the family, even if that means beating her, she must be supportive of him, even if that means allowing herself to be abused repeatedly."[10]

Sex roles learned through process of socialization is major factor contributing in wife battering particularly in Indian context.

Sex Role

Sex role plays major part in domestic violence as it is found that in most reported wife battering cases husband commits wife abuse by physical, psychologic and economic abuse of wife. Men learn to be aggressive, dominant and expect women to be feminine and passive. With changing social structure in which women do not consider themselves subordinate and weaker, participating in the political and socio-economic sphere of society. Of course many men and women adjust to changing sex role without violence but major chunk of male element of society are not adjusted to this changing societal phenomenon. Those who continue to hold traditional sex role differentiation may be more likely to explode resulting into physical abuse.

The whole societal construction is male dominated and determined, what is the position, values, rights and duties of women all are decided by male elements of society. Universally women have been placed in subordinate position, it is more true particularly in India. Thinkers and scholars belonging to dominant sex tried to institutionalize and perpetuate this trend. The whole teaching of society concentrates on the point that woman ought to be relative to man. "To please them, to be useful to them, to make themselves loved and honoured by them, to educate them when young, to care then when grown, to counsel them, to consol them and to make life sweet and agreeable to them–these are duties of woman at all times and what should be taught them from their infancy."[11] A man is the right in being a man, it is woman who is in the wrong. Due to socio-economic and cultural deprivations for such a long time there is some type of indifference and lack of awareness in intellectual masses about the oppression of woman. Women are reared in atmosphere which slowly but positively helps in development of inferiority. They become used institutional legitimation of their low status and find nothing wrong in crimes and exploitation committed against them. Therefore in domestic violence they bear the toll as their fate and duty to be chasticised by husband and never complain. Male are reared with attitude that they should be aggressive, violent and use every means to dominate over female. Indian society is religion ridden society, therefore sex role plays very crucial role in wife abuse cases. In every religion particularly in Hindu and Muslim religion husband is depicted as sole owner of life of wife, he has authority to discipline and chasticise the wife and wife is indoctrinated to obey and sustain the discipline and not to resist against the husband. This miraculous position and role created by religion play very crucial role in wife abuse in India. It is also the reason behind not reportig the malady to law enforcement agency. This religious carving of sex role is the main reason because of which intellectual, legalist, jurist and common mass think it as no problem at all, if reported whether through media or any other channel it is considered only as domestic adjustment problem Domestic violence has never been treated as crime and criminality.

LEGAL REGIMENTATION OF PROBLEM

Law is an important instrument for tackling social problems, curbing social vices and advancing social change. Law is norm setter, when state wishes to make social change it enacts a new statute. Report of the Committee on the status of women in India points out this quality of law and observed:

"It can act directly, as a norm-setter or indirectly, providing institutions which accelerate social change by making it more acceptable."[12]

Domestic violence particularly wife battering is major problem before the society, which is not only affecting the women but society as whole. The children reared in such weakening family are more violence prone, indulge in domestic violence when grown up and also drift towards delinquency. Domestic violence creats unjust situation to the victims which is against the principle that the society has undertaken responsibility to impart justice to every person. Looking to magnitude and effect of the problem, it is inevitable to take steps for curbing this problem, state has attempted in this regard by legislative measures by which executive and judicial measures to tackle the problem have been envisaged. Wife battering is not a localized problem but found whole through the world therefore for tackling this problems attempt has been made by International community by convening various conventions at International Forum as well as by states in municipal regime.

International Conventions

Wife battering is a universal phenomenon, existing whole through the world. Several International Conventions have attempted to check the problem and evolve the values against the wife battering by which real equality should be manifested and family atmosphere should become free from violence, denial and neglect in which child should be reared and socialized properly ultimately by which crime and criminality may be tackled appropriately.

Charter of United Nations

United Nations was constituted in 1945, which is grounded on very much humanitarian ground. Its very purpose is to provide equality and good treatment to every person of world community. The very words in preamble of charter "We the people" give clear message that United Nations represents every person, irrespective of his nationality and gender. The main moto of United Nations is to protect human rights of every person - whole through world. Art 55 of United Nations charter stipulates that United Nations "shall promote respect and observance of human rights and fundamental freedoms". Under Art 56 all member states pledge themselves "to take joint and separate action in connection with the organization for the achievement of the purposes set forth in Art 55." United Nations Organisation has acted and organized many conventions for the protection of human rights of every person and with particular concern to violence against women.

Universal Declaration of Human Rights (UDHR) was initial step towards protecting the women in marriage and family institution. UDHR's first Article makes clear, "All human beings are born free and equal in dignity and right. ....." This clearly manifest that female being has the same rights and dignity as male being is having. The declaration makes attempt to protect women in marriage institution as in this institution she being victim of violence and neglect and her human dignity has been violated from time immemorial. UDHR further proclaims that she has ".... equal rights as to marriage, during marriage and at its dissolution" (Art 16). Thus UDHR has effectively delegitimised violence against women within the marriage institution.

International Bill of Rights

The International Bill of Rights consists of the pertinent articles of UN Charter, UDHR, International Covenant on Civil and Political Rights (CCPR), International covenant on Economic Social and Cultural Rights (CESCR) and the Optional Protocol to the CCPR that allows individual to make complaints to the Human Rights Committee.

CCPR enunciates the equal rights of men and women and provides a clear non-discrimination clause directing to state parties that:

> "the state parties ...... undertake to ensure the equal rights of men and women to the enjoyment of civil and political rights set forth in the present covenant."[13]

CCPR specially gives direction to state parties for protection of human rights of wife by which violence free equalitarian society should be realized:

> "(1) No marriage shall be entered into without the free and full consent of the intending spouses.
>
> (2) State parties ...... shall take appropriate steps to ensure equality of rights and responsibilities of the sources as to marriage, during the marriage and at its dissolution ....".

In tackling the problem of violence against women of which wife battering is major problem, the provisions of the CCPR has created an atmosphere against this menace but after all it is soft law not providing clear-cut mechanism to execute the law. Particularly in realm of wife battering it not provides any express provision.

The Convention on the Elimination of All Forms of Discrimination Against Women 1981

The Convention on the All Forms of Discrimination Against Women has developed the legal norms on non-discrimination of women by state instrumentalities. The convention moves from a sex-neutral norm that requires equal treatment of men and women. It progresses beyond the earlier human rights conventions by addressing the pervasive and systematic nature of discrimination against women and identifies the need to confront the social causes of women's inequality by addressing "all forms" of discrimination that women suffer. CEDAW marks a conscious intention to place discrimination against women prominently on the world's human right's agenda and to remove obstacles in making really egalitarian society. It provides that:

"State parties shall take all appropriate measures:

(a) to modify the social and cultural patterns of conduct of men and women with a view to achieving the elimination of prejudices and customary and all other practices which are based on the idea of the inferiority or the superiority of either of the sexes or on the stereotyped roles for men and women."[14]

The main reason behind domestic violence is sex role and socialization process in which male is taught to be aggressive, dominant and claimed as super being and female is nurtured in the process to become docile, submissive and to become inferior being. CEDAW strived to rectify this situation and given direction to state parties for tackling this discrimination. CEDAW is useful instrument in tackling cultural norms that subject women to spousal violence.The main attribute of CEDAW which differentiate it from other conventions is to make it binding to implement the convention at the national level. State parties undertake to submit reports on the legislative, judicial and administrative measures they have adopted to give effect to the convention and the difficulties they may have encountered in implementing its provisions. These reports are to be submitted to the Secretary-General who forwards it to the CEDAW Committee for consideration. After initial report, state parties must submit periodic reports at least every four years or whenever the committee requires. The reporting obligation is currently the convention's implementation mechanism.

Declaration on the Elimination of Violence Against Women, 1993

Declaration on the Elimination of Violence Against Women was passed unanimously by General Assembly of United Nations. Although declaration is not a convention therefore not binding on the governments, it is groundbreaking instrument for protecting women by showing world community's determination to eradicate the violences against women. Declaration observed why the violence against women is there, it is very important situation, without knowing causation the problem cannot effectively be tackled. It has recognized that violence against women is manifestation of historically unequal power relations between men and women which have led to discrimination and domination against women by men and the prevention of the full development of women. In its preambular part it has been observed that:

> "..... the urgent need for the application to women of the rights and principles with regard to equality, security, liberty and dignity of all human beings......"[15]

> "...... that violence against women is a manifestation of historically unequal power relations between men and women, which have led to domination over and discrimination against women by men and to prevention of the full advancement of women is one of the crucial social mechanism by which women are forced into subordinate positions compared with men."[16]

In Declaration international community shown its determination to eradicate violence against women:

> "..... there is need for a clear and comprehensive definition of violence against women, a clear statement of the rights to be applied to ensure the elimination of violence against women in all its forms, a commitment by states in respect of their responsibilities and a commitment by the international community at large to the elimination of violence against women......."[17]

Article 1 defines violence against women that the term violence against women means:

> "any act of gender-based violence that results in or likely to result in physical, sexual or psychological harm or suffering to women including threats of such acts, coercion or arbitrary deprivation of liberty whether occurring in public or in private life."

In this definition violence occurring in the family has also been taken into consideration, it shows the increasing consciousness of world community regarding domestic violence. Domestic violence is that sort of violence against women traditionally which never been considered as violence or crime and at the same time it is difficult to tackle it as it occurs within the family and committed by that person against whom victim usually has no willingness to file the case and pursue the case for imposition of punishment on them. Declaration further in quite comprehensive terms explain violence against women in which explicitly domestic violence has been enumerated:

> "Violence against women shall be understood to encompass but not limited the following:
>
> (a) Physical, sexual and psychological violence occurring in the family including battering, sexual abuse of female children in the household, dowry related violence, marital rape, female genital mutilation and other traditional practices harmful to women, non spousal violence and violence related to exploitation........"[18]

Art. 1 and 2 are directive in nature directing the state policy for eradication of violence against women and Art. 4 is creating state responsibility to make attempt for effectively tackling the problem:

> "States should condemn violence against women and should not invoke any customs, tradition or religious consideration to avoid their obligation with respect to its elimination. State should pursue by all appropriate means and without delay a policy of eliminating violence against women ....".

The wording of Article 4 clearly makes binding and obligatory for state parties to eradicate violence against women expressly referring battering, dowry related violence and marital rape which are major types of violence coming under purview of domestic violence. The Declaration on elimination of violence against women 1993 is manifestation of world community's rising consciousness to eradicate violence against half of world citizenry and for maintaining real equality between male and female. The declaration recognizes that violence against women is the manifestation of historically unequal power relations between men and women.

State responsibility is a fundamental principle of International law. It provides that a state is legally accountable to breaches of international obligations and this principle of state responsibility has recently taken unavoidable shape particularly in its goal to protect women against discrimination and violence. It now requires governments to take preventive steps to protect the exercise and enjoyment of human rights, to investigate alleged violations, to punish proved violations and to provide effective remedies including provisions for compensation to victims. International legal regime provides direction to municipal legislative body to enact the law in those areas where law is lacking or not effective. Protection of women's human rights is mainly coming under jurisdiction of municipal law, for which International Law provides directions. In modern era of globalization now state parties are bound by international law and its creation of atmosphere for that and evolving of international norms. Whole through the world state's initiative for coping domestic violence is only due to the International conventions creating environment against this universal social menace.

Indian Law

International instruments calling action against violence against women and providing protective umbrella to women for their malady and directing to states for penalising male hunches, induces us to analyse our legal arena to find out whether our legal regimentation is sufficient enough to tackle the problem of domestic violence committed against women.

Constitutional Law

Constitution is the fundamental legal document and the supreme law of the land in a democratic society. The framers of the Indian Constitution were aware of the sociology of the problem of emancipation of the female sex and various other social problems. They well knew that gender justice and elimination of gender discrimination and violence were crucial for the national development. The Constitution of India has taken positive steps for the protection of weaker section of society.

The constitution of a country provides not only the structure of governance, but also the legal, political and social frameworks within which individuals and groups subsist and interact with each other. Wife battering is criminality existing and continuing in the society mainly due to socio-politico-economic reasons therefore situated within our constitutional framework. A society governed by the rule of law must seek to set out the goals that it strives to attain and the mechanisms through which these will be attained. Indian Constitution set out the goals to be strived in preamble are fraternity assuring the dignity of the individual and the integrity of the nation. Domestic violence is the told violation of fraternity and dignity of individual committed by stronger sex against the weaker section of society, therefore, it is against the lofty goals of Constitution. For attaining this Constitutional goal Constitution has provided way in Part-III and Part-IV of Constitution. Part-III of Indian Constitution which enshrines fundamental rights and Part-IV directive principles and Part-IV-A fundamental duties specially provides protection to the women. These provisions provide directions for new legislations for elimination of violence and protection of women.

Fundamental Rights

Art. 14 makes every person equal and Art. 15 expands this horizon by explaining the situation how equal treatment will be given and how the person will be made equal. Art 15 dealing with right to equality refers women as equal citizens. It lays down:

> "15(1) the state shall not discriminate against any citizen on ground only of religion, race, caste, sex, place of birth or any of them."

Every person is not equal in reality therefore legislations passed to make them equal with others or for providing special treatment, are not considered to be violative of the equality principle.

Equality based on 'gender neutral approach' shows clear cut limitation in tackling domestic violence. If women are not provided with special protection and treatment the problem cannot be coped with. For checking this menace a 'special treatment approach' is needed which is embodies in Art. 15(3) of Constitution of India.[19] Art. 15(3) provides that:

"15(3) nothing in this Article shall prevent the state from making any special provision for women and children,"

Thus constitution enjoins equal status to women, as citizens, but also takes into consideration some speial disabilities which state shall endeavour to rectify by affirmative action through special enactments. Domestic violence is problem because of socio-eonomic weaker position of women, which can effectively be tackled through making special enactment for empowering them and socio-politico economic strengthening, by which real equality between male and female be made ultimately resulting into elimination of domestic violence.

Directive Principles

The Directive Principles of State Policies serves as the guidelines for social welfare legislations and steps to be taken for the welfare of citizens by the state. Directive Principles makes it prime responsibility of state to emancipate its citizens from social injustices and cruel atmosphere of exploitations. Social inequality and economic dependence of women have created circumstances in which women may be abused physically, sexually, psychologically and economically in the home setup, for eliminating this situation directive principles of state policy enshrined in Part-IV of constitution gives guideline to state instrumentalities and affirmative action thereon. Art. 38 states that–

"(1) The state shall strive to promote the welfare of the people by securing and protecting as effectively as it makes a social order in which justice, social, economic and political shall inform all the institutions of the national life."

Domestic violence which creates unjust situation for woman in which she is deprived of her socio-politic rights and economic hurdles are created. Art.39 manifests certain objectives for making available economic opportunities to women as economic dependence is the root cause of the problem. It provides that the state should direct its policy towards securing:

"(a) That the citizens, men and women equally, have the rights to an adequate means of livelihood."

In domestic violence the major cause is inequality between men and women, from time immemorial male are socialized to be aggressive and fate determiner of women, disciplining women by physical and psychological violence. Male being are having full liberty to have discretion either to love and care or hate and neglect his dependant wife. Realising this fact constituent assembly placed this provision in the constitution that the state shall make strive for making equality particularly in economic arena which is sole determining factor of real equality by which wife battering may effectively be tackled.

Fundamental Duties

Part-IV-A of the constitution deals with fundamental duties.[20] Fundamental duties are intended to serve as a constant endeavour to remind every citizen that while constitution specifically conferred on him certain fundamental rights, equally citizen is required to observe certain basic norms of democratic conduct and behaviour. Art. 51-A(e) seeks to renounce practices derogatory to the dignity of women. The provisions of Art. 51-A provides that:

"It shall be the duty of every citizen of India :

(a) ....

(b) ....

(c) ....

(d) ....

(e) to promote harmony and the spirit of common, brotherhood amongst all the people of Indian transcending religious, linguistic and regional and sectorial diversities; *to renounce practices derogatory to the dignity of women.*"

Wife battering is a social problem and derogatory to the dignity of women. Art. 51-A(e) directs to the citizens that they should not indulge and promote such derogatory practices.

Indian Penal Code

Criminal law of any nation manifests norms and values of the society. Indian Penal code is major Penal statute of India, it denounces practices derogatory to the dignity of women. It seeks to upheld woman's dignity by making provisions against obscenity, kidnapping, abduction, prostitution and violence against married women. At the moment one can identify three modes of legal intervention which are available to victims of domestic violence.

Criminal law, civil remedies and matrimonial relief. Of these criminal law provides remedy to women victims of physical abuse. In criminal law, provisions on general assault, battery, grievance hurt, manslaughter and murder particularly provision for cruelty and dowry death provide remedies to women in cases of domestic violence. Except general provisions for penalizing criminal activities, there are some special provisions in penal code which protects women in marriage institution from physical and psychological violence committed by husband and his relatives.

Cruelty by Husband and Relatives

The provision contained in S. 498-A punishing cruelty is major provision to punish the act of domestic violence particularly wife battering. In order to combat the barbaric violence occurring in marriage set up committed by husband and his relatives, the legislature enacted S.498-A[21] of the IPC and S. 113-A[22] of the Indian Evidence Act. In order to convict a person for committing cruelty against wife, it is needed to prove that the accused committed acts of harassment or cruelty as contemplated by the section. The term cruelty U/s. 498-A of the IPC includes both mental and physical cruelty. Cruelty means any willful conduct that is of such a nature as is likely to drive the woman to commit suicide or to cause grave injury or danger to life, limb, health (mental or physical) or harass or coerce her or any other person related to her to meet any unlawful demand.

Wife beating is mainly dealt in criminal law as offence of cruelty and it is most common crime which cuts across all social barriers of castes, class, education and religion, yet it is not recognized as crime by society a large occurring in private life within the four walls behind the closed doors and considered a private matter so the police are reluctant to intervene. Women from all sections of society, all income groups, educational levels and socio-economic strata get beaten. But reporting is made mostly by lower class women getting battered because they have lesser sense of privacy and police usually intervene in the matter but in case of upper class women police does not intervene. Along with it after reporting the case to police surviving of marriage comes to nugatory and creates problem of marriage tie breach up which is problematic to her and her children. Battered women are reluctant to report that they have been beaten up. It is their feeling of guilt and shame and fear of breach up marriage as well as socio-economic position prevent them from reporting the crime.

Considering these problems legislature has enacted presumption clause in evidence Act. The offences against married women are committed normally in circumstances in which direct evidences are not available. Therefore S. 113-A makes provision to check the harassment of married women. This section raises a presumption that where court is faced with a question, whether the commission of suicide by a woman had been abetted by her husband or any relative of her husband and evidence has been produced to show that (a) she had committed suicide within a period of seven years from the date of the marriage and (b) the husband or such relative of her husband had subjected her to cruelty, then court is enabled to presume, having regard to all the circumstances of the case that such suicide had been abetted by her husband or by such relative of her husband. This is a rebuttal presumption and the burden shifts to the husband or his relatives to show that they had not abetted the suicide. The presumption reverses the normal rule of prosecution in criminal cases. Once the circumstantial evidence is brought in the court that cruelty or in some cases of treatment bordering cruelty was mated out by wife before suicide, the court is free to draw the presumption U/s. 113-A Evidence Act.

Law has been made very meticulously to prevent wife battering in S. 498-A of IPC and S. 113-A Evidence Act, it has some lacunae which check its effectivity. Women usually not reports, if reported, police commonly not intervene, if intervened then another problems come forth: surving of marriage become nugatory and marriage tie comes to an end. During the trial prosecution is required to establish specific cruelty which should be in accordance with provisions of S. 498-A IPC and have nexus with some objectives given in that section only after that presumption clause of Evidence Act Works and court will presume cruelty and resultant suicide. If death of wife is not caused, presumption clause is not applicable meaning that in wife battering not resulting into death of wife, prosecution is needed to establish the case beyond all reasonable doubts. Therefore these provisions of criminal law are not in position to check domestic violence.

Dowry Death

Most heinous and extreme nature of domestic violence is causing of death of wife, which is punishable under IPC in provisions contained for punishing murder and culpable homicide. Dowery death occurs within the four walls of the house, therefore considering the situation of lack of direct evidences and lesser punishing rate in wife death, one new provision has been added in Criminal Law in S.304-B of IPC to punish causing death of wife where reason of such death is dowry demand. In 1987 304-B[23] was incorporated in IPC, this section provides for tiding over various difficulties that were faced by prosecution for proving wife battering resulting into death and getting culprits punished. This section is attracted when the death of a woman is caused by burns or bodily injury or occurs otherwise than under normal circumstances and this occurrence is preceded by cruelty or harassment by the in-laws in connection with a demand for dowry. According to this provision and related provisions[24] whenever a married woman dies within seven years of her marriage under suspicious circumstances and it is proved that she was harassed for dowry then it shall be presumed that the in-laws or the husband are responsible for the dowry death. It is immaterial whether she committed suicide or was murdered, both type of death are covered under dowry death U/s. 304-B IPC.[25] In *Mst. Premwati Vs. State of M.P.*[26] court observed that:

> "The framers intend and contemplate the liability of the occurrence of death of the bride to be fastened on the in-laws though they did not cause it, by creating a fiction. If the husband or his relations create such circumstances as would compel a person to choose death as the only way of getting out of the misery, such treatment would also attract section 304-B."

The introduction of Sec. 304-B in IPC and Sec. 113-B in the Evidence Act has shifted the burden of proving the innocence on the person against whom there is an allegation of causing dowry death. This was specially to combat the difficulty in adducing evidences for the crime of dowry death and to overcome legal hassles in coping the menace of wife-battering.

Sections 304-B and 498-A of I.P.C. are mutually exclusive these provisions deal with two distinct offences. Under S. 304-B it is dowry death within the time period of seven years. There is no such time limit has been given within which the offence would have to be committed to attract the provisions of S. 498-A IPC. Sec. 498-A deals with offence of cruelty committed by husband or his relatives Sec. 304-B deals that stage of cruelty in which cruelty has resulted into death of victim either that is murder of bride or suicide. Where dowry death takes place after seven years of marriage, then other provisions of IPC would be applicable viz. provisions relating to murder and culpable homicide. Sections 304-B and 498-A of IPC read with Sections 113-A and 113-B of Indian Evidence Act provide major protection to women under criminal law from wife battering and resultant situations.

Protection of Women from Domestic Violence Act, 2005

Women make the most vulnerable group of the society destined to be inferior sex determined by male element of the society. Various type of atrocities are committed against them out of which wife battering is most glaring form of crime committed against them since time immemorial. In domestic violence mainly civil rights of victims are affected particularly when she has willingness to raise her voice against cruelty of husband and his relatives, she faces problem of shelter, economic deprivations, absence of supply of feeding materials and clothings, and protecting herself from continuing violence. Now in modern era it is responsibility of state to protect the weaker section of the society. Various laws are trying to ameliorate the situation, but till recently it was evident that full proof remedy was not available to victims of domestic violence, civil actions apart from being lenthy and cumbersome procedure have not proved to be equally efficacious remedies, criminal law having various lacunas particularly to prove specific type of cruelty and in case of dowry death to establish nexus between death and cruelty created situation in which batterer may not be punished in most of the cases. Consequently on this subject appropriate legislation having more teeth and sanctions against perpetrators of domestic violence was needed particularly to provide civil remedies. Therefore Indian legislature enacted a statute–Protection of women from Domestic Violence Act in 2005 in accordance with the direction given by world community in Convention for Elimination of Discrimination Against Women (CEDAW). Prefatory note of the Act very lucidly clears the need of having such Act:

"1. The phenomenon of domestic violence is widely prevalent but has remained largely invisible in the public domain. Presently, where a women is subjected to cruelty by her husband or his relatives, it is an offence under S.498-A of Indian Penal Code. The Civil Law does not however address this phenomenon in its entirety.

2. It is, therefore, proposed to enact a law keeping in view the rights guaranteed under Art.14, 15 and 21 of constitution to provide for a remedy under the civil law which is intended to protect the women from being victim of domestic violence and to prevent occurrence of domestic violence in the society."

Protection of women from Domestic Violence Act 2005 is a civil enactment but it envisages criminal procedure for disposal of cases under the Act. It empowers criminal court to dispose the cases by using criminal procedure code by which speedy and just remedies could be provided to aggrieved person.[27] Act of 2005 expands the arena of domestic violence in comparison to Indian Penal Code, where only two situations have been thought to be remedified one in S. 498-A and other in S. 304-B. Section 3 of Act defines domestic violence not only completed act but even threat to commit violence. Domestic violence may be physical abuse, sexual abuse,[28] verbal and emotional abuse and economic abuse. Therefore the ambit of legal protection to wife has been widely expanded.

Existing state instrumentalities have completely failed to provide protection to women from battering, that's why this enactment creates and establishes some new agencies having responsibilities to make attempt to check the problem of wife battering by assisting aggrieved person to file the case before law courts. The major problem felt by law enforcement agencies have been that aggrieved persons not usually report the case and problem is going an unchecked, this situation has been considered and protection officers have been appointed under this enactment. Protection officer is very key agency created by the Act who will after getting information about wife battering immediately inform to magistrate and police officer.[29] For reporting purposes it is not necessary that information should be given by aggrieved person, any person knowing about commission of domestic violence incident may inform to protection officer, police or magistrate. As it is reality that due to various impediments wife usually not resort to legal remedies available to her, therefore law enforcement agencies were not in the situation to protect her, this innovation might prove protective to women by curing this lack of information situation. Under this enactment court may pass order for counseling, taking assistance of welfare experts and various types of other protective orders. Speedy remedy is the main objective of Act of 2005, the battered wife is in need of immediate protection and remedy. She is usually deprived from shelter and not having economic avenues available to her, therefore Act provides that as soon as prima facie case proves domestic violence court will pass protection order prohibiting batterer to continue in wife battering further any more, residence order will also be passed in her favour and, compensation and monitory reliefs are provided her by the court.[30]

The Act of 2005 is very progressive and modern enactment attempting to provide complete protection to women from domestic violence but only be good enactment not fulfills its objective unless its enforcement is proper. Domestic violence is very different type of problem in which aggrieved person and aggressor have very intimate relationship therefore prosecution agency and judiciary are usually not in situation to provide justice to victim and in proper handling the problem by punishing batterer due to lack of reporting and evidences. This problem may affect enforcement of this Act of 2005 also. Domestic violence is as one of the most difficult types of crimes to investigate and prosecute. Because physical abuse typically occurs inside the home, rather than in public, the victim and the victim's children are often the only witnesses to the crime. Consequently, the prosecution's case typically relies heavily on the victim testifying. But getting victims to testify can be a monumental challenge. In majority of domestic violence cases, victims recant the testimony that was given to law enforcement immediately following the violent event and many victims refuse to continue co-operating with the prosecution. These situations give rise to dismissal of the case. A number of reasons why victims so frequently recant testimony or refuse to co-operate may be given. In domestic violence cases, unlike most crimes, the victim and batterer are or were involved in an intimate relationship. The victim may still care for the batterer and feel obligated to try to protect the batterer from prosecution, which is more prevalent reason in

India where husband is worshiped and wife dedicates her life to husband in this world and also beyond this world. The victim and batterer may have children and for the future of children she wants to continue in marriage with batterer. Victims of domestic violence are often financially dependent on the batterer.

All these factors contribute to the unique difficulty for domestic violence prosecution. Protection of Women from Domestic Violence Act 2005 is very sound and progressive Act but still the problem of lack of direct evidences, victim's full cooperation and recant testimony may affect its proper enforcement and create probability for its failure.

CONCLUSION

Wife battering is a social vice creating problem to women, family system and prospective progeny. It is in existence from time immemorial and still continuing in the era of liberalization, globalization and equalization, showing that there is unjust and injustice situation with half of the world population by another half of the world, evoking to think its cure and remedy. In this regard legislature, law enforcement and judiciary should think about every facet of problem therefore causation and prevention should be considered at the same time. Personality traits of batterer and battered women, strain situation of the society, Intoxication, social role assignment to sexes and socialization process are prevalent causes of wife battering. Analysis of these causes shows that behind all these causes most important factor is faulty notion of male superiority resulting into distorted social norms and values. For prevention of wife battering situation social reconstruction is needed in which social norms and values should be such by which real loving atmosphere in the family be created. Law is main instrument having two pronged action one immediately checking the problem by penalizing batterer and providing remedy to the victims. Another action of law is teaching to coming generation by socializing in new norm and value atmosphere. International Community has given directions by various conventions to state parties for proper legislation to prevent wife battering. In India various laws have been made accordingly. Out of these the provisions of Indian Penal Code and Protection of Women from Domestic violence are commendable.

Community has given directions by various conventions to state parties for proper legislation to prevent wife battering. In India various laws have been made accordingly. Out of these the provisions of Indian Penal Code and Protection of Women from Domestic Violence Act are commendable.

Legislations are there to protect women, but women have no willingness to file the case, if filed to pursue the case. Greatest problem before the legal system is due to the retracted testimony by which law is not properly enforced and becomes only paper tiger resulting into loss of faith and respect in legal system. When case of wife battering is filed by wife, she sustains loss of reputation while husband losses nothing but his masochism is acclaimed. Filing of case becomes decisive factor in breaking of marriage and prospect of remarriage and other supports are nil to the wife. In these circumstances for proper tackling the problem of wife battering we should think about social awakening, social reconstruction and changing of social norms and values alongwith legal protection to women. Without social change the dream of society free from wife battering cannot be realized.

Legislations are there to protect women, but women have no willingness to file the case, if filed to pursue the case. Greatest problem before the legal system is due to the retracted testimony by which law is not properly enforced and becomes only paper tiger resulting into loss of faith and respect in legal system. When case of wife battering is filed by wife, she sustains loss of reputation and husband losses nothing but his masochism is acclaimed. Filing of case becomes decisive factor in breaking of marriage and prospect of remarriage while other supports are nil to the wife. In these circumstances for proper tackling problem of wife battering we should think about social awakening, social reconstruction and changing of social norms and values along with legal protection to women. Without social change the dream of society free from wife battering cannot be realized.

NOTES

1. S. 3. Protection of women from Domestic Violence Act, 2005.
2. S. 2(a) PWDV Act, 2005.
3. Leory G. Schultz, The Wife Assaulter, *Corrective Psychiatry and Journal of Social Therapy*, (6th Feb., 1960) pp. 103-111.

4. Bonnie E, Carlson Battered Women and their assailants in Delos H. Kelly (ed.) *Deviant Behaviour,* St. Martin's Press, New York, 1979, p. 540.
5. *Id* at p. 546.
6. Sue Titus Reid, *Crime and Criminology* (5th ed.), p. 247.
7. Bonnie E. Carlson, *Op. cit.,* p. 540.
8. *Id* at p. 543.
9. Maura O'Keefe and Shirley Lebovics, Adolscents from Mantally Violent Homes, Domestic Violence: Definition and Much more available on *http://www.Answer.com.*
10. Reid, *Op.cit.,* p. 247.
11. Jean Jacous Rousseau cited in Indu Prakash Singh, *Women's Oppression Men Responsible,* Renaissance Publishing House, New Delhi, 1988, p. 30.
12. Report of the Committee on the status of Women in India, p. 102.
13. Art. 3 CCPR.
14. Art. 5 CEDAW, 1981.
15. Paragraph 1 of Preamble of DEVAW 1993.
16. Paragraph 6 of Preamble of DEVAW 1993.
17. *Id* at paragraph 12.
18. Art. 2 of DEVAW.
19. Court applies this special treatment approach when women before the court fulfls the requirement of sex stereotype. Neither protective nor corrective approaches have been applied by courts when women before the court did not meet the sex stereotypes. In *state of U.P., v. Kaushiliya,* AIR 1964 SC 416 the apex court negative the challenge by a sex worker to the law on immoral traffic which conferred unfettered discretionary power on the magistrate to deal with prostitutes.
20. Added to the Constitution of India, by 42nd Amendment of Constitution.
21. Inserted by criminal law (2nd amendment) Act 1983. Sec. 498-A reads as:

    498-A Husband or relative of husband subjecting her to cruelty- whoever being the husband or the relative of husband of a women, subjects such woman to cruelty shall be punished with imprisonment for a term which may extend to three years and shall also be liable to fine.

Explanation: For the purpose of this section, cruelty means–

(a) any willful conduct which is of such nature as is likely to drive the woman to commit suicide or to cause enjury or danger to life and limb or health (whether mental or physical) of the woman; or

(b) harassment of the woman where harassment is with the view to coercing her or any other person related to her to meet any unlawful demand for any property or valuable security or is on account of failure by her or any other person related to meet such a demand.

22. Section 113-A Evidence Act reads as:

When the question is whether the commission of suicide by a woman had been abetted by her husband or any relative of her husband and it is shown that she had committed suicide within a period of seven years from the date of her marriage and that her husband or such relative of her husband has subjected her to cruelty the court will presume having regard to all the circumstances of the case, that such a suicide had been abetted by her husband or by such relative of her husband.

Explanation: For the purpose of this section 'cruelty' shall have the same meaning as in S.498-A IPC.

23. Ins. By Act 43 of 1986, Sec. 10 (w.e.f. 19.11.1986).

24. S.304-B IPC, S.113-A and S.113-B Indian Evidence Act.

25. *Soni Babubhai vs. State of Gujarat* (1991) 4 SCC 298.

26. (1991) Cr. L.J. 268 (M.P.).

27. Section 28 of Protection of Women from Domestic Violence Act, 2005.

28. By giving protection to wife from sexual abuse Act of 2005 has introduced the concept of marital rape in legal protection arena. Traditionally Rape within marriage is not an offence in Indian. There is some limited recognition of rape within marriage, in as much as it is recognized as an offence, if the wife is below 15 years of age (Sec. 375 IPC) or if the parties are separated by an agreement or by custom: Explanation of S.375 of IPC provides:

Explanation: "Sexual act of a man with his own wife will not amount to rape unless the wife is below the age of 15. Sec. 376-A of Indian Penal Code Provides that: "376-A Intercourse by a man with his own wife, who is living separately from him under a decree of separation or under any custom or usage without her consent shall be punished with imprisonment of either description for a term which may extend to two years and shall also be liable to fine."

29. SS. 4 & 5 of Protection of Women from Domestic Violence Act, 2005.
30. SS. 17-22 of Protection of Women from Domestic Violence Act, 2005.

REFERENCES

Carlson Bonnie E. (1979), Battered Women and their assailants in Delos H. Kelly (ed.) Deviant Behaviour, Sr. Martin's Press, New York.

Keefe Maura O' and Shirley Labovics, Adolscents from Maritally Violent Homes, Domestic Violence and Much More available on *http://www.answer.com.*

Reidsue Titus Crime and Criminology (5th ed.), Hold Rinehart and Winston, New York, 1988.

Singh, Indu Prakash (1988), Women's Operation Men Responsible Renaissance Publishing House, New Delhi.

Schultz Leory G. (1960), The Wife Assaulter, Corrective Psychiatry and *Journal of Social Thereapy,* 6th Feb., p. 103-111.

Human Rights and Children in India

ARUN KUMAR SINGH*

INTRODUCTION

Children are the supreme assets of any nation.[1] They being the great gift to humanity are the potential and useful human resources for the progress of the country.[2] Children are innocent but defenceless. They are burdened by prejudice fears and hypocrisy. They need appropriate attention and proper support to grow well.[3] If we neglect and do not provide bare needs of food health and education, heavy price will have to be paid in future. Neglecting the children means loss to the society as a whole. If children are deprived of their childhood, socially economically, physically and mentally, the nation gets deprived of potential human resources for social progress.[4] Abandoning children and excluding food foundation of life for them is a crime against humanity. Millions of children live in difficult circumstances, such as orphans, refugees, street children, children working in hotels, tea stall etc. Van Bueren argues that children's right can be distilled down to four core elements identified as protection, precaution, provision and participation which she calls the four P.[5] GandhiJi said about the children and their role in peace and human development that "if we are to reach real peace in this world, and if we are to carry on real war against war, we shall have to be with children. And if they will grow up in their natural innocence, we won't have to struggle, we won't have to pass fruitless, idle resolutions, but we shall go from love to love and peace to peace, until at last all the corners of the world are

* *Lecturer, Department of Law, North Eastern Hill University, Shillong.*

covered with that peace and love for which consciously or unconsciously, the whole world is hungering"[6]. India is home to almost nineteen per cent of the world children.[7] More than one third of the countryy's population around forty four million are below eighteen years.[8] About forty per cent of those children are in need of care and protection which indicate the extent of the problem.[9] Children are the most vulnerable section of the society. This paper aims to high light the problems of children, national and international provisions regarding children and role of judiciary. The problems and issues like child abuse, malnutrition, children neglect, child education, health protection and development, child discrimination, child marriageand trafficking of children.

STATUTORY PROVISIONS IN INDIA

Article 21 of the Constitution of India includes right to life with human dignity[10]. This right to life includes right to live with human dignity enshrined in Article 21, derives its life breath from the Directive Principle of State Policy and particularly clause (e) and (f) of Article 39[11] and Article 41[12] and Article 42.[13] Article 21 A[14], Article 45[15]and Article 51-A[16] of the Constitution of India, ensures free and compulsory education for the children. Apart from the above legislations, The Prohibition of Child Marriage Act, 2006 and The Commission for the Protection of Child Rights Act, 2005 also provide protection to childhood. The Prohibition of Child Marriage Act, 2006 provides that every child marriage is voidable. The Commission for the Protection of Child Rights Act, 2005 provides for the constitution of National and State Commission for the protection of children.Some states have formulated state specific legislation to deal with child abuse e.g. Goa and Tamil Nadu[17]. Even then minimum requirements to enable a person to live with human dignity are not fulfilled. The first Act dealing with child labour was the Employment of Children Act, 1938 which prohibited the child labour by the children below the age of fourteen years in railway. . After the independence many other enactments came in to force which prohibited employment of children in different occupations[18]. Thereafter in 1986 Child Labour (Prohibition Regulation) Act came in to force. This Act repelled the Employment of Children Act 1938. Part A of the Schedule to the Act 1986 mentions the name of the occupations where no child can be employed or permitted to work. They are the occupation connected with (1) transport of passengers, goods or mail by railway, (2) cinder, picking, clearing of an ash pit or building operations in railway premises, (3) work in catering establishment at railway station involving the movement of vendor or any other employee of the establishment from one platform to another or into or out of moving trains, (4) work relating to construction of railway station or with any other work where such work is done, enclose proximity to or between the railway live. Part B of the schedule contains name of the process where no child can be employed or permitted to work. They are, beedi making, carpet weaving, cement manufacturing including begging of cement, cloth printing, dying and weaving, manufacturing of matches, explosive and fins work, mica cutting and splitting shellac manufacture, soap manufacture, fanning wool, cleaning, building and construction industry. Section 3 of the Act prohibits children in employment of certain occupation but has certain exceptions.[19] Such as children can continue to work if they are part of the family which is doing labour. Further the children may continue in the industries which are not specified in Part A or Part B of the schedule. The children can be employed in any school which is established by the Government. If any person employs any child or permits to work in contravention of the provision of section 3,of Child Labour (Prohibition) Act,1986, shall be punished up to one year imprisonment which will not be less than three-months and fine up to 20,000 which will not be less than 10,000.[20]

INTERNATIONAL PROVISIONS

Childhood is the most sensitive part of life of every human being. The identity of the individual is formal during childhood. Children comprise about 50 per cent of earth's population and are most vulnerable component.[21] A number of conventions have been concluded under the auspices of the United Nation and other International organization to protect human rights of children. These are in the form of treaties. But the problem is that these treaties shall be binding only on the parties to the treaties not on third parties. This customary rule is based on the maxim *pacta tertis nec nocent nec prosunt.* This rule has been incorporated in Vienna Convention 1969.[22] India has become party of same by ratification.[23]

The concept of equality of all human being as embodied in the Universal Declaration of Human Rights, 1948, recognizes a standard in the field of treatment of the child. The Convention on the Rights of Child was initiated from the period of league of Nation on 'Declaration of the Rights of Childs in 1924.[24] This Declaration is also known as Geneva Declaration on the Rights of Child. Meanwhile, in 1946 the Temporary Social Commission of Economic and Social Council decided that terms of Geneva Declaration should be binding on the peoples of the world. Subsequently, the Social Commission in 1950 adopted a draft of Declaration on the Rights of Child on the line of Geneva Declaration.[25]Thereafter the same was forwarded to ECOSOC. ECOSOC considered the Commission's opinion and sent it to General Assembly. General Assembly adopted and proclaimed the Declaration to the Child on 20th November 1959.[26] The Declaration contains 10 Articles called ten principles.[27] It has 10 values of human rights.[28]

But on 20th December 1989, U.N. General Assembly adopted a convention known as the Convention on the Rights of child, 1989. The preamble of the convention affirms that:

(i) The children require special emphasis on the primary care and protective responsibilities of the family.

(ii) The need for legal and other protection of child before and after birth.

(iii) The need for respect for cultural values of the child's community, and

(iv) It requires international co-operation in achieving realization of the children's rights.

The Convention recognizes that every human being below the age of 18 years can be called a The Convention recognizes that every human being below the age of 18 years can be called a child.[29]All the rights of children are interrelated. One right will be useless without other right. Likewise, right to life is inherent right of every human being.[30] Right to freedom of expression[31] and right to education[32] are closely related. Same thing is applied in case of right to health[33] and right to social security.[34] Article 14 deals with the child's right to freedom of thought, conscience and religion. Every child has the right to standard of living adequate for his/her development.[35] Children should not perform any work which may be hazardous or interfere with education, or which may be harmful to their development and health. That is why children have been protected from economic exploitation.[36] Besides above rights, the Convention provides some other rights to the children.[37] The Convention has some legal protective guidelines in ensuring harmonious family relation.[38] The Convention has also prescribed certain positive regulations for protecting children from exploitive labour and abuses. The state parties are under the obligations to ensure these rights.[39] These rights are enforceable directly against the state.

Apart from the provisions of the Universal Declaration of Human Rights[40] and International Covenant on Civil and Political Rights,[41] Article 2 of the Declaration on Protection of Persons from being subjected to Torture or Degrading Treatment or Punishment, 1975 declares torture as an offence against human dignity which is violation of human rights and fundamental freedoms.[42] The states are directed not to promote and not to tolerate any form of torture even in exceptional circumstances as State of War or internal political instability or emergency.[43]

It also mandates the state parties to take effective measures to prevent all forms of torture.[44] In order to make it more effective the struggle against torture continued with the result that a convention was adopted by the General Assembly on December 10, 1984, which is known as the Convention against Torture and Other Cruel, Inhuman or Degrading Treatment or Punishment. This is also known as United Nation Convention against Torture, 1984. It came into force on June, 26, 1987. In this Convention state parties are obligated to prevent and punish not only act of torture but also other acts of cruel, inhuman, degrading treatment or punishment.[45] Each state party shall ensure that all acts of torture and its attempt are an offence[46]. These offences are made punishable according to its gravity.[47] The state shall not expel, return or eradicate any person to another state where there are substantial grounds for believing that he would be in danger or being subjected to torture. The Convention was signed by India on 14th October 1997, however it has not been ratified till now.

PROBLEMS AND ISSUES REGARDING CHILDREN

One of the characteristics of modern society is heavy reliance on law to bring about social change. The task of social reconstruction, development and nation-building all call for major changes in the social order, to which legislation is one of the main instruments. But legislation cannot by itself change society. To translate these rights into reality is the task of other agencies. The judiciary and the executive have a major role to improve the status of children. Mass media is used for publicity of certain measures taken up by the government. There is a wide gap between promise and performance[48]. Following are the major issues which are needed to be discussed.

(a) Malnutrition: Nineteen per cent of world's children are living in India. According to 2001 census, 44 million people of the country are aged below eighteen years. But position of children are terrible. According to the recently released National Family Health Survey - 3 for 2005-2006, 46% of children below seven years are underweight down from 47% in 1998-1999.[49] It is disappointing that despite the acceleration in economic growth in the country there has been only one per cent reduction in the proportion of underweight children at the end of seven years.[50] Three out of four children in India are anaemic children[51] .Under 3 of the age are 79%.[52] According to National Health Survey – 3, 2005-2006 child born with low birth weight are 46%.[53] The most crucial factor regarding malnutrition is that the public health messages are not reaching to the families and children. Doctors always suggest breast feeding during first six months of baby's life. Despite that in 2005-2006 only 23 per cent of infants up to five months old were exclusively breastfed. [54] Apart from the above child malnutrition are closely linked with the care of women receive during pregnancy and thereafter. NHF – 3, reveals that there is marginal progress from 1998-1999 to 2005-2006. The proportion of birth assisted by doctor, nurse or health workers went up 42 to 48 per cent while birth rate went up from 36 to 41 over the same period. Working Group Report on Women and Children for the Eleventh Five Years Plan (2007-2012) revealed that 2.5 million children age in India every year, accounting for one in five death in the world with girls being 50% more likely to die.[55] One out of 16 children die before they attain one year of age and one out of 11 die before they attain five years age. India accounts 35% of the developing worlds low birth weight babies and 40% of child malnutrition in developing countries one of the highest level in the world. A high India's neo-natal mortality rate declined in 1990 from 69 per 1000 live birth in

1980 to 53 per 1000 live birth in 1990. It remained static dropping only four points from 48 to 44 per 1000 live births between 1995 and 2000. From the above study it becomes important to focus on improving intent feeding and carrying practices as well as nutritional well being of mothers because intergenerational transfer of malnutrition from mother to child captured in the high proportion of low birth weight babies. It is essential to be checked. New born babies and children under the age of 3 years needs top most attention.

(b) Problem of Child Education: In 1974 National Policy for Children came into existence, which declared that children are the most important assets of the Nation. It pleaded that measures and safeguards are needed to protect them. But unfortunately ten Five Year Plans have not allocated adequate resources to meet the needs of the children. However, Article 21 A[56], Article 45[57] and 51-A[58] of the Constitution of India, ensures for free and compulsory education for the children. But insensitivity of the Government is a hindrance to achieve this goal. Total expenditure on children in 2005-2006 on health, education, development and protection together amounted to a mere 3.86% which in 2006-2007 reached 4.91%.[59] Let alone others even available resources have also not been utilized effectively for achieving UNESCO report. Only 29% of pre-primary age children are enrolled in educational institution in India. [60] Spending money on child education is not expense on public exchequer but asset in the long run. It is the best infrastructure that could be laid for the prosperity of a nation. About 42 million children in the age group of 6-14 do not have access to basic education. [61] Female education which famous jurist Palkiwala called priority of priorities is hampered not only by deep-rooted prejudice culture but also due to lack of real concern. According to the stastics provided by UNICEF, out of India's 7 lakh rural primary and upper primary schools only one in six have toilets, which deter girls from attending school.[62] Initiatives like operation blackboard, *Sarva Shiksha Abhiyan* and mid-day meal scheme have been running so that school drop out rate can be curtailed. But the policies and efforts to serve the proposes are not consistent.

(c) Problem of Child Labour: Problem of child labour is not only a disgrace to generation but also a problem of future generation.[63].It is violation of their childhood also. As a consequence of development

child labour is a symbol and symptom of inequality in which hundreds of children are excluded from a normal childhood and denied their fundamental rights in India[64]. Considering the perpetuation of the practice of bonded labour in the agrarian rural structure in India such development is adversely affecting the children belong to the deprived communities[65]. Millions of half fed, half naked and illiterate children contribute 20% of total income of Gross National Product to a nation of one billion people.[66] It is one of the most pressing problems which the International Community is facing. According to ILO estimated 2000, 211 million children between 5 to 14 years of age work in developing countries, and 50 to 60 million children between the age of 5 to 11 are working in hazardous activities.[67] The Employment of Children Act, 1938 which prohibited the child labour by the children below the age of fourteen years in railway. But the Act did not apply to the other industries though these are hazardous. If any person employs any child or permits to work in contravention of the provision of section 3,of Child Labour (Prohibition) Act,1986, shall be punished up to one year imprisonment which will not be less than three-months and fine up to 20,000 which will not be less than 10,000.[68] But Act did not lay as to rehabilitation of the child once the employer is prosecuted.

From above problems it appears that following issue is needed to be discussed.

(d) Child Abuse: Child abuse is a series issue of the society. It is gross violation of human rights of children. The National Child Abuse Study carried out by *Prayas* Institute of Juvenile Justice as part of global study on child violence by the United Nation has revealed that close 5% of the children in the country face some form of abuse.[69] The term child abuse may have different connotations in different cultural milieu and socio-economic situations. A universal definition of child abuse in the Indian context has not been defined.[70] The working definition of child abuse as is as follow .[71] 'Child abuse refers to the intended, unintended and perceived maltreatment of the child, whether habitual or not including the following:

'Physical and psychological abuse, neglect, cruelty, sexual exploitation and maltreatment. Any act, deed or word which debases degrades or demeans the intrinsic worth and dignity of a child as a human being. Unreasonable deprivation of his or her basic needs for survival, such as food and shelter or failure to give timely medical treatment to an injured child resulting in serious impairment of his or her growth and development or in his/her permanent incapacity or death.'

Child abuse can be classified in the following categories.

(1) Physical abuse: Physical abuse means inflicting physical injury upon a child. This may include hitting, shaking, kicking, beating or otherwise harming a child physically. The parent or caretaker may not have intended to hurt the child but some time over discipline is inappropriate to the child abuse.[72]In Indian society like most of the societies across the world is patriarchal in structure where the chain of command is definite and unavoidable.[73] In such power structure parents and teacher adopt harsh method of disciplining children.[74] Severe physical maltreatment also takes place outside the family and forms of it are corporal punishment in school and physical abuse at workplaces. The indication for identifying physical abuse is, physical indication in the child, behavioral indication in the child and parental indication in family where abuse is going on . About 76.7% of subjects reported physical abuse. The most common perpetrators of physical abuse are father (55.2.%) followed by policemen (29.7%).[75] Physical abuse was found to be significantly associated with domestic violence use in family, step parent. Apart from this physical abuse in school also referred corporal punishment. About 65% of children get beaten at schools across the country.[76] Out of those 54.28% were boys and 45.42% were girls.[77]Older children were beaten more in school as compared to younger ones.[78] The very high percentage of corporal punishment was reported in government and municipal schools.[79] Despite the ban on corporal punishment in Andhra Pradesh, Delhi, Madhya Pradesh, Maharashtra, Goa, and West Bengal the high rate of incidence from these states is a matter of concern.

Apart from above physical abuse of children in institutions is also a major violation of human rights of children. If is found that there are large number of people without parental care, vulnerable and need of care and protection. The states set up the institutions to provide food shelter clothing and education to children who were not living in the family environment. But the standard of care in these institutions are very low. Children are often subjected to physical abuse within and out side of the institutions by care givers, peers, police staff, and members. It is found that about 56.37% of abuse is in correctional institutions.[80] Among them girl's physical abuse is very high.

Besides above the child domestic workers are also physically abused. The children who work as domestic workers are the most vulnerable and exploited. The works are like carrying babies, handling fuel , work for long hours without rest with little or no remuneration. They are deprived of schooling, play and social activities. They do not get affection from friends and their families. A study conducted by Save the Child and Tulir in 2006[81] reveled the position of the West Bengal that 31% of child domestic workers did not get any rest during the day while 41% had only two or less than two hours rest in a day.[82] About 50.2% of the domestic workers worked seven days a week[83] out of total working children 23% child domestic workers among these 81.16% were girls. Among total number of working children 11.2% children were at tea kiosk and restaurants.[84] Out of total children working in tea kiosks and restaurants 22.55% reported physically abuse, among then 91.94% were boys.[85] Out of total number of working children, 7.8% were involved in bidi rolling, among them 83.33% girls.[86] Besides above the position of street children are not good. One of the study conducted by Human Rights Watch in 1996 reported that the street children in India were routinely detained, illegally beaten and tortured and sometime killed by police. About 66% per cent of street children living with their parents but only 58.8% were provided food by them. About 20% children brought their food by themselves.

(2) Sexual abuse: Sexual abuse means inappropriate sexual behavior with a child. It includes fondling a child's genitals, making the child fondle the adult's genitals, intercourse, incist rape, sodomy, exhibitionism and sexual exploitation. To be considered that these acts are generally committed by person responsible for the care of child like baby sitter, parents or related to the child. If a stranger commits these acts it would be considered as sexual assault and solely will be handled by police and criminal Courts.[87] Child sexual abuse includes, inducement or coersion of a child to engage in any unlawful activities, the exploitative use of child in prostitution or other unlawful sexual practices, the exploitative use of children pornographic performance and materials. But it is not

limited up to the above only. It also includes some severe form of sexual abuse. These are assault including rape and sodomy, touching or fondling a child, exhibitionism (forcing a child to exhibit his/her private body parts), photographing a child in nude. There are some other forms of sexual abuse also likewise (a) forcing kissing (b) sexual advances forwards a child during marriage situations (c) sexual advances towards a child during travel (d) exhibitionism (e) exposing a child to pornographic materials. The National Child Abuse Study carried out by Prayas Institute of Juvenile Justice as part of global study on child violence by the United Nations has revealed that close to fifty per cent of the children in the country face some form of abuse.[88] The Study on Child Abuse India, 2007, a study conducted by Ministry of Women and Child Development. In which the questionnaire administered to 12,447 children. Out of total child respondents 53.22% reported having faced one or more forms of sexual abuse. Among them 52.94% were boys and 47.06% girls.[89] Out of total child respondents 20.90% were subjected to severe forms of sexual abuse which include sexual assault, making the child exhibit private body and being photographed in nude. Out of these 57.30% were boys and 42.7%were girls.[90] Besides it out of 12447 child respondents were 51%, reported being subjected to other forms of sexual abuse that included forcible kissing exposure of pornographic materials. [91]

(3) Emotional Abuse: It is also known as verbal abuse, mental abuse and psychological maltreatment. It includes act or failure to act by the parents, caretakers which cause or can cause serious behavioural cognitive emotional or mental trauma. This can include parents caretakers using extreme and/or bizarre forms of punishment, such as confinement in closet or dark room or threatening or terrorizing child.[92] According to World Health Organization Report,1999 of the Consultation on Child. Abuse Prevention, Geneva, emotional abuse includes the failure to provide appropriate supportive environment including availability of primary attachment figure so that the child can develop a stable and full range of emotional and social competencies commensurate with her or his personal potential and in the context of society in which the child dwells.[93] There are various forms of emotional abuse like, humiliation, comparison, etc. Humiliation of a child refers to degradation of the self esteem of a child by parents, caretaker or

any other persons in presence of others. Some time parents or caregivers compare one child with others in terms of their physical appearance. It mentally affects the children.

A research conducted by Ministry of Women and Child Development in 2007 resulted that out of 12447, 48.37% children reported emotional abuse of one form or other among them 49.99% are boys and 50.1% are girls. Out of total number of children 44.13% reported facing humiliation, and out of all the child respondents 20.06% reported emotional abuse through comparison. Out of which 48.86% were boys and 51.4% girls.[94] Apart from this girl children are neglected. This is failure to provide all round development of a girl child. Suggestions from the above study point out that there is need to discuss the critical issues of child abuse and child protection so that we can resolve the problem of human rights violation of children. Government agencies themselves cannot deal with it. While dealing with the issue of abuse, it is imperative to identify the forms of abuse.The way in which the funds allocated to it are used and to empower the child to resist abuse. The understanding must be translated in to action not only central or state government but civil society families and children themselves, to need and to understand the human rights. It is also important to create atmosphere wherein child is protected from exploitation and abuse.

(e) Child Neglect: Child neglect is an act or omission or commission by any person denies child's basic needs. Neglect can be (a) Physical neglect (b) Educational neglect (c) Emotional neglect.

(a) Physical neglect: Not to provide adequate food or clothing, appropriate medical care, supervision or proper weather protection like heat and cold are covered in the purview of physical neglect. It may indeed abandonment of child from liability. Somehow Constitution of India tries to provide protection under article 39(e).[95]

(b) Educational neglect: It includes failure to provide proper schooling or special educational needs. Though the Constitution of India guarantees fundamental rights to free and compulsory education to the children.[96]But it is not sufficient. Apart from above Article 45 of the Constitution of India provides, about the facility for the education of the child under six years of age.[97] Besides it part IV-A of the Constitution of India imposes obligations on each and every parent/guardian to provide education.[98] But it is found

neither the State nor the (guardians are performing their duty properly and child neglect is going on continuously.

(c) *Psychological neglect:* Psychological neglect includes lack of any emotional support and love, never attending to the child substances abuse including allowing the child to participate in drug and alcohol use, to take them part in right and cabret dance[99]. These problem generally comes from high society or the children from slum areas. The problem of child abuse which is a major problem regarding the human rights of children is spread not only on National levels but also on International levels. That is why the U.N. Secretary General has given following view regarding violence against children across the world: [100]

(a) According to WHO in 2002, 530 children died due to child homicide. In the Global School Based Health Survey carried out in wide range of developing countries between 20% and 65% of school going children reported having been verbally or physically bullied in school in the previous 3 days. Similar rates of bullying have been found in industrialized countries also. (b) An estimated 15million girls and 73 million boys under 18 year of age have been undergoing forced sexual intercourse or other forms of sexual violence involving physical contact. (c) ILO estimates that 218 million children are involved in child labour in 2004 of whom 126 million were involved in hazardous work. Estimates from 2000 suggest that, 5.7 million were in forced or bonded labour, 1.8 million in prostitution and pornography and 1.2 million were victim of trafficking. (d) Only 2.4 of the world's children are legally protected from corporal punishment.

JUDICIAL APPROACH

Indian Judiciary as protector of civil liberties has been guardian of human rights. The Supreme Court through wisely and in statesman like manner adopted strategies which ensured that human rights are accessible to the poorest of the poor and commonest of the common[101] But these rights are not properly enforced and protected. That is why the Judiciary through judicial activism has tried to protect the human rights of children and whenever called upon gave full protection to the rights of children in consonance with the international commitment. However the problems like child labour and their exploitation is still going on.

Considering the problem of child exploitation, Kerala High Court in the case of *Sathyavan Kottarakkra v State*[102] held that– "Exploitation of children in any form which has the tendency to exploit them either physically, mentally or otherwise is objectionable. Any attempt in this direction should be put an end to achieve the goals enshrined by the Indian Constitution, namely Articles 21, 39, 41 45 and 46. In a civilized society the importance of child welfare cannot be over emphasized because of the welfare of the entire community. Its growth and welfare depends on the well being and health of children. Children are supremely important national asset and the future well being of nation depends on how its children grow and develop. Children need special protection because of their tender age and physique, mental immaturity and in capacity to look after themselves. Children must be brought up in an atmosphere of love and affection".

The Supreme Court in respect of child labour gave liberal interpretation in term of 'hazardous employment'. The Supreme Court directed that the schedule to the Employment of Children Act, 1938, should be amended because the term 'employment' is wide and it includes employment in construction work. It was held by the Court that the construction work is clearly hazardous occupation and it is absolutely essential that the employment of children under the age of 14 years must be prohibited in every type of construction work. This is Constitutional prohibition which even if not followed up by appropriate legislation must operate propriovigour.[103]

In another case *Laboratories working and Salal Hydro Project v State of J & K.*[104], Supreme Court held that construction work is hazardous. It is against the goal of Article 24of the Constitution of India.[105] The Court said that:" We are aware that the problem of child labour is difficult problem and is purely on account of economic reason. Parents often want their children to be employed in order to be able to make two ends meet. This is an economic problem and it cannot be solved merely by legislation so long as there is poverty and destitution in the country. It will be difficult to eradicate child labour. But even so an attempt has been made to reduce if not eliminate. Because a child should be able to receive proper education so that he can play vital role in the construction of the society. It is not possible to prohibit child labour together but Article 24 of the Constitution prohibits working in hazardous employment".

In *M.C. Mehta v State of Tamilnadu*[106] the Supreme Court discussed the problems of children employed in match factory of Shivakashi. Public Interest Litigation was filed before the Supreme Court to prevent such type of appointments. The Court opined that, as regards to the welfare of child labour in the factories, insurance scheme should be provided. The Court held that children can be employed in process of packing done in area away from the manufacturing and minimum wages should be fixed. The Supreme Court laid down exhaustive guidelines so that State authorities may protect economic, social and humanitarian rights of the millions of children who are working either in hazardous or non hazardous jobs. The Court directed that for the hazardous job the employer of the factory where the children are working must be asked to pay compensation for every child employed in contravention of the Act a sum of Rs. 20000 which would be deposited in a fund to be known as Child Rehabilitation-cum Welfare Fund. The Court also directed that the liability of employer would not cease even if he would desire to disengage the child previously employed. The Court directed the government to ensure that an adult member of the family whose child is employed in a factory or in mine or in hazardous work gets a job any where in lieu of the child. If it is not feasible the appropriate government as contribution would deposit Rs. 25,000 for each child appointed in the factory. So Authority concerned will have two alternatives, either he should provide job to the guardian or he should deposit Rs. 25000 in Child Welfare Fund.

Apart from the above judgment Supreme Court in *Bandhua Mukti Morcha v State of U.P.*[107] held that State is obliged to render socio economic justice to the child and provide facilities and opportunities for development of their personality. In this case public interest litigation was filed alleging that in U.P. most of children under the 14 years of age are being employed in the carpet industry. Supreme Court appointed Committee to confirm it. The Committee confirmed that forced labour in U.P. carpet industry is going on. The Court observed that the child of today cannot develop to be a responsible and productive member of tomorrow unless an environment which is conducive to his social and physical health is assured to him. Neglecting children means loss to society as whole. If children are deprived of their childhood socially, economically, physically and mentally, the nation gets deprived of the potential human resources for social progress, economic empowerment and good citizenry.

The Court opined that various welfare enactments made by Parliament and appropriate legislations are only on paper and illusory unless they are effectively implemented and the right to life of the child driven to labour is made a reality.[108] A well planned and focus alleviation programme may eradicate child labour.

Besides above, in *Narendra Malva v State of Gujrat*[109] through Public Interest Litigation Supreme Court was asked to pay attention on the plight of child labour in various self mines in the State of Gujrat. It was alleged that minors were being employed in these mines and they were subjected to all kinds of exploitation. The Court requested the *amicus curiae* and SEWA a social action organization to inquire and investigate with regard to the welfare and well being of the self workers and their family with reference to education facilities of the children of the self workers and availability of adequate and proper housing and medical facilities, and submit the report with the Court within three months.

Apart from the above child education is an issue which is needed to be discussed. Supreme Court looked forward in *Mohini Jain's case*[110] and held that right to education is an unremunerated right. Without education the fundamental freedom in Article 19 and dignity of the individual under Article 21 cannot be assured. The Court also observed that "dignity of man is inviolable. It is the duty of the State to respect and protect the same. It is primary education which brings forth the dignity of a man. The Court further observed that right to life is the compendious expression for all those rights which the Court must enforce because they are basic to the dignified enjoyment of life. Considering above judgment Article 21 -A is included in the Constitution of India, and a duty is imposed upon the parents to send their children for education who are between 6 to 14 years of age.

Sexual abuse of children is a major problem of present scenario. *Vishal Jeet v Union of India*[111] is the case in which some seminal questions relating to the sexual exploitation of children have been dealt with and decision have been given by the Supreme Court. The Court in this case observed that it is highly deplorable and heart rending to note that many poverty stricken children and girls are taken to the flesh market and forcibly push in to flesh trade which is being carried in an utter violation of morality, decency and dignity of mankind. The Court held that states should direct their law enforcing authorities to take appropriate and speedy action to eradicate child prostitution and other kind of sexual abuse. The Court also held that the Union and State Government should set up an advance Advisory Committee within their respective zone to look after whether the social welfare programmes to be implemented for the care and protection of young, specially girls, have been implemented or not.

In the case of *Gaurav Jain v Union of India*[112] regarding the protection of basic human rights and dignity of life of the children and prevention of sexual abuse of female children, Supreme Court has pronounced its landmark judgment. It has been held that right of the child is the concern of the society so that the children have the right to equality of opportunity, dignity, protection and rehabilitation by society with both hands open to bring them in to mainstream of social life without pre stigma affixed otherwise for no fault of her/his. It has been also held that State parties shall take all appropriate measures to protect the child from all form of physical or mental violence, injury or abuse including sexual abuse, and State parties shall according to their national laws ensure alternative case for such children. The Court also held that State parties should recognize that every child has the inherent right to life which is already granted by Article 21 of the Constitution of India to make the right to life meaningful even to the deprived segment of the society with dignity of person and in pursuit of happiness.

Supreme Court took into consideration of welfare of child regarding his custody. The Court held that the custody of child may be refused to father if the interest and welfare of the children is better looked elsewhere like a maternal uncle.[113]

From above discussion it appears that the Court being guardian of the Constitution of India looking forward towards interest of children.

CONCLUSION AND SUGGESTIONS

Childhood which is the vital part of the life is required to be protected. But at present it is not safe. Although laws are existing but they are not implemented properly. Child abuse including child labour and child neglect is consistently going on and no response come from the side of the children. This is because they are unable to understand the different dimension of child abuse. Indian Judiciary from time to time is issuing directions and guidelines towards safeguards of children, but it is not implemented in properway. The present National Policy on Child, 1974 needs revision. Every State should establish State Commission for the protection of children to enhance the care and protection of children in country. There is need to develop standards, protocols on child protection at district levels, village levels. Adequate financial and human resources should be allocated and there is need of strong machinery to create a protective environment for children. Apart from this, gender equality should be maintained. Discrimination of girls resulted in their lower enrolment in the schools.Higher levels of malnutrition, trafficking of girls for sexual exploitation, child marriage and their non-participation in decision making in the family should be avoided. The attitude of people towards the value of girl child should be changed to avoid imbalance in the society. Media may be used to spread awareness on human rights of children. The schools are safest for children and therefore efforts should be made to increase the enrolment of children in the school by adopting innovative child friendly methods of teaching. Adequate infrastructure including sanitation facilities with special facilities to the girls can encourage the enrolment of girl children in school. There is also need for a central legislation banning corporal punishment .Besides forgoing there should be better co-ordination at National, State, District and Block levels for the rrescuing children from banned occupation, the reasons must be considered why children are nagging in child labour and hazardous activates.The guidelines should be formulated not only on national levels but on state levels for the rescue, repatriation and rehabilitation of child domestic workers.

Apart from the above the children in institutions need high care. Some other suggestions may be incorporated like Juvenile Justice Board, Child Welfare Committee and Special Juvenile Police

Unit should be setup. In existing institutions standards of care should be established and maintained. The behaviour of care givers of institution some time destroys the faith and trust because they often abuse the children. It should be prevented.There should be uniform definition of child for all legislations relating to employment of children and a child should be construed as a person below 14 years of age. One more thing which is important is to set up night schools so that poor workers and children get opportunity to have at least primary education. India wants to show the world community that it had faith to protect human rights, but is not prompt for that.[114] In India treaty making power is the executive power of Union Government while the law making power for implementing the treaty or convention is vested in parliament.[115]

This distinction makes discrimination and treaties unable to acquire the same status and force as enacted laws have. Simply ratification is not sufficient for the Courts to enforce the provisions of international treaties and conventions. They are required to be transformed in municipal laws. India has enacted a few legislation to give effect to the conventions. For example Immoral Traffic Prevention Act 1987 was enacted to give effect to the Convention for the Suppression of the Traffic in Person and Exploitation of Prostitution of Others of 1949. Juvenile Justice (Care and Protection of children) Act 2000, has been enacted to give effect to the Convention on Rights of Child, 1989 etc. Though Courts had tried to incorporate the international treaties without incorporation in domestic laws but the International provisions should be consistent with domestic laws.

So, from above discussion it is clear that the time has com to pay more attention for the protection of their human rights.

NOTES

1. Justice Shivraj Patil 'Children Supreme Asset of the Nation' in *All India Reporter*, 2005, p. 5.
2. *Ibid.*
3. *Ibid.*
4. *Ibid.*
5. Deirdre Fottrell, 'Children's Right' in Angella Hegarty and Sheobhan Leonard, *Human Rights an Agenda for Twenty First Century* 1999, London, Cavendish Publication Ltd. p. 167.

6. Infra note 174, p. 72.
7. Smt. Deepa Jain Singh in *Study on Child Abuse in India* 2007, p. III.
8. *Ibid.*
9. *Ibid.*
10. Article 21 provides 'No person shall be deprived of his life or personal liberty except according to the procedure established by law'.
11. Article 39(e) provides that the state shall in particular direct its policy towards securing that health and strength of workers men and women and the tender age of children are not the abused and that citizens are not forced by economic necessity to enter avocation unsuited to their age of strength. Article 39(f) provides that the state shall in particular direct its policy towards securing that children are given opportunities and facilities to develop in a health manner and in conditions of freedom and dignity and that childhood and youth are protected against exploitation and against moral and national abandonment.
12. Article 41 provides the state shall within limits of its economic capacity and develop make effective provisions for securing the right to work, education and to public assistance in care of unemployment old age sickness and disable3ment and in other case of undeserved want.
13. Article 42 provides that the state shall make provision for securing just and human condition of work and for maternity relief.
14. Article 21 A, provides, The State shall provide free and compulsory education to all children of the age of six to fourteen years in such manner as the state may be law, determine.
15. Article 45 provides, "the State shall endeavor to provide early childhood care and education for all children until they complete the age of six years"
16. Article 51- A (k) of the Constitution of India provides, "It shall be the duty of every citizen of India who is parent or guardian to provide opportunities for education to his child or as the case may be ward between the age of six and fourteen years."
18. The Factory Act, 1948, Indian Mines Act, 1952, Motor Transport Workers Act, 1961, Beedi and Cigar workers (Condition of employment) Act 1966 and Apprentice Act, 1961.
19. Section 3 of the Act provides, "No one shall be employed or permitted to work in any of the occupations set forth in part A of the schedule or any workshop wherein any of the process set forth in Part B of the schedule is carried on provided that nothing in this section shall apply to any workshop wherein any process is carried on by the occupier

with the aid of his family or to any school established by receiving assistance or recognition from the Government."

20. Section 14 of the Child Labour (Prohibition and Regulation) Act, 1986.
21. Yuri Kolosov, 'The Right of the Child' cited in Janusz Symonides '*Human Rights Concept and Standards*, 2002 New Delhi, Rawat Publication , 259.
22. Article 34 of Vienna Convention 1969.
23. (a) International Convention on Elimination of All Forms of Racial Discrimination 1965 was ratified on 3rd December 1968.

    (b) International Convention on the Suppression and Punishment of the Crime of Apartheid 1973 was ratified on 22nd September 1977.

    (c) International Convention against Apartheid in Sports 1985 ratified on September 12, 1990.

    (d) Convention on Prevention and Punishment of Genocide (1951) ratified by India 27 August 1959.

    (e) Convention on Right of Child (1989) ratified by India in on 11 December 1992.

    (f) Convention on the Elimination of All Forms of Discrimination Against Women (1979) was ratified on July 1993.

    (g) Convention on the Political Rights of Women 1952 was ratified on November 2, 1961.

    (h) Convention for the Suppression of the Traffic in Person and of the exploitation of the Prostitutions of others 1949 was ratified on January 9, 1953
24. Sorabji 'The United Nation and Human Right", Quoted in Sorabjis *Law and Justice*,(ed.) Universal Law Publishing Co. Ltd., p. 19
25. Dr. Baidyanath Choudhary 'Laws Concern on Children on International and National Standard' cited in Dr. Nirmal Kanti Chakraborty, Prof. M.K. Nag (edited) *Law and Child*, 2004, Kolkata, R. Cambray and Co. Private Ltd. p. 3.
26. *Ibid.*
27. *Ibid.*
28. These principles are:

    Principle 1 Right against discrimination in the enjoyment of rights prescribed in the Declaration.

    Principle 2 Right to facilitates and opportunities for development, physically mentally morally, spiritually and socially.

Principle 3 Right to social endurance by birth.

Principle 4 Right to social security for protective care and basic needs.

Principle 5 Right to special treatment and education for physically and mentally retorted children.

Principle 6 Right to full and harmonious treatment and development in loving care of responsive parents in the absence of State.

Principle 7 Right to free and compulsory education in furtherance of general culture and ability to become responsive citizen of tomorrow.

Principle, 8. Right to provides protection and relief.

Principle 9 Right to protection against neglect, cruelty and exploitation.

Principle10 Right to protection against racial, religious and other forms of discrimination.

29. Article 1 of the Convention on Rights of Child, 1989.
30. Article 6 of the Convention on Rights of Child, 1989.
31. Article 13 of the Convention on Rights of Child, 1989.
32. Article 28 of the Convention on Rights of Child, 1989.
33. Article 24 of the Convention on Rights of Child, 1989.
34. Article 26 of the Convention on Rights of Child, 1989.
35. Article 27of the Convention on Rights of Child, 1989.
36. Article 32of the Convention on Rights of Child, 1989.
37. Article 2-Right against all forms of discrimination; Article 16-Right to protection of privacy.
38. (i) Article 5 provides for State's duty to respect parental guideline.

    (ii) Article 9 provides not to be separated from the parents.

    (iii) Article 20, provides for protection of children without family.

    (iv) Article 22, provides for special care for refugee children.
39. (i) Article 32 provides Protection from Child Labour

    (ii) Article 33 provides Protection the Children from drug abuse

    (iii) Article 34 provides Protection against sexual exploitation

    (iv) Article 35 provides Protection against trafficking

    (v) Article 36 provides Protection from all forms of exploitation

    (vi) Article 37 provides Protection from torture and inhuman treatment

    (vii) Article 40 provides Administration of Juvenile Justice, Article 39 provides Prohibition of Cruel treatment and rehabilitative treatment

40. Article 5 of the Universal Declaration of Human Rights, 1948 provides, "No one shall be subjected to torture or to cruel or inhuman or degrading treatment or punishment.

41. Article 7 of the International Covenant on Civil and Political Rights (1966) provides, "No one shall be subjected to torture or to cruel, inhuman or degrading treatment or punishment. In particular non one shall be subjected without his free consent to medical or scientific experimentation.

42. Jitendra Mishra, 'Custodial Atrocities Human Rights and the Judiciary' *Journal of the Indian Law Institute,* Vol. 47, 2005 ,p. 512.

43. Article 3 of the 'Declaration on Protection of All Persons from being Subjected to Torture and other Cruel, Inhuman or Degrading Treatment or Punishment, 1975.

44. Article 4 of the Declaration on Protection of All Person from being Subjected to Torture and other Cruel, Inhuman, Degrading Treatment or Punishment.

45. Article 2 of the U.N. Convention against Torture , proclaims that the prohibition against torture is absolute and no exceptional circumstances, what so ever, including war or public emergency or order from superior authority or public servant can be invoked as Justification of torture.

46. Article 4 the U.N. Convention against Torture, 1984.

47. *Ibid.*

48. Tapti Bose, "A Comparative Study of the U.N. Convention on the rights of the Child and Indian Laws", in N.K. Chakrabarti, M.K. Nag and S.S. Chatterjee, *Law and Child,* 2004, Kolkata, R. Cambray and Co. Pvt. Ltd., p. 68.

49. A. K. Shiva Kumar 'Why are Child Malnutrition not improving in' *'The Hindu'* June 23, 2007.

50. *Ibid.*

51. 'Study on Child Abuse India 2007', Ministry of Women and Child Development, Government of India, 2007, p. 6.

52. *Ibid.*

53. *Ibid.*

54. *Ibid.*

55. Working Group Report on Women and Children for Eleventh Five Year Plan(2007-2012) in *Study on Child Abuse India* ,2007, Ministry of women and Child Development, Government of India. p. 7.

56. Article 21 A, provides, The State shall provide free and compulsory education to all children of the age of six to fourteen years in such manner as the state may be law, determine.
57. Article 45 provides, "the State shall endeavor to provide early childhood care and education for all children until they complete the age of six years".
58. Article 51- A (k) of the Constitution of India provides, "It shall be the duty of every citizen of India who is parent or guardian to provide opportunities for education to his child or as the case may be ward between the age of six and fourteen years."
59. Supra note 51 p. 6.
60. *Ibid.*
61. Supra note 1.
62. *Ibid.*
63. Suresh Babu GS 'Child Labour in India', *Think India' Quarterly Vol-9 No. 3* July-September, 2006 p. 47.
64. *Ibid.*
65. *Ibid.*
66. Latika Srivastava 'Child Labour and Adjudicatory System in India' *Delhi Law Review*, Vol. XXVI, 2004, p. 214.
67. Dr. H. O. Agarwal *Human Rights* 2005,Allahabad Central Law Publication, p. 112.
68. Section 14 of the Child Labour (Prohibition and Regulation) Act, 1986.
69. *The Hindu*, April 14, 2007.
70. World Health Organisation(1999), Report of the Constitution on Child Abuse Prevention, Geneva, *www.who.int/ violence – injury – prevention / violence / neglect / in*
71. *Supra note* 52.
72. *Ibid.*
73. *Supra note* 52 p. 43
74. *Ibid.*
75. *Supra note* 52 p. 44.
76. *Supra note* 52 p. 52.
77. *Ibid.*
78. *Ibid,* p. 54.
79. *Ibid.*

80. *Ibid.*, p. 57.
81. *Ibid.*
82. Supra note 52 p. 58.
83. *Ibid.*
84. *Ibid.*
85. *Ibid.*
86. *Ibid.*
87. Supra note 52.
88. *The Hindu*, 14 April, 2007.
89. Supra note 52 p. 74.
90. *Ibid.*
91. *Ibid.*
92. *Ibid.*
93. *www.who.int/volence injury-prevention/violence/neglect/en*
94 Supra note 52 p. 110
95. Smt. Deepa Jain Singh in *Study on Child Abuse in India* 2007, p. III.
96. Supra note 51.
97 *Ibid.*
98. *Ibid.*
99. *Ibid.* p. 4.
100. Pinherio P.S. ,World Report on Violence Against Children ; United Nations Secretary Generals,2006, Study on Violence against Children, United Nation New York, in Study on Child Abuse India, 2007, Ministry of Women and Child Development Government of India, p. 4.
101. Gitanjali Nain Gill 'Human Rights in India Some reflection' in *Civil and Military Law Journal*, Vol. 37, 2001 p. 34.
102. AIR 1997 Ker 133.
103. *People's Union of Democratic Rights v Union of India* (1982) 3 SCC 235.
104. (1983) 2 SCC 181.
105. Article 24, No Child below the age of 14 years can be allowed to employee in hazardous activities.
106. (1992) 1 SCC 283.
107. (1997) 10 SCC 549.

108. Mamta Rao, '*Law relating to Women and Children*', 2005, Lucknow, Eastern Book Company, p. 433.

109. (2004) 10 SCALE 12.

110. *Mohini Jain v. State of Karnataka* (1992) 2 SCC 66 See also *Unnikrishnan v State of AP* (1993) 1 SCC 645.

111. AIR 1990 SC 1413.

112. AIR 1997 SC 3021.

113. *Kirit Kumar Mahashankar Joshi v Pradip Kumar Karuna Shankar Joshi* AIR 1992 SC 1447.

114. India is signatory to the convention on the Elimination on All Forms of Discrimination Against Women. It is the first country whose report had become due for submission to the committee in 1994, but report was submitted in 2000, similarly India was to place its first report before the committee of Convention on Rights of Child in 1995, but that report was filed in July 7, 1997.

115. Article 73 of the Constitution of India Provides (1) Subject to the provision of this constitution to executive power of the Union shall extend;

    (a) to the matters with respect to which Parliament has power to make law.

    (b) to the exercise of such rights authority and jurisdiction as are exercisable by the Government of India by virtue of any treaty or agreement.

    Provided, that the executive power referred to in subsection (a) shall not save as expressly provided in this constitution or the law made by the parliament extend in any state to matter with respect to which the legislature of the state has also power to make laws.

Implementation of Economic, Social and Cultural Rights in India: Some Reflections

B. C. NIRMAL*

M. K. Sinha's[1], *Enforcement of Economic, Social and Cultural Rights* is important for two reasons: its subject matter and its method. In dealing with human rights, it adopts what one may call the comparative analysis process to assess the implementation and realization of social and economic rights in India. Before coming to the contents of the books it is necessary to put its subject matter in a proper perspective. Human rights[2] are a great idea of our time. Louis Henkin in the "*The Age of Rights*" said that the concept of human rights is "*the only political-moral idea that has received universal acceptance*"[3]. Human rights are also seen today as the central moral issue in contemporary relations–as the '*currency of the international moral discourse*'[4] or as the '*modern tool of revolution*'[5] in the struggle for human dignity in our time. Some contemporary commentators go further and convincingly argue that '*the language of human rights has become the dominant mode of moral discourse of the last fifty years, edging out moral topics such as distributive justice, the common good, and solidarity*'[6]. While such claims to universality and dominance may be overstated, the increasing national and international acceptance of human rights as a universal secular ideology with its attendant consequences for law, politics and morality cannot be denied. The development of an international regime of human

* Professor of Law, Banaras Hindu University, Varanasi, UP, India; Member, Governing Body, Indian Society of International, New Delhi.

rights, the proliferation in the past twenty five years of domestic bills of rights[7] and the spread of democracy across the globe especially after the collapse of communism' symbolized by the fall of the Berlin have provided further strength and vigour to the human rights movement and transferred human rights standards into an yardstick against which the legitimacy of national governments will be judged[8]. At the same time human rights discourse finds itself in the midst of a variety of philosophical and theoretical challenges like belief pluralism[9], cultural relativism[10], appropriation of the politics of human rights by powerful corporations[11], lack of the appropriate criteria for distinguishing between appropriate and inappropriate usages of human rights discourse[12], severe and serious implications of globalization process[13] for human rights[14] and the nearly exclusive focus of existing legal theories on anthropocentric as opposed to ecocentric views[15]. Overcoming these problems and challenges not only require a clear understanding of the issues involved, and the legal status of human rights but also the development of appropriate legal and philosophical framework which could accommodates diverse theories of rights[16].

It has been said that 'human rights are the rights of human being to live according to their nature and with other human beings[17]'. They are attributes of human dignity, and embody 'a common and unifying expression of all people's deepest aspirations to live freely and securely in a just and peaceful world[18]'. They are international norms that help to protect all people everywhere from all types of severe political, legal and social abuses'. They exist as moral and/or legal rights and are regarded as high priority norms. Maurice Cranston states that human rights are matters of 'paramount importance' and their violation 'a grave affront to justice'[19]. Human rights have also been characterized as 'personally oriented, normatively necessary moral requirements, entitlements, justified claims, or more property of individuals', or as 'indispensable valuable possessions'[20], or as 'a claim to something' (freedom, good or benefit) of crucial importance for human life[21]. Human rights are supposed to be inherent in human nature and essential for a man/ woman to live a dignified life. They are based on human kinds' increasing demand for a life in which the inherent dignity and worth of each human being will receive respect and protection. It is also believed that these rights enable us to develop fully and use our human qualities, intelligence our talents and our conscience and to satisfy our spiritual and other needs.

One most important aspect of human rights to be recognized is that they are rights, though not in a strict sense. Gewirth argues that the human rights are primarily claim rights[22], in terms of Hohfeld's famous classification of four different categories of rights[23], held by all human beings against all human beings 'although in certain respects governments have special duties to secure the rights'. Their objects are 'certain important kind of goods'. But the justifying bases or grounds of these rights is uncertain and problematic[24]. Nonetheless, human rights differ considerably from other kinds of rights and practicability, universality, being of paramount importance and immediacy or urgency[25] is some of the criteria which distinguish these rights from those that are merely desires or wants best pursued outside the human rights framework.

Rights, according to Dworkin, are not gifts from God'[26], this institution, in his view is 'a complex and troublesome practice that makes the government's job of securing the general benefit more difficult and more expensive, and it would be a frivolous and wrongful practice unless it served some point. For Feinberg also rights are not 'mere gifts with favours'. 'A right is something which a man can stand on, something that can be demanded or insisted upon without embarrassment or shame... A world with claim rights is one in which all persons, as actual or potential claimants, are dignified objects of respect ... No amount of love or compassion, or obedience o higher authority or noblesse oblige, can substitute for those values'[27]. For these reasons, rights have, to use Rawls expression, 'lexical priority'[28]. This means that they are to be promoted above all other considerations. Moreover, they are to use Dworkin's expression 'political triumphs[29] held by individuals' and as such should not be traded off to attain the policy goals of society. To say so does not imply that they are absolute or exception less or 'resistant to trade-offs'.

One important aspect of these rights is that they only lay down minimal standards and as such their focus is merely on protection of minimally good lives for all people[30]. These rights concern, in words of Henry Shue, 'the lower limits' on 'tolerable human conduct' rather than 'great aspirations and exalted ideals'. This minimal standards approach means that 'not all problems delving from inhumanity or selfishness and stupidity are human rights problems'. This approach also allows national governments to accommodate a great deal of cultural and institutional variations in their quest for the realization of human rights and defence of human dignity[31].

While human rights are generally seen as constitutive of universal standards to be achieved by all nations and peoples across the globe, there is a very attractive suggestion to conceive them as providing a useful framework for negotiating claims between different interest groups. The only caveat is that in this the substances of the claims are not taken into literally[32]. On these understanding human rights emerges only as a language for expressing claims and arguments, rather than an abstract set of universal standards[33].

There is also an interesting suggestion from John Rawls according to which human rights "specify limits to a regime's internal autonomy" and that 'their fulfillment is sufficient to exclude justified and peaceful intervention by other peoples, for example, by diplomatic and economic sanctions, or in grave cases by military force'[34]. But this proposal seems to be debatable, especially in view of Rawl's narrow and limited list of human rights–"the rights to life (to the means of subsistence and security); to liberty (to freedom from slavery, serfdom and forced occupation and to a sufficient measure of liberty of conscience to ensue freedom of religion and thoughts); to property (personal property); and to formal equality as pressed by the rules of natural justice (that is, that similar cases be treated similarly"

It is a also a well known fact to be overemphasized that the list of human rights have expanded since the 18th century and the pressure to expand it further goes unabated leading to the risk of 'human rights inflation'. Central to this phenomenal growth of human rights are not only new threats to human dignity and commission of a new variety of human wrongs but also an increasing use of the rights language by the political movements and campaigners for different causes for assertion, publicity, promotion and legitimation of their claims, demand and concerns at the international level. The growing recognition of symbiotic linkages of human rights with self-governance and self management[35], gender justice and women empowerment and now with environmental justice, reinforced and buttressed by the ongoing processes of globalization and finally the advent of modern technologies, including information technologies continue to inspire and instigate these movements and human rights activists to put pressure on national governments and the international community to accord recognition to new concerns as matters of human rights. T.H. Marshall, a distinguished British sociologist explains this evolution and development of human rights by relating it to elements of citizenship–civil, political and social and forcefully and convincingly argues that full citizenship requires not only the guarantee of civil and political rights but also the protection of social rights[36]. Martin Loughlin's analysis[37] also underscores the breadth of claims currently made in the name of human rights and highlights the major trends in human rights movements each of which promotes an increasing 'politicization of rights'[38]. According to the learned author the rights movement should be seen 'as an evolutionary process' marked by four trends: "*generalization*' (as greater numbers of political claims are expressed in the language of rights), *institutionalization* (as such claims increasingly require recognition in positive law); *collectivization* (as claims extend, beyond the abstract individual to embrace social groups), and *internationalization* (as rights discourse, enter the domain of international relations)."[39]

There is a tendency among scholars to classify all human rights in terms of generations of rights[40] and to put civil and political rights as well as economic, social rights on the same pedestal by advancing the indivisibility and interdependence of human rights[41]. It is argued in particular that the guarantee of certain economic and social rights is a *sine qua non* for enabling an individual to enjoy civil and political rights. No wonder then, the historic priority accorded to civil and political rights is under a scathing attack and prioritizing the first is seen as a ploy to universalize the first generation civil and political rights to universalize western values in the name of human rights[42]. There is also a strong view that to regard right as claims by individuals made against the state 'fosters an atomistic view of society, and obscures the systematic widespread abuse of rights often visited on groups, for example, the millions of humans, who are denied the basic right to food'[43]. So if human rights are to become universal in the real sense of the term, non-western traditions of rights, which reflect more organic notions of socially need to be recognized internationally[44].

Although social, economic and cultural rights have received international and constitutional recognition of course with weaker enforcement machinery and the United Nation's policy is to accord equal status to both categorize of human rights, the former receive lesser importance than the civil and political rights on the basis of supposed deficiencies. In particular, it is argued that social and economic rights are mere programme rights or promotional rights and as such are not enforceable and justifiable[45]. Further, they promote more politicization than civil and political rights because being positive rights their implementation involves the allocation of resources that affect the whole population and there can only be politically preferably solutions to it[46]. It is also argued that social rights are more overtly concerned with questions of distributive justice[47]. This had led some scholars to claim that 'to the extent that social rights can be perceived as more political than legal, this often works to enhance the higher institutional standing of civil and political rights'[48].

The foregoing discussion of jurisprudential questions relating to the existence, content, nature and universality of human rights makes usefulness of a work like the book under review which appears to be a sequel to the author's earlier work[49], self-evident. This book aims to explore the various international and regional mechanisms available for enforcement of economic, social and cultural rights and give an informed account of the jurisprudence of the Indian judiciary in the field of economic, social and cultural rights Chapter I provides an informative and descriptive account of the meaning, definition, evolution and development of the concept of human rights and the place of human rights in international law and the Indian Constitution[50]. The next chapter (Chapter II) begins with matters such as submission of state party report, and the nature of obligations under the International Covenant on Economic, Social and Cultural Rights and then gives an account of the right to development and ends with a narrative of regional mechanisms for implementation of economic, social and cultural rights[50a]. Here the absence of any background to different spectrum of the economic, social and cultural rights may cause avoidable inconvenience to the reader in understanding the existing implementation mechanisms.

It is worthy of note here that economic, social and human rights have a recent but illustrious history[51]. All major religions manifest concern for the poor and oppressed. Thus, Papel Encyclicals emphasized the importance of the right to subsistence while liberation theology has sought to build upon this preferential option for the poor. Thomas Paine, Kant, Marx, John Rawls, Chancellor Bismark in Germany (who introduced social insurance schemes in 1880) all expressed their empathy with social and economic concerns of people[52]. Social and economic rights first found their way into national constitutions and then gained recognition in regional and international institutions[53]. Article 23 of the Covenant of the League of Nations required member states to 'endeavour to secure fair and human conditions of labour'. The Constitution of the International Labour Organization, a part of the Versailles Peace stressed that all industrial communities should endeavour to apply certain agreed methods and principles for regulating labour conditions. From 1919 onwards, the ILO adopted a considerable number of conventions on various aspects of labour, relations and working conditions President Roosevelt in his 1941 address to the U.S. Congress referred to freedom from hunger along with freedom from fear, freedom of speech and freedom of religion as human rights. In his 1944 State of the Union address the said: "We have come to a clear realization of the fact that true individual freedom cannot exist without economic security and independence. Necessitous men are not free men. People who are out of a job are the stuff of which dictatorship are made. Social and economic rights were also set forth in the Draft Bill of Rights compiled in 1914 by a committee appointed by the American Law Institute.

The adoption of the UN Charter marked the beginning of a new stage in international regulation of economic, social and cultural rights. Article 55(a) of the UN Charter states that the UN shall promote higher standards of living, full employment and conditions of economic and social progress and development. The Universal Declaration of Human Rights, 1948 contains an extended and specific list of economic, social and cultural rights. These rights are regulated in more detail in the International Covenant on

Economic, Social and Cultural Rights which is designed to create binding obligations for States Parties to it. These rights are also recognized in a number of regional instruments viz., European Social Charter, American Declaration on the Rights and Duties of Man, Inter-American Charter of Social Guarantees, Arab Labour Standards Convention, Arab Social Security Convention, Protocol of San Salvador.

Social, economic and cultural rights established by the International Covenant on Economic, Social and Cultural Rights are as follows: right to work (Art. 6.1), the right of everyone to just and favourable conditions of work (Art. 7); trade union rights (Art. 8); right to social security (Art. 9); right to protection of and assistance to the family and others (Art. 10); right to an adequate standard of living (Art. 11); right to everyone to the highest attainable standard, the physical and mental health (Art. 12), right to education (Art. 13); cultural rights (Art. 15) and the right to equality in the enjoyment economic, social and cultural rights (Art. 2). All these rights are discussed in some detail in *chapter 3* of the book under review, yet two points need to be highlighted here. *First,* no clear division can be made among the different rights declared in the Covenant. *Secondly,* cultural rights set forth in Article 15 (1) have tended to be dealt with in relation to ICCPR under its non discrimination clause (Art. 2.1), the minorities provision (Art. 27) or specific rights such as freedom of expression, religion, and association and the right to 'take part in the conduct of public affairs[54]. And there has been neglect of the specifically economic and social rights aspects of the cultural rights by the UN human rights bodies'.

While the international community has repeatedly proclaimed the indivisibility and interdependence of all human rights, one can still find statements according to which civil and political rights can be satisfied by state abstention alone but economic and social rights require state intervention. A distinction is also very often made between civil and political rights on the one hand and economic, social and cultural rights on the basis of the notion of immediacy with regard to former and of progressiveness in relation to social rights[55]. But as Theodoor C. van Boven rightly points out that this distinction cannot be taken categorically because the possibility of progressive realization of civil and political rights is also recognized in Article 2(2) of the Civil rights Covenant and is an underlying element of the reporting system under the Covenant[56]. In addition to this, these two categories of rights cannot be logically or practically separated in watertight compartments. The Civil and Political Rights Covenant contains certain provisions which are promotional provisions rather than rules of immediate obligation[57]. On the other hand, there are a good many provisions in the Economic Covenant which are capable of immediate obligations[58]. Again, there are many provisions in the Civil Covenant which have social and economic dimensions and as such depend for their implementation on the realization of some of economic and social rights[59].

The so called difference between civil and political rights on the basis of the notions of enforceability and justiciability is also not a clear but rather a question of gradation. As aptly stated by the former Secretary-General of the UN 'their effective transformation into directly applicable and enforceable legal rights may require time'[60]. This statement implies that social and economic rights may also be enforceable and justiciable rights or may become so in due time. It is true that the Economic Covenant does not require states parties to develop the possibilities of judicial remedies but as aptly pointed out by the Committee on Economic, Social and Cultural Rights, the right to an effective remedy, required under the ICESCR, does not always require a judicial remedy. Further, there are some obligations such as (but by no means limited to) those concerning non-discrimination in relation to which the provision of some form of judicial remedy would seem indispensable in order to satisfy the requirements of the Covenant[61]. In other words, whenever a Covenant right cannot be made fully effective without some role for the judiciary, judicial remedies are necessary. Further, the CESCR is of the view that many provisions of the Covenant could be considered to be justiciable in domestic courts:[62]

'In relation to civil and political rights, it is generally taken for granted that judicial remedies for violations are essential. Regrettably, the contrary, presumption is too often made in relation to economic, social and cultural rights. This discrepancy is not warranted either by the nature of the rights or by the relevant covenant provisions. The committee has already made clear that it considers many of the provisions in the Covenant to be capable of immediate implementation. Thus in general comment no. 3 it cited by way of example: articles 3, 7(a), 8, 10(3), 13(2)(a), 1393), 13(4) and 15(3) ... While the general approach of each legal system needs to be taken into account, there is no Covenant right which could not, in the great majority of systems, be considered to possess at least some significant justiciable dimensions'.

Studies show that social and economic rights may become justiciable through their interaction and interdependence with civil and political rights. For example, based on the so called integrated approach the Human Rights Committee, the European Court of Human Rights and the European Court of Justice have held that the right not to be discriminated applies also to the right to social security and that this aspect of the right to social security is a justiciable part of the right[63]. Again, adopting the inter-dependency and indivisibility of all human rights the Human Rights Committee, the European Commission on Human Rights (now defunct), and the European Court of Human Rights have approached the issue of the right of indigenous peoples to enjoy a distinct culture and such diverse rights as cultural rights, property rights, the right to privacy, participatory rights, and express minority rights[64]. One obvious inference from these facts is that bodies other than those mentioned in Chapter II of the book under review are also engaged in the implementation of social economic and cultural rights in their own way and hence they too could have been discussed in that chapter.

Contrary to the view of some scholars like Robertson, according to which the Economic Covenant only establishes standards to be attainted, the Covenant establishes legal obligations for the States parties to it. It is true that under Article 2.2 of the Covenant, the commitment of states to these rights is limited, where a state 'undertakes to take steps ... to the maximum of its available resources with a view of achieving progressively the full realization of the rights recognized in the ... Covenant'. The Covenant nonetheless 'imposes an immediate and readily identifiable obligations upon states parties'[65]. The obligations of immediate effect include *inter alia* the non discrimination provisions, and the undertaking to take steps which should be taken within a reasonably short time after the Covenant has entered into force for the state concerned and which should be deliberate, concrete and targeted as clearly as possible towards meeting the obligations recognized in the Covenant. Steps to be taken towards the realization of these rights include legislative measures but are not confined to them, other appropriate measures administrative, financial, educational and social measures could also be adopted. The states parties are under an obligation to move as expeditiously and effectively as possible towards the gradual realization of all economic, social and cultural rights. Any deliberate retrogressive measures in this regard would require the most careful consideration and would need to be fully justified. Even in time of severe resources constraints the vulnerable members of society must be protected by the adoption of relatively low cost targeted programmes. Further, a minimum core obligation to ensure the satisfaction of minimum essential levels of each of the rights is incumbent upon each state party. Most importantly, the obligations of the states parties under the Economic Covenant have three components, namely, the duty to respect, the duty to protect and the duty to fulfill. In addition to all these, the Economic Rights Committee has also emphasized that international cooperation for development and thus for the realization of social, economic and cultural rights, is also an obligation for the States Parties to the Covenant[66].

The implementing machinery under the Economic Covenant is discussed in some detail in chapter II of the book under review. What emerges from the discussion in this chapter is the limited competence of the Economic Rights Committee and its relatively inferior status *vis-à-vis* treaty bodies like the Human Rights Committee, the CEDAW and the Committee on the Rights of the Child[67]. Nevertheless, the Committee has through its General Comments and analysis of state reports, made a valuable contribution in the interpretation of the social, economic, social and cultural rights set forth in the Economic Covenant and its work has provided the international community with an analytically helpful interpretive glass on the normative characters of economic, social and cultural rights[68].

The reasons for poor implementation of the Economic Covenant include inter-alia the perceived vagueness of many of the principles contained therein, 'the relative lack of legal texts and judicial decisions; 'the ambivalence of many states in dealing with economic, social and cultural rights[69]; continuous and sustained adverse impact of globalization on the economic and social rights[70]; scant regard of the major agents of globalization for these rights and hijacking of the human rights agenda by the powerful multinational corporations for advancing their interests through the trade related market-friendly paradigm of human rights[71]. In addition, problems faced by the Economic Rights Committee in obtaining relevant and precise information are acute, especially because relatively few non-governmental organizations focus on this area. But what is more worrisome and challenging for the implementation of the economic, social and cultural rights is the attitude of tolerance of states and the international community towards the serious breaches of these rights. While the breaches of civil and political rights generally provoke expressions of horror and outrage and lead to concerted call for immediately action, the sustained and constant denial or deprivation of the economic and social rights are tolerated with attitudes of resignation and helplessness[72] which is certainly a matter of deep anguish and regret for all those who believe in the indivisibility and interdependence of all categories of human rights.

The remaining three chapters (Chapters 4-6) deal with social, economic and cultural rights from the national perspective. In particular, these chapters aim (i) to compare and contrast the constitutional provisions relating to economic, social and cultural rights with the provisions of the International Covenant on Economic, Social and Cultural Rights, (ii) to discuss legislative, administrative and other measures which have been adopted by the government during the last five decades in response to the constitutional mandate to give effect to Directive Principles of State Policy and (iii) to examine and assess the role of the Indian judiciary in the implementation of economic, social and cultural rights.

Chapter 4 which is essentially an introduction[73] to the discussions in chapters 5 and 6, covers a wide range of sub-themes such as the constitutional regime, drafting debate principles of governance under the Directive Principles of State Policy, justiciability of Economic, Social and Cultural Rights, fundamental rights versus Directive Principles of State Policy, international obligations under Indian Constitution and due process of law, implementation mechanism at national level, access of public interest litigation, role of the National Human Rights Commissions, NGOs and media in promotion, protection and implementation of human rights. It may be observed that this chapter being adaptations of a chapter from the authors' earlier work is not organically integrated with the earlier chapters of the present study[74].

Chapter 5 discusses economic rights with the help of constitutional provisions and relevant legislations and schemes[75]. Although the discussion in this chapter is very illuminating the use of sub- head 'conclusion' after each right and the long discussion of some legislations like the National Rural Employment Guarantee Act, 2005 and a relatively brief discussion of other laws tend to affect the quality of discussion in the chapter. The next chapter deals with social and cultural rights[76].

It needs to be recognized that the Indian model of human rights has three pillars, fundamental rights, directive principles of state policy and fundamental duties[77]. While the purpose of the fundamental rights is to create an egalitarian society, to free all citizens from coercion or restriction by society and to make liberty available for all[78], the purpose of the Directive Principles is to fix certain social and economic goals for immediate attainment by bringing about a non violent social revolution[79]. In this unique model of human rights certain rights which belong to the category of economic, social and cultural rights enjoy the status of fundamental rights and as such are enforceable and justifiable. Thus the abolition of the system of bonded labour, right against exploitation, prohibiting all forms of bonded labour, child labour and trafficking in human beings and linguistic and minority rights find place in part III of the Indian Constitution and as such are enforceable[80]. In addition, there are certain directive principles of state policy which have been elevated to the status of fundamental rights by the judiciary[81]. Displaying a remarkable degree of judicial statesmanship and judicial pragmatism, the apex judiciary has also sought to put the directive principles and fundamental rights on the same pedestal by holding that both of them are supplementary and complimentary to each other[82] and by assenting that provisions in Part III of the Indian Constitution should be interpreted having regard to the Preamble and Directive Principle of State Policy[83].

Most significantly, the Supreme Court has observed that the Directive Principles of State Policy are forerunner of the Convention on the Right to development and asked the state to provide facilities and opportunities to ensure all round development of we the people of India[84]'. Finally, it seems to be more willing to enlarge the province of the domestic human rights jurisprudence by adopting a liberal, progressive, policy science oriented integrated and holistic approach to human rights and interpreting the provisions of the Constitution in the light of the standards and norms set out in international treaties, covenants and declarations[85].

But the constitutional provisions relating to economic and social rights and an impressive body of homespun human rights jurisprudence alone are not the surest guarantee for realization of these rights unless they are not backed by adequate resources, good governance practices[86] and effective and efficient implementation of the appropriate policies, programmes and measures designed to carry out constitutional commitment and international undertakings regarding the realization of these rights. No wonder then despite great strides made by the successive governments towards the realization of these rights there is still a huge gap between the pledge and performance so far as the implementation of the Directive Principles of State Policy is concerned. Thus, we are at the halfway point in the quest to achieve the Millennium Development Goals but we have not been able to remove the scar of poverty and achieve the goal of education for all. The country still faces a number of challenges, including unsustainable development[87], poor governance, poor access to health care and reproductive health services, rapid and unplanned urbanization, massive youth unemployment, deforestation, water scarcity, gender inequalities, HIV/AIDS infection, energy crisis, food insecurity, rapid population growth, threats of various types of climate change. But the challenges are neither insurmountable nor are the Millennium Development goals non achievable with the sustained economic growth of around 9 per cent, good policies and practical strategies and optimum use of existing tools and resources and good governance techniques we cannot only eliminate the age old curse of poverty but can also move ahead towards meeting the basic needs of the poor and disadvantaged sections of society. Though the book under review does not delve deep into the causes of poor implementation of economic, social and cultural rights, the author touches upon this issue in his own way in the analysis of the rights in chapters 5 and 6.

Coming to the concluding chapter of the book under review, it does not add anything new to what has already been discussed or said in the early chapters. It gives an erroneous impression that human rights are still a doctrine[88] even after the development of a rich corpus of international human rights law in all these years. In addition, the assertion of the author that the judges have to only interpret the constitution in terms of what the constitution makers wanted or that the main emphasis of the apex judiciary has been on making basic civil and political rights in meaningful for the large masses of the people[89] go against his own assessment of the role of the judiciary in the implementation of economic, social and cultural rights in chapters 5 and 6.

In conclusion, the book under review is a useful addition to existing literature on the subject of economic, social and cultural rights. It should hopefully encourage further studies on the subject with a comparative analysis perspective and stimulate studies on specific rights such as right to health, right to education, right to work. The book successfully explodes the myth that human rights fall nearly into two or three neat categories[90]. The comparative analysis process adopted in the book has also a potentiality to demonstrate that despite the claim of universality of human rights protections, individuals may enjoy different levels of protection depending on whether they happen to live on the planet earth[91]. For these reasons this book is highly recommended as a new acquisition for any comprehensive collection of international and comparative law books.

NOTES

1. M. K. Sinha, Enforcement of Economic, Social and Cultural Rights: International and National Perspectives, Manak Publications Pvt. Ltd, New Delhi, 2006, pp. 354, Price 700/- (Hereinafter referred to Enforcement).
2. For discussion on human rights see P. Alston, *The United Nations and Human Rights: A Critical Appraisal,* New York, Oxford University Press, 1990;T. Buergenthal, *International Human Rights in a Nutshell,* Saint Pual, Minnesota, West Publishing Co, 1995;L. Henkin, *The Age of*

Rights, New York, Columbia University Press, 1990; T. Meron, *Human Rights in International Law: Legal and Policy Issues,* Oxford, Clarendon Press, 1987; F. Newman and D. Wessbrodt, *International Human Rights: Law, Policy and Process,* Cincinnati, Anderson Publishing Co, 1990;Karel Vasak, *International Dimensions of Human Rights,* Paris, UNESCO, 1978; Mahoney and Mohoney (eds) *Human Rights in the Twenty First Century: A Global Challenge,* Netherlands, Martinus Nijhoff, 1993; Asbjorn Eide *et al* (eds) *The Universal Declaration of Human Rights: A Commentary,* Oslo, Scandinavian University Press, 1992; Matthew Crawen, *The International Covenant on Economic, Social and Cultural Rights,* Oxford, Clarendon Press, 1995;John Humphrey, *Human Rights and the United Nations: A Great Adventure,* New York, Transnational Publishers, 1984; Janusz Symonides (ed) *New Dimensions and Challenges for Human Rights,* Rawat Publications, New Delhi, 2003; Janusz Symonides (ed) *Human Rights Concept and Standards,* Rawat Publications, New Delhi, 2002;

3. Louis Henkin, *The Age of Rights,* IX, New York, Columbia University Press (1990)
4. Martin Shupack, 'The Churches and Human Rights: Catholic and Protestant Human Rights Views as Reflected in Church Statements', *Harvard Human Rights Journal,* 6 (1993),127
5. Irwin Cotler, 'Human Rights as the Modern Tool of Revolution', in Kathleen E. Mahoney and Paul Mahoney (eds.) *Human Rights in the Twenty-First Century,* 1993, cited in Joy Gordon, 'The Concept of Human Rights: The History and Meaning of its Politicisation', *Brook J. Int'l Law,* XXIII, 1998, 691.
6. William Twining, 'Law, Justice and Rights: Some Implications of a Global Perspective' (draft, 2007), Professor Twining has written extensively on interface of globalization, legal theory, law and human rights. For a partial list see: *Globalization and Legal Theory* (2000); *Law in Context: Enlarging a Discipline* (1997); 'Reviving General Jurisprudence' in *The Great Juristic Bazaar,* 2003, 335-363.
7. Twining, n. 6; C. Gearty, *Can Human Rights Survive?* (2006) at 63-64
8. Twining, n. 6, at p. 16.
9. B. C. Nirmal, *Right to Self-determination in International Law,* 1999, Deep and Deep, New Delhi, Chapter x, pp. 254-264.
10. See generally An Naim, Toward *An Islamic Reformation, Civil Liberties, Human Rights and International Law* (1990); An Naim and Deng, *Human Rights in Cross-Cultural Perspectives* (1992).
11. 'Relativism' is a highly ambiguous term. Susan Hack, *Manifesto of A Passionate Moderate* (1998). Gordley and Nussbaum merely insist on

the universality of underlying principles. See Martha Nussbaum, *Women And Human Development: The Capabilities Approach* (2000). Alan Gewirth, a prominent universalist argues that universalism can justify certain kinds of ethical particularism, in the sense that ' one ought to give preferential consideration to the interests of some persons against others, including not only oneself but also , other persons with whom one has special relations'. According to him, '(T)he ethical particularism with which I am concerned here, then, is confined to preferences for a particularity towards various groups, ranging from one's family and personal friends to larger pluralities of one's community, nation , and so forth . In the view of Joseph Raz, the Universal and the particular are to be seen as complimentary rather than antagonistic. Raz, 'Multiculturalism', Ratio Juris, 11 (1998) 193. He acknowledges that morality can change, but not radically. 'Since radical moral change is impossible, it follows that social relativism is untenable', he argues. Raz, Engaging Reason', (1999) at 180. For a brief but interesting account of universality vs. cultural relativism debate, see B.C.Nirmal, 'An Ancient Indian Perspectives of Human Rights and its Relevance', IJIL,43,(2003)p 452-458; Baxi Upendra, The *Future of Human Rights* (2006).

12. Twining, note. 6 at 17.
13. For meaning, definition and consequences of globalization, for state sovereignty and international law, see B.C. Nirmal, Sovereignty in International Law, *Soochow Law Journal,* 3,(2006), pp. 1-51 at 41-48.
14. B.C.Nirmal, Globalization and International Human Rights Law, International Conference on International law in the New Millennium: Problems and Challenges Ahead(4-7 Oct, 2001) New Delhi, *Souvenir and Conference papers,* Vol. 2, pp. 575-612
15. Twining, note. 6, 1 et seq. According to Donnelly and Bishop: 'An anthropocentric action is taken to be one in which the reason to act is the provision for a benefit to human beings. An ecocentric action is taken to be one in which the reason to act is the provision of a benefit to the environment.' Quoted in Twining note. 6, p. 19.
16. B. C. Nirmal, An Indian Perspective of Human Rights and Its Relevance, *IJIL,* 43 (2003), 445 et seq.
17. According to Maurice, a human right is something that every body has. They are not rights a man acquire by doing, certain work, enacting a certain role, or discharging certain duties, they belong to him simply because he is a human being. Maurice Cranston, 'Are There Any Human Rights?' Daedalus, 112(4), 1983, p11 cited in Alice Tay, Human Rights and Human Wrongs, *Adelaide Law Review,*21,1999,pp. 1-18,at 9. According to Gewirth, 'Human rights are rights which all persons

equally have simply in so far as they are human.' Gewirth, The Epistemology of Human Rights, Social Philosophy and Policy, Vol. I, 1984, pp. 1-24, excerpted in Lloyd and Freeman, Lloyd's Jurisprudence, Fifth ed. 1985, 229.

18. UNHCR, *Human Rights and Refugee Protection* , October, 1995, p. 15.
19. Cranston, note. 17, at 12
20. Gewirth, note. 17, at 230
21. Susan Moller Okin, Liberty and Welfare: Some Issues in Human Rights Theory, in Nomos XXIII, cited by Gewirth, note. 17, at p. 230.
22. Gewirth, note. 17, at p. 234.
23. Wesley N. Hohfeld, *Fundamental Legal Conceptions,* New Haven: Yale University Press, 1964.
24. Gewirth, note. 17, at p. 236, et seq
25. Cranston, note, 17, at pp. 13-15
26. Dworkin, *Taking Rights Seriously,* 1978, pp. 198-199
27. Feinberg, Duties, Rights and Claims, *American Philosophical Quarterly,* 3, 1966, at 137.
28. Rawls, *A Theory of Justice,* 1971, 42-45; Rawls, *The Law of People* (1999); Collected Papers (1999 ed S. Freeman); *Political Liberalism* (1993): 'Justices as Fairness: Political not Metaphysics,' reprinted in Papers, Chapter 18.
29. Dworkin, no.26 at p. ix, see particularly pp. 232-238, 272-78, 357-58
30. See generally, James Nickel, *Making Sense of Human Rights: Philosophical Reflections on the Universal Declaration of Human Rights* (1987) p. 3-4, cited in Alice Tay, note. 17 at p. 6.
31. Alice Tay, note. 17 at p. 6.
32. Yash Ghai, Universalism and Relativism: Human Rights as a Frame work for Negotiating Interethnic Claims, *Cardozo Law Review,* 21, 2000, pp. 1095-1114.
33. Twining, note. 6, at p. 16
34. Rawls, *A Theory of Justice,* 1971, 42-45; Rawls, *The Law of People* (1999); for scholarly critique of John Rawls' conceptions of Human Rights see Rex Martin, *Rawls and Rights,* second reprint, 1986. see alsoWilliam N. Nelson "Special Rights, General Rights, and Social Justice" *Philosophy and Public Affairs,* 3 (1974): 410-30; Frank I. Michael, "In Persuit of Constitutional Welfare Rights: One View of Rawls' Theory of Justice," *University of Pensylvania Law Review,* 121 (1973): 962-1019; H.L.A.Hart, "Rawls on Liberty and Priority."In *Reading Rawls,* ed.

Norman Daniels, 230-52. New York: Basic Books,1975. Reprinted from University of *Chicago Law Review*, 40 (1973): 534-55.

35. B. C. Nirmal, *Right to Self-Determination in International Law*, 1999, Deep and Deep, New Delhi, pp 254-264, 297-308; B. C. Nirmal, Autonomy and Self-Government in International Law, in TPPRC, Tibetan Autonomy and Self-government: Myth or Reality?, 2000, New Delhi, pp. 17-69.
36. T. H. Marshall, *Citizenship and Social Class*, 1992.
37. M. Loughlin, *Sword And Scales*, 2000.
38. *Ibid*.
39. *Ibid*, at p 208 (emphasis is original).
40. See Jermey Waldron, Liberal Rights, 1993, pp 3-5. For an interesting discussion on the third generation human rights, see Stephen P. Marks, Emerging Human Rights: A New Generation for the 1980's, *Rutgens Law Review*, 33, 1981, 435 et seq; See also P. Alston, Conjuring up New Human Rights: A Proposal for Quality Control, *AJIL*, 78, 1984, 607.
41. Indivisibility of human rights thesis has also been recognized by the Vienna Declaration and Programme of Actions, 1993. The relevant paragraph of the Declaration runs: All human rights are universal, indivisible and interdependent and interrelated. The international community must treat human rights globally in a fair and equal manner on the same footing and with the same emphasis. While, the significance of national and regional particularities and various, historical, cultural and religious backgrounds must be borne in mind. It is the duty of States, regardless of their political, economic and cultural systems to promote and protect all human rights and fundamental freedoms.
42. S. Veith, E. Christodaulidis, and L. Farmer, *Jurisprudence: Themes and Concepts*, 2007, 33.
43. *Ibid*.
44. *Ibid*.
45. Boven, infra note 56, at p. 51.
46. Veitch *et al*, note. 43, at 31
47. *Id*. at p. 33.
48. *Ibid*.
49. Manoj K. Sinha, *Implementation of Basic Human Rights*, 1999, Manak Publications, (Hereinafter referred to Implementation)
50. Sinha, note. 1, at pp. 1-41.

50a. Sinha, note. 1 at pp. 42-100.

51. For historical origins of Economic and Social Rights, see Steiner and Alston(eds.), *International Human Rights in Context, Oxford*, 1999, 242

52. Vladimir Kartashkin, Economic, Social and Cultural Rights, in Karel Vasak (ed) *The International Dimensions of Human Rights*, Greenwood Press, 1997, III.

53. See Steiner and Alston, note. 53, at pp. 247-248.

54. *Id.* at p. 248.

55. Theodoor C. Van Boven, Distinguishing Criteria of Human Rights, in Karel Vasak ED, note. 54, at 51-52.

56. *Ibid.*

57. See Article 23, para 4 (equality of rights and responsibilities of spouses to marriage), Article 24, para 1 ICCPR (right of a child to have measures of protection on the part of the family etc), Boven, *ibid*, 52.

58. For example, right form and join trade unions, (Art 8), marriage must be entered with the free consent (Art. 10.1),the prohibition of employment of children in harmful practices (Art 10.1), liberty of parents to choose for their children schools and other than those established by the public authorities (Art. 13.3), and the understanding to restrict the freedom indispensable for scientific research and creative activity (15.2), ICESR.

59. Boven, note. 56, at 52 on interdependence of both categories of rights, see Steiner and Alston, note. 53 at p. 247.

60. UN doc. E/CN.4/988, para 75, and paras 31 and 154, cited in Boven, note. 57 at p. 53.

61. UN doc. E/C.12/1998, General Comment no. 9 (19th session), The domestic application of the Covenant , adopted on 1 December, 1998, para 9.

62. *Id.* para 10.

63. See Catarina Krause and Martin Scheinin, *The Right not to be Discriminated Against: The Case of Social Security*, in Theodore S. Orlin, Allan Rosas and Martin Scheinin, *The Jurisprudence of Human Rights Law: A Comparative Interpretive Approach* (2000), 253-286, at 285.

64. Martin Scheinin, The Right to Enjoy a Distinct Culture: Indigenous and Competing Uses of Land, in Orlin *et al*, note. 64, at 159-222, particularly, pp. 217-222

65. Committee on Economic, Social and Cultural Rights: General Comment no. 3, 1990, UN Doc E/1991/23, Annex III.

66. See HRI/GEN/Rev1, p.48. Other important General Comments are: G.C.4 (1991)on the right to adequate housing; G C., 5 (1995) on the right of persons with disabilities, G.C.6 (1996) on the economic and Cultural rights of older persons. In 2006, the ESCR Committee adopted General Comment no. 17 on the Right of Everyone to Benefit from the Protection from Scientific, Literary or Artistic Production of which he or she is the Author. General Comment No. 17, ESCOR, Comment on Economic Social and Cultural Rights , 35. See UN/Doc. E/C. 12/ Gc/17(2006). See also Philippe Cullet, Human Rights and Intellectual Property Protection in the TRIPS Era, *Human Rights Quarterly*, 20, 2007, pp. 403-430, particularly pp. 420-430.

67. The ESCR Committee Commenced its operation in 1987. It consists of 18 members, who are independent experts and are elected by the ECOSOC. It is not responsible to states parties but to the Economic and Social Council.

68. See, Phillip Alston, The Committee on Economic, Social and Cultural Rights, in Alston (ed) *The United Nations and Human Rights,* (1992), 473-508.

69. M. N. Shaw, *International Law* (Fifth Ed., 2005).

70. B. C. Nirmal, *Sovereignty in International Law,* note. 13; Globalization and International Human Rights Law, note. 14.

71. U. Buxi, *The Future of Human Rights,* (2002).

72. Statement of the ESCR Committee to the Vienna World Conference, UN Doc. E/1993/22, Annex III, paras 5&7.

73. Manoj Kumar Sinha, note. 1, Chapter 4, pp. 157-204.

74. The discussion on Fundamental Rights vs. Directive Principles of State Policy is just in one page (pp. 167-168) which is surprising in view of one of the stated objectives of the book to present an analysis of the relationship between the two. Furthermore, a detailed account of due process was perhaps not necessary, in the context of economic, social and cultural rights. Besides, the discussion in this chapter does not closely correspond with its title which is Implementation Mechanism Available at National System: The Indian System. Further, the discussion of National Human Rights Commission is more about its organization and structure and less about its activities in the field of economic, social and cultural rights. Moreover, the author has drawn inferences and conclusions from the 1993-1994 annual report of the National Human Rights Commission leaving its subsequent reports ignored or unnoticed. The discussion on the role of NGOs and media is also too brief. But what is most surprising is the lack of a separate chapter on the role of the executive and the legislature in the

implementation of economic, social and cultural rights in India. This is more so because the author has himself acknowledged the need to take account of the role played by these organs of the state in the implementation of these rights.

75. Manoj K Sinha, note. 1, Ch. 5, pp 205-242 (dealing with jurisprudence of Economic, Social and Cultural rights).

76. *Ibid,* Chapter 6.

77. See Nirmal, An Ancient Indian Perspectives of Human Rights and Its Relevance, *IJIL,* 43,2003, 445, at 274-476.

78. See B. C. Nirmal, Poverty and Human Rights: An Indian Context, *IJIL,* 46, 2006, 187, at 189-90.

79. Observation of Justice K. S. Hedge, quoted in S.C. Kashyap, Our Constitution, 2007, 131-132.

80. Nirmal, note. 78, at 475; For different spectrum of human rights law in India, see Nirmal, 'Human Rights and Their Derogation Under the Indian Constitution, in B. P. Panda (ed) *Current Law Issues,* 2003, 1-27; 'Refugees and Human Rights', *ISIL Year Book of International Humanitarian and Refugee Law,* 1, 2001, 94-117;Nirmal, 'Crimes within the Jurisdiction of the International Criminal Court and the Indian Response', *ISIL, Year Book of International Humanitarian and Refugee Law,* 6, 2006, pp106-125; 'Genocide in International Law and Indian State Practice: A Comparative Panorama' , in Mohammad Shabbir (ed) *Human Rights in the 21st Century,* Rawat Publications, 2008, pp 67-90; ' Taking Violence Against Women Seriously: International and National Human Rights Jurisprudence', in Bimal N Patel (ed.) *India and International Law,* Vol. 2, 2008, Konanklije, pp 413-452; B.C.Nirmal, 'Counter Terrorism Legislations Vis-à-vis Human Rights: A Comparative Legislation', in *Indian Law Institute Golden Jubilee Volume,* 2007, pp 246-261; For human rights dimensions of sentencing policies and practices in India, see B. C. Nirmal and Prakash C. Shukla, 'Sentencing Polices and Practices in India: Need for Reform', *Soochow Law Journal,* 4, 2007, pp 1-70

81. Nirmal, note. 79, at pp. 192-193

82. *Keshvanand Bharati Vs. State of Kerala,* (1973) 4 SCC 225; *Unni Krishnan vs. State of A. P.* (1993) 1SCC 645.

83. See *Grih Kalyan Kendra Workers Union Vs. Union of India* (1991) 1 SCC 611, para 6; *Literary Association Vs. State of Karnataka* (1990) 2 SCC 396

84. *All India Statutory Corporation Vs. United Labour Union,* AIR 1997 SC 645, para 38.

85. *Visaka & Others Vs State of Rajasthan* (1997) 2 SCC 241; *Apparel Export Promotion Council Vs. A.K. Chopra,* (1999) 1 SCC 759, discussed in B.

C. Nirmal, The Legal Status of Refugees in India, in Bimal N. Patel (ed) *India and International Law,* 2006, Martinus Nijoff, p. 175-188. For an interesting account of constitutional provisions having bearing on implementation and enforcement of international law, see, Nirmal, Cession of Territory and Its Validity: An Appraisal of the Supreme Court Contribution, *Banaras Law Journal,* 10, 1974; Nirmal, An Introduction to International Law (in Hindi, 1998), 68-72, ISIL; See also, A.K.Ganguli, Interface between international and Municipal Law: Role of the Indian Judiciary, in Bimal N. Patel (ed) *India and International Law,* Vol. 2, 2008, Konanklije, pp. 11-47.

86. For an interesting account of good governance practices, see B. C. Nirmal and P. C. Shukla, ' Sustainable Development , Human Rights and Good Governance, in J.L.Kaul and M.K. Sinha (eds) *Human Rights and Good Governance: International and National Perspectives,* 2008, Satyam, pp. 1-31.

87. For the meaning and definition of sustainable development, see, Nirmal and Shukla, note. 87; Nirmal, 'Book Review of S. Bhatt, *Environment Protection and Sustainable Development, Banaras Law Journal,* 32,(2003-2004), of related interest, see, Nirmal, 'Overview of Bio-safety Protocol', *Journal of Indian Law Institute,* 46, 2004, pp. 373-392; From Vellore to Nayadu: The Customary International Law Status of the Precautionary Principle, *Banaras Law Journal,* 30, (2001), 58-99; Nirmal, 'Environmental Law,' *Annual Survey of Indian Law,*(2004); Nirmal, 'Farmers' Rights: International and National Perspectives,' *Journal of Judicial Research and Training Institute,* 2004.

88. Manoj Kr. Sinha, note.1 at p. 302.

89. *Id.* at pp. 312-313.

90. See A. Eide *et al.* (eds), *Economic, Social and Cultural Rights: A Text book,* 1995.

91. Orlin& Scheinin, 'Introduction' in Orlin *et al.* (eds) *The Jurisprudence of Human Rights Law: A Comparative Interpretive Approach,* 2000., pp. 1-26.

Individual Property Rights, Economic Inequalities and Moral Obligations

JAGAT PAL*

We may think that our own labour and the labour of our ancestors entitle us to own what we now own. And what we now own rightfully, no one has any moral right to use or take it away from us. These claims we make on the grounds of the following two principles assumed to constitute valid grounds for holding property rights: the principle of labour and the principle of ancestral relationship. In this paper an attempt has been made to show that both of these principles lead to economic inequalities over a period of time among the people within the society and economic inequalities are morally unjust because ownership of one's property rights does not justify one to morally put others in hardship and disadvantageous position. No doubt, we do have the moral right on what we earn by our labour. We also do have the legal right on what our ancestors had earned by their labour, but we do not have any moral right to own abundance individual properties beyond our needs when other people suffer within the society from poverty and lead a miserable life for no faults of their own. When many people face injustices, discriminations, exploitations, mistreatments and obstacles etc. resulting from the fact of past institutional economic imbalances, discriminations, political and social structures of the society, it is our moral obligation to give economic aids to empower them to develop economically according to their own abilities so that they can eliminate poverty from their life which

* Department of Philosophy, North Eastern Hill University, Shillong, (Meghalaya).

we consider as a social evil. If we do it, I am sure, we would greatly reduce, if not eradicate, the problem of economic inequalities existing between the rich and the poor within our Indian society. To establish these points, let me first begin with the principle of labour which we use to justify ownership of property rights.

According to the principle of labour, if we have done some labour to earn something, then our labour entitles us to own what we have earned; and what we labour entitles us to own rightfully, no one has any moral right to interfere in it, at least where our choices and labour do not harm other persons of the society. If we are forced to labour without getting any entitlement to the fruit of our labour, we do have the moral right to resent and fight against the injustices resulting from it simply because our labour entitles us to own what we deserve and what we deserve, we must get it. If we do not get what we morally deserve, it amounts to mean the violation of the principle of labour and to violate the principle of labour is morally unjust. In other words, if we think and feel that we do have the moral right to own our individual properties simply because we have earned them by our labour, then it is morally wrong or unjustified to violate one's individual property rights. And if it is morally wrong to violate one's individual property rights, and then it is also morally wrong to use or take them way from us even if it is the only way to bring economic equality among people within a society. Why is it so? The reason is just this. If we have property rights on this ground because we have earned by our labour, then our property rights give the right to us to exclude others from using or taking them away from us. Our property rights also give us the right to donate or transfer our properties to others the way we like. If so, then no one has any moral right to harm or interfere in other's property rights because to harm or interfere in other's property rights would amount to mean the violation of property rights and to violate property rights is morally unjustified. One's property rights also morally bind others to respect property rights and to respect property rights means not to use or harm or take them away from us which we are morally entitled to own. All this is analytically true from the very meaning of the word 'right' itself because one cannot have a 'right' without having corresponding 'duties' when one is capable of discharging them. But to say this does not mean to say that no one can have any moral right without corresponding 'duties'. One can have moral rights without corresponding 'duties' in certain contexts. For example, infants, minor children, physically and mentally handicapped people do have the moral right to own properties according to their needs without corresponding 'duties' simply because they do not have the capacity to discharge them. 'Rights' and 'duties' are co-relative terms but only in those contexts where individuals are capable of discharging the corresponding 'duties'. If so, then in those contexts where ownership of one's property rights implies other's moral obligations we are morally bound to respect other's property rights and to respect other's property rights means not to use, harm or take them away which they have earned rightfully by their labour. Not only this, respecting individual's property rights also mean to defend them from others who cause harms against them. The concept of property rights, thus, morally binds others to respect property rights both positively as well as negatively.

Now if we hold this view that we do have the moral right on what we earn by our labour, then from this it also follows that we do not have any moral right on what we do not earn by our labour, that is, ancestral properties because it is our labour which gives us the right for the entitlement of property rights and none else. If so, then property rights based on the principle of labour are incompatible with those property rights which rest on the principle of ancestral relationship because what the principle of ancestral relationship affirm, the principle of labour denies. Both the principles we cannot hold as valid principles of moral rights in the same breath because they are mutually contradictory principles. So if we have the moral right to own our properties on the ground that we have earned them by our own labour, then on the same ground we do not have any moral right on the properties earned by our ancestors because the labour of our ancestors does not morally entitle us to own what they had earned by their own labour. We cannot say that the labour of our ancestors is our labour because what we do only that counts as our labour, and what we do not do that does not count as our labour. But to say this is not equivalent to saying that one cannot have property rights on more than one ground. One can have property rights on more than one ground. For example, we do have the legal right on the properties of our ancestors. The legal laws of our country entitle us to own what were earned by our ancestors, and any attempt to use or to take our ancestral prosperities away from us amounts to mean the violation of law and the violation of law is illegal and unjust. But property rights which we enjoy on the ground of legal law are conceptually quite different from those property rights which we enjoy on the ground of moral law because legal laws are not moral laws. Moral laws are not framed and promulgated by any legal authorities, while legal laws are framed and promulgated by the legal authorities. Legal laws are implemented and governed by the Government agencies of the respective societies which is not the case with moral laws. Moral laws are not implemented and governed by any Government agencies. They are self-determined and self-regulated laws. They are not arbitrary and subjective laws. Moral laws are universally valid laws. But to say that legal laws are different from moral laws is not to say that what is legally permissible that cannot be morally permissible. It is perfectly quite possible that what is legally permissible is also morally permissible because there is no contradiction between the two. That is why we can have property rights on both the grounds without facing any logical difficulty. When there exists any conflict between the two, the moral rights always override the legal rights because moral rights do have relatively a greater weightage. Moral laws are more fundamental than legal laws. Moral laws constitute the foundation of legal systems. It is because of this reason the legal systems are always justified ultimately by referring to the system of morality when the question of justification about them is raised. And to say this is not to say that our own labour and the labour of our ancestors both can be used as a moral ground to justify what we now own. Both cannot be used as a moral ground to justify ownership of property rights because they are mutually contradictory.

Nonetheless, individual property rights no matter whether we base them on labour or on ancestral relationship do give rise to economic inequalities over period of time within a society due to the differences existing in the physical and mental capacities of the individuals and their birth-conditions. Different people have different physical and mental capacities to labour. So we cannot be equal in our labour even if we wish given our nature. Besides, our social, economic and physical conditions etc. also vary since the birth. If we do have different levels of physical and mental capacities to labour, we will naturally labour differently; and if we labour differently, our material conditions such as resources, facilities, wealth and income etc will also differ drastically. Not only this, our birth-conditions also vary and birth-conditions do determine our educational, economic and social conditions of life. All people do not get same kind of food, education and training which matter in the economic development of their life. We do not inherit equal amount of properties from our ancestors. Some people inherit abundant of properties from their ancestors which put them in advantageous position economically and socially over others who do not get even that much property which they require to fulfill their basic needs of life. This gap between the rich and the poor keeps on perpetuating from generation to generation simply because of the birth-conditions. But we cannot surely hold advantageous people morally responsible on the ground of their birth-conditions because they had no control over their birth-conditions and we can hold people morally responsible only for those things over which they have control. If birth does not result from the act of one's choice, how can anyone be held morally responsible on this ground? We can hold people morally responsible only for that what they do. We cannot hold people morally responsible for that what they do not do by their choice. If economic inequalities exist and persist among people of the same society because of the birth-conditions, then how can marginalized groups of people play same kind of economic games on an equal foot against unmarginalized ones who enjoy advantageous position since the birth even if they are provided with same kind of opportunities by the society? To avail equal opportunity always requires leveling of the playing field of all the people marked by inequalities within a society. We differ in our wealth and income, and wealth and income generate properties. Since the very fact that property generates property, economic inequalities are bound to incur, perpetuate and increase within a society marked by inequalities. If there existed inequalities among people within a society since the birth, all people cannot play economic games on the same foot even if they are physically and mentally capable of doing so against their counter parts because economic inequalities put them in disadvantageous position since the beginning compared to their counter parts. In fact, economic inequalities which were existing and also continue to exist even now within our society do exist not only because of our different labour capacities, inherited ancestral properties but also do exist because of our historical, social, political and economic institutional structures of the society. This is a naked truth which no one can deny. Economic inequalities resulting from the above mentioned factors we cannot, thus, simply brush aside because these factors do matter in moral considerations.

So if we think and feel seriously that poverty is a great moral and social sin, then ownership of one's property rights does not justify one morally to make the economically and socially marginalized groups of people to suffer or to put them in disadvantageous position, voluntarily or involuntarily, to fulfill their own ulterior ends. There is no doubt about it that we do have the moral right to own property what we earn by our labour rightfully simply because our labour entitles it. We also do have the legal right on what were earned by our ancestors rightfully by their labour. But it is also equally true at the same time that we do have certain moral obligations and responsibilities towards economically and socially marginalized groups of people, at least those who live below the poverty line even if it is true that we are not morally responsible and accountable for their poverty just because of being human, and morality deals with the well-beings of humanity as a whole. The criterion of labour, no doubt, does constitute a rational moral ground to hold one's property. But the criterion of need also constitutes a rational moral ground to hold property even if someone is not physically and mentally capable to labour against their counter parts, for example, physically handicapped people. The criterion of need also constitutes a rational ground to justify that no one has the moral right to own excessive properties more than what one needs to live well or flourish. Morality demands that one should give up excessive material goods which one does not morally deserve and give to others who morally deserve them. No one is morally entitled to own surplus properties at the cost of the needs of others. No one has the moral right to own properties which he does not morally deserve even if he has the legal rights on them. When we judge the issues pertaining to individual's property rights and economic inequalities resulting from these on a moral basis, we will have to take into account everyone's interests, needs and aspirations, that is, both beneficiaries and non-beneficiaries. As a human being we not only have certain moral duties and responsibilities towards one's own but we also do have certain moral duties and responsibilities towards others who belong to the class of economically and socially marginalized groups within a society. We cannot escape from our moral duties and responsibilities even if we assume that certain economic inequalities are morally permissible and unavoidable because of the differences existing in our needs, aspirations, physical and social conditions etc. Everyone's needs are morally valuable but everyone's needs may not be equally valuable. This is perfectly quite possible because of the morally relevant variations found among us. When there exists a conflict between the principle of labour and the principle of need, one has to go by the merit of the case and the merit of the case will have to be decided on the basis of relatively weightier morally good reasons and these reasons may differ, and do vary, from one context to another because of the variations found in our human nature, characteristics, social, economic and geographical conditions etc.

Further, if we are morally entitled to own only that which we earn rightfully by our labour, then we have no moral right to make any claim on what we do not earn by our labour. We do not earn our physical characteristics and bodies by our labour. We just happen to own them without any choice because of certain antecedent conditions. If we do not own our physical body on the ground of our labour, we have no moral right to claim anything based on it. If some people cannot compete with their counter parts because of their physical and mental incapacities without any fault of theirs, it does not mean that they do not have any moral right to live well. If right to life is a fundamental moral right of any individual, and the only way to save one's life is to infringe property rights, then one is morally justified to do so because the right to life overrides property rights and ownership of property rights does not morally justify that his or her act of the violation of property rights is morally wrong. If ownership of property rights is causing threat to the life of others by creating morally undesirable economic inequalities among people of the society, a society has the moral right to abolish the institution of property rights or to re-allocate properties among its citizens on the basis of their needs. The arguments for property rights do not, and cannot, morally justify people's having an over-abundance of economic goods even if they do not voluntarily harm others because they do create such conditions that harm others. If people who are living below the poverty line are given economic aids over the others who are not living below the poverty line to develop economically according to their own capacities, we would surely to a great extent reduce, if not eradicate, the existing phenomena of economic inequalities from our country. When we do it, we do not thereby vitiate the principle of the individual's property rights nor do we vitiate the principle of justice to equality because it is intended to level the playing field for all individuals which is morally justified. The policy of giving economic aids does not involve in it any kind of stigma on its beneficiaries that they are less capable of; nor does it impose any costs on its non-beneficiaries. It is a rational and morally justified policy because it rests on the principle of equitable playing field for all individuals in a social context. When we see the policy of giving economic aids to those who are living below the poverty line from the point view of equalizing opportunity for them to participate in economic field, it is not morally wrong. It is morally justified which any society like India requires to become a healthy and prosperous society.

It might be argued that we cannot hold the present generation of beneficiaries morally responsible for the poverty of others which result from the ownership of inherited properties and the past institutional imbalances. We can hold them morally responsible only for the deeds done by them. But if we go by this line of argument, then on the same ground beneficiaries do not have any moral right to enjoy the benefits which result from inherited properties of their ancestors even if it is legally permissible because inherited properties put them in advantageous position against the marginalized groups of people. If we cannot hold beneficiaries morally responsible on the ground of their birth-conditions over which they had no control, then on the same ground they do not have any moral entitlement on those properties which were earned by their ancestors. And if we think and feel that they do have the moral right on what were earned by their ancestors, then on the same ground they also do have certain moral responsibilities towards those people who suffer from economic inequalities resulting from inherited properties and the past institutional imbalances without any fault of theirs. Not giving special considerations to the economically marginalized groups of people which they morally deserve amounts to mean allowing the past economic imbalances to perpetuate within the society and that is morally unjustified.

In short, we can thus conclude that both the principles, that is, the principle of labour and the principle of ancestral relationship lead to economic inequalities among people over a period of time within the society and the ownership of property rights does not entitle one morally to own excessive amount of properties beyond one's needs when the economically marginalized groups of people suffer from poverty resulting from the institution of individual's property rights and the past institutional economic imbalances without any fault of theirs. If individual's property rights cause sufferings to the marginalized groups of people, a society has the moral right to abolish the institution of property rights or to give special privileges to the marginalized groups of people in different forms to develop and grow according to their needs and merits by introducing the policy of affirmative action. But all these things will have to be done in a rational and morally justified manner keeping in view the interests of all those individuals and societies who figure in moral considerations.

Juvenile Justice Administration in Nigeria

Hakeem Ijaiya*

INTRODUCTION

Juvenile justice system is an integral part of the criminal justice system[1]. It is guided by a philosophy of concern, care and reformation for persons under the age of seventeen years.[2] Juvenile justice administration is a system of justice world over which is applicable to juveniles and which is different from the justice system applicable to adults. Today, there are more than one million children in detention worldwide most of whom have committed only minor offences.[3]

The juveniles like adults accused of crimes have certain rights. These rights are guaranteed by the constitution of the Federal Republic of Nigeria. Such rights include proper and prompt notification of charges, private trial trail, impartial adjudication, adequate defence, examination of prosecution witnesses etc.

The Nigerian juvenile justice are grossly inadequate in quantitative and qualitative terms to meet the rights of the juveniles. These inadequacies impair the capacity of the courts, police, remand homes, approved institutions and borstal to meet the United Nations Rules and Guidelines as well as other international standards on the treatment of juvenile offenders. The inadequacies which are due to policy defects, inadequate funding, incoherent and punitive programme reduced these institutions to fortresses of punishment instead of correctional and rehabilitation

* Law Faculty of Law, University of Ilorin, Nigeria E-mail: hakeemijaiya@yahoo.com

institutions. The study will examine the inadequacies in the juvenile justice system in Nigeria. It will focus on the age and criminal responsibility of the juvenile, bail of juvenile offenders, pre-trial custody and detention of the juvenile, the constitution and procedure of the juvenile courts, and the juvenile custodial institutions.

THE AGE AND CRIMINAL RESPONSIBILITY OF THE JUVENILE

There is differences in the age and criminal responsibility of the juvenile in Nigeria. For instance section 30 of the Criminal Code Act[4] and section 50 of the Penal Code Act[5] establish that a child under the age of seven years does not have criminal responsibility. From 7 to 12 years, a child can only be found responsible if it can be proved that he/she had the capacity to know that the act or omission should not have been carried out. Above the age of 12 years, the person is deemed as fully responsible for the act or omission.

Contrary to the position of the Penal Code Law and the Criminal Code Law, the Children and Young Persons Act[6] defines a child as a person under the age of 14 years and a young person as a person who has attained the age of 14 years and is under the age of 17 years.

Under the Islamic or Shari'ah Law[7], the age of criminal responsibility is taken to be either 18 years or puberty. In cases involving fornication or adultery, which may attract flogging or the death penalty, the age of criminal responsibility is 15 years. The implication is that, in cases where, children reach puberty earlier than 18 years, no distinction is made between them and adults in dispensing Shari'ah punishments.[8] The age of criminal responsibility under the Shari'ah law allows for discrimination against girls because they often achieve puberty earlier than boys, as well as among Muslim and non-Muslim children.[9] Also it creates discriminatory treatment among girls, as the menstruation is often considered as the achievement of "*maturity*" or "*puberty*". Hence, onset of menstruation is not the same for all. [10]

BAIL OF JUVENILE OFFENDERS

Section 3 of the Children and Young Persons Act[11] provided for the release of a juvenile offender, apprehended with or without warrant by a police officer. Such release may be on "*a recognizance entered into by him or by his parents or guardian, with or without sureties, for such an amount as will in the opinion of the officer, secure the attendance of such person upon the hearing of the charge"*. This bail condition, however, does not apply to a person: (a) accused of homicide or other grave crime or (b) to situation where *"it is necessary in the interest of such person to remove him from association with any reputed criminal or prostitute"* or (c) to situation where "the officer has reason to believe that the release of such person would defeat the ends of justice". The last condition (c) appears too vague and may be abused to unnecessarily deny bail to young offenders.[12]

PRE-TRAIL CUSTODY AND DETENTION

There is a wide consensus amount the human rights organizations that Nigerian Policemen exhibit brutality and incivility in their relationship with juvenile offenders.[13]

The Children and Young Persons Act prohibits detention of a child in prisons, but that of young person is subject to exceptional circumstances.[14] A juvenile offender may be detained in remand homes, approved institutions including borstal institutions and prisons. A native or local authority or a Local Government Council with prior approval of competent authority.[15]

Contrary to statutory provisions on the matter, Nigerian prisons contain a large number of young offenders, who are often not separated from adults inmates.[16]

Juvenile offenders often complain of the poor condition while in police custody[17]

THE CONSTITUTION AND PROCEDURE OF THE JUVENILE COURTS

The procedure for the trial of juvenile offenders are provided under section 8 of the Children and Young Persons Act. The section regulates the trail procedure of juvenile courts in Nigeria including the right of juvenile offenders to due process. This provision satisfy the requirements of Article 40 of the Convention on the Rights of the Children and section 36 of the Nigerian Constitution.

Section 29 of the Children and Young Persons Act made provision to the effect that only juvenile courts can try juvenile offenders. It provides;

Where a persons, whether charged with an offence or not, is brought before any court otherwise than for the purpose of giving evidence and it appears to the court that he is a child or young person, the court shall make due inquiry as to the age of that persons, and for that purpose shall require the production of a birth certificate or other direct evidence as to the date of birth and in the absence of such certificate or evidence, a certificate signed by a medical officer in the service of the government giving his opinion as to such age.

The constitution of juvenile courts is provided under section 6 of the same law, which states that;

A juvenile court for the purpose of hearing and determination of cases relating to children or young persons shall be constituted by a magistrate sitting with such other persons, if any, as the Chief Justice of the region shall appoint.

It appears from the provision of sections 6 and 29 of the Act that two approaches were given to the establishment of juvenile courts in Nigeria. The first approach which is adopted in Lagos State envisaged a visible structure of juvenile justice administration. In most of the other states in Nigeria the second approach is popular. The magistrates hear cases involving juveniles outside the normal courtrooms or outside normal court session either in the courtrooms or in their chambers. The second approach often results to some difficulties because magistrate in the process of handling adult offenders and juvenile delinquents may lost sight of the procedure to be adopted.

In addition to the procedural inadequacies, the international standards enshrined in the Convention on the Rights of Children and other instruments such as the Administration of Juvenile Justice are not reflected in the Nigerian system of juvenile justice. For instance the judges, police and other personnel handling cases involving juvenile offenders in Nigeria have little knowledge on how best to handle juvenile cases.[18] In Nigeria, female police officers are often deployed to juvenile welfare departments in divisional and state police command headquarters. They are not given specialized training, assignment to the unit and in most cases they are frequently transferred in and out of the unit.

THE JUVENILE CUSTODIAL INSTITUTIONS

Juvenile Custodial Institutions are homes built to correct, reform and rehabilitate juvenile offenders. The institutions are meant to bear upon the inmates every good influence which may establish in them the will to lead a good and useful life when they are released from custody. The institutions are expected to provide vocational training in tailoring, photography, welding, building (masonry or bricklaying), electrical installation etc. as well as formal educational institution up to General Certificate of Education.

There were very few custodian institutions in Nigeria. In many cases they exist within the premises of the prisons. For instance the first juvenile justice custodial institution established in 1937 is a wing of the Enugu Prison. The goals of the institution are not realized in Nigeria due to lack of proper policy, legal and institutional framework for juvenile offender correction and juvenile delinguency prevention. Also the objectives of the institution are compromised by the lack of proper planning and implementation, gross under founding, inadequate staff, and lack of necessary training facilities. Most of these institutions are not provided with enough fund to provide quality accommodation, food, sleeping materials, medical care, hygiene, education, vocational training, recreation and leisure.

Another problem is that in most institutions inmates are not adequately protected against physical and verbal abuse by officials and fellow inmates. According to Ahire *"There was near complete absence of medical and educational facilities at both the Yola and Bauchi remand homes"* [19]. As Ogbonna put it;

> *The so-called objectives of the institutions–correction, rehabilitation and reformation of young offenders are not been realized. There are numerous factors militating against proper and efficient functioning of the institutions. They include shortage of personnel, lack of fund, inadequate facilities–it is noteworthy as well that due to the poor conditions of these institutions, juvenile offenders are now kept in prisons with adult criminals and under the same facilities. For instance, at Owerri prison there are many young offenders in their custody.*[20]

The inadequacy of the conditions and facilities in Nigerian juvenile institutions militate against the realization of the objectives of the institutions. [21]

Workshop facilities in the Nigerian juvenile institutions are in a state of obsolescence and unserviceability[22]. The workshops lacked serviceable equipment, and those available are obsolete and often cannot be used because of poor maintenance and under-funding.

The problem of inadequate staff to teach as well as overcrowding also militated against the effective utilization of the obsolete facilities in the workshops[23]. In some cases, inmates were allowed to continued their education through attendance at any nearby school, or if not, through non-formal classes organized within the institutions. These are clearly inadequate and unsatisfactory arrangement through which the children/juveniles can receive and acquire proper education[24].

The conditions in the juvenile custodian institutions in Nigeria have deteriorated. These inadequacies led the Nigerian Law Reform Commission to observed that;

> *From all indications, the Nigerian Prison system as at present, is not geared towards the reformation of prisoners to enable them live a more useful life – instead our prison system appears more punitive and retributive–*[25].

CONCLUSION

The juvenile justice system in Nigeria interm of facilities and services in the system are grossly inadequate. These inadequacies impair the capacity of the institutions to meet the obligations under the Convention for the Rights of the Children, the United Nations Rules and Guidelines, as well as other international standards on the treatment of juvenile offenders. The inadequacies, which are due to policy defects, inadequate funding, incoherent and punitive programme reduced these institutions to warehouses, or human cages and fortresses of punishment instead of correctional and rehabilitation institutions. To eradicate these inadequacies the Federal Government of Nigeria should address the following situations.

Firstly, the government should amend the age of criminal responsibility as provided under the applicable laws. The Penal Code Law and the Criminal Code provision on the age of criminal responsibility should be increased from 7 years to 14 years and also the age of penal majority should be fixed at 18 years. The government should in addition amend the Children and Young Persons Act and all other legislations in the country to comply with the international standards as contained in the Convention on the Rights of the Children.

Secondly, the government should looked into the situation of juvenile children detained in the Nigerian prisons to ensure that they are not fixed up with the adult inmates. The Government must ensure that every child kept in prison detention is separated from adult inmates, in line with Article 37(c) of the Convention on the Rights of the Children. There is no doubt that inadequate remand carters, approved schools and borstal institution in the country contributed to the urgly situation, however the government must concentrate on improving the existing institutions for juvenile offenders and in addition creates new ones in all the states of the federation.

Thirdly, the Government should create special courts for the trial of juvenile offenders. Well trained judges should be assigned to try juvenile offenders. The Government should establish new training programmes for the police, courts, remand homes, approved institutions, borstal and prison personal, as well as for every other person involved in handling of juvenile offenders. The Government should create special unit for the police, in line with the section 207 of the Child Rights Act[26].

In addition the Government should concentrate on building institutions that will cater for the juvenile offenders. The institutions should be adequately funded and manned by trained staff. The inmates should be exposed to vocational training. The provision of educational, vocational and religious or moral training for juvenile offenders are considered as a viable measure for the correction, reformation and rehabilitation of juvenile offenders. In essence, the provision of education, vocation training, and moral/religious education along with the safe custody of the juvenile offenders are considered the primary responsibilities of juvenile correctional and penal institutions in Nigeria. But in reality, these facilities and opportunities are grossly inadequate both in quantitative and qualitative terms, within the Nigerian juvenile institutions[27] and the wide criminal justice system[28].

Furthermore, the Nigerian juvenile justice agencies such as the police, courts, remand homes, approved schools, borstal and prisons lacks adequate and qualified workers that are able to meet the needs, concerns and aspirations of the juvenile offenders.

The Nigerian civil society should concentrate on the provision of facilities and services for the development and welfare of young persons, and be active in the monitoring of conditions in juvenile justice institutions, advocacy for progressive correctional, rehabilitation and non-custodial programmes for the treatment of young offenders in the country. The Government should in its development planning, policies and programmes, and in resource allocation be guided by what the UNICEF prescribed as the principle of "First Call" [29]. In addressing the problems above, it is recommended as follows;

1. The Government should embark upon a thorough reform of the juvenile justice system in accordance with the provisions of the Child Rights Act. In particular, the Government should develop a system of non-custodial education measures and alternatives to imprisonment for children, adequately chosen and monitored by specialized personnel, trained in children's rights and restorative justice practice and principles. Juvenile detention facilities should take into account the specific needs of children and focus on strategies aiming at their effective and long-term reintegration into the community.
2. The sounding factor in all aspects of the child justice system should be to promote, enshrine and enforce the rights of the juvenile offenders.
3. The Government should collaborate with specialized international organizations and their special mechanisms, as well as with national and international NGOs in the establishment, monitoring and the implementation of a comprehensive system of administration of juvenile justice in Nigeria.
4. The Government must ensure that juvenile offenders are separated from the adult inmate in the Nigerian Prisons, in line with article 37 (c) of the CRC. Also the existing specialized institutions for juvenile offenders must be improved and new ones established in all the states of the federation.
5. The Government should embark on a national campaign to promote non-custodial treatment of juvenile offenders. They should also promote measure to reduce the sigma attached to child offenders in the country and develop

programmes to encourage and assist reintegration of child offenders into their community.

6. The children in Nigeria are subjected to all forms of abuse and cruel in human or degrading treatment and punishment. The structural causes of the violation of children's rights require, economic and special change. Therefore, there is need for fundamental legislative and administrative changes in Nigeria that would facilitate the implementation of the children's rights. The Government should adopt and implement the rights of the children enshrined in the Child Rights Act 2003 in all the states of the Federation and in addition ratify the Optional Protocol to the Convention on the Rights of the Child as well as the African Charter on the Rights and Welfare of the Child.
7. The Government should improve on the facilities in juvenile custodial institutions and also organize training programmes for the staff of these institutions. The Government should organize regular in service educational programmes for the police, courts, remand homes, approved institutions, borstals and prisons in order to make them aware of the needs of the children in Nigeria.
8. The Government should establish special unit of the Nigerian Police Force in line with section 207 of the Child Rights Act. The unit would focus on the investigations of juvenile offenders.
9. The Government should amend the existing laws so as to increase the minimum age of criminal responsibility from 7 years to 14 years and also fix the age of penal majority at 18 years.

NOTES

Juvenile justice system may be regarded as a tract within the criminal justice system of a society. The criminal justice system consists of several tracts–adult and juvenile process, and the rich and poor tracts to justice. Adult and juvenile tracts of justice administration were purposively designed and officially organized. However, the differential tracts for the poor and wealthy are invisible and formally unorganized, indeed denied, because to recognize class-based of justice, will negate the ideology of equality of all (poor and rich) before the law. But in all societies, the poor are more likely to be arrested, detained, denied bail, convicted and sentenced to severe or hash terms of punishment more than their wealthy and politically influenced counterparts.

2. There is no universal definition of a juvenile. The laws of different nations stipulate different age brackets for the juvenile. The concept of juvenile is sometimes used interchangeably with other concepts like a child, an adolescent and a youth. For instance the children and young persons Act defines a child as "a person under the age of 14 years" Also, the law defines a young person as "a person who has attained the age of 14 years". The law did not define a juvenile. However other indicators in the law show that the term refers to a person under the age of 17 years. Juvenile justice system has been influenced by the activities of humanitarians and penal reformers who protested cruelty to children under the guise of administering justice before children were harshly punished for even petty offences. The juvenile justice system is concerned about handling of juvenile offenders.

3. UNICEF (2006) Children in Conflict with the Law , Child Protection Information Sheet.

4. Criminal Code Act Laws of the Federation of Nigeria 1990 Cap. 77 Chap. 77. Section 30 provides that "a person under the age of 7 years is not criminally responsible for any act or omission. A person under the age of 12 years is not criminally responsible for an act or omission, unless it is proved that at the time of doing the act or making the omission he has capacity to know that he ought not to do the Act or make the omission. A male person under the age of 12 years is presumed to be incapable of having carnal knowledge" The Criminal Code Act is applicable to the Northern parts of Nigeria.

5. The Penal Code Law which is applicable to the Southern parts of Nigeria made similar provisions on age of criminal responsibility of children as discussed under the Criminal Code Act.

6. The Children and Young Persons Act, is the most important legislation in Nigeria dealing with the treatment of juvenile offenders. The Act was first enacted as an ordinance in 1934, it has been subsequently amended through several legislation (i.e. Ordinances 44 of 1945; 27 of 1947; 16 of 1950 as well as the Laws of Nigeria 131 of 1954; 47 of 1955 and Order in Council 22 of 1946). Intended as a national law (Cap. 32 Laws of the Federation of Nigeria and Lagos 1958), provisions were made for their adoption as Regional Laws and subsequently as state laws. As a result, the law was extended to the Eastern and Western Regions of Nigeria in 1946 by Order-in- Council, No. 22 of

1946. The law was enacted for the Northern Region in 1958 and constituted the Children and Young Persons Law, Cap. 21 of the Laws of Northern Nigeria 1963 Lagos State also adopted the law in 1970 – Children and Young Persons Law (Chap. 26 of the Laws of Lagos State). The law was enacted to make provision for the welfare of the young person and the treatment of young offenders and for the establishment of juvenile courts.

7. The introduction of Islamic or Shari'ah legal system in the northern parts of Nigeria has created new dimension in the administration of juvenile justice in Nigeria. The Shari'ah Code made fixed the age of criminal responsibility of a child at either 18 years or puberty. This is quite different from the provision of the Penal Code Act and the Criminal Code Act discussed above.

8. Integrated Regional Information Networks (IRIN), Nigeria: Focus on the Administration of juvenile justice, August 26th 2002. Available under *http://www.irinnews.org/report.asp?* Report ID = 29531.

9. The Sharia Penal Code only applies to persons of Muslim faith. It does not apply to the Christians living in the Shariah compliance states of Northern Nigeria.

10. Okoli, B. Nigeria: The Constitution and Child Rights, 19th October 2007. Available under *http://allafrica.com/stories/200710190453html.*

11. Section 3 provides that "where a Person apparently under the age of seventeen year is apprehended with or without warrant, and cannot be brought forthwith before a court of summary jurisdiction, the police office in immediate charge for the time being of the police station to which the person is brought, shall inquire into the case and may in any case, and shall (a) unless the charge is one of homicide or other grave crime or (b) unless it is necessary in the interest of the person to remove him from association with any reputed criminal or prostitute; or (c) unless the officer has reason to believe that the release of the person would defeat the ends of justice.

12. *Ibid.*

13 Ahire, P. T., "Native Authority Police in Northern Nigeria: End of an Era?" in Tamuno, T. N. and Bashire, I. L. and Alemika E.E.O. and Akano A. O. Policing Nigeria: Past, Present and Future, Malthouse Press Ltd., Lagos, 1993, Ahire, P. T. Imperial Policing, Milton Keynes, Open University Press, 1991; Alemika, E.E.O., Policing and Perception of Police in Nigeria" in Socio-Economic and Criminological Attributes of Convicts in Two Nigerian Prisons" in Journal of Criminal Justice, Vol. 16 (3), 1988 pp. 197 – 207; Alemika E.E.C. & Chukwuma T., Police-Community Violence in Nigeria Center for Law Enforcement

Education (CLEEN), Lagos 2000; Odekunle, F. "The Nigeria Police Force: A Preliminary Assessment of Functional Performance in *International Journal of Sociology in Law*, Vol. 6, 1979 pp. 73–78. Ohonbamu, O. "The Dilemma of Police Organization under a Federal System: the Nigerian Example" in The Nigerian Law Journal Vol. 6, 1977 pp. 73 –78; Tamuno, T. N. The Police in Moderns Nigeria, Ibadan University, Ibadan, 1970; Ayua, I. A. and Okagbue I. E., The Rights of the Child in Nigeria, Nigerian Institute of Advanced Legal Studies, Nigeria, 1996, CLO Annual Reports 1988 and 1996.

14. Children and Young Persons Act Section 7 deals with the remand or committal of custody of juvenile offenders. It provides that "A court on remanding or committing for trial a child or young person who is not released on bail, shall instead of committing him to prison, commit him to custody in place of detention provided under this ordinance and named in the commitment, to be there detained for a period of which he is remanded or until he is thence delivered in due course of law, provided that in case of a young person it shall not be obligatory on the court so to convict him if the court certifies that he is of a unruly a character that he cannot be safely so committed, or that he is of so, depeared a character that he is not a fit person to be so detained".

15. The Children and Young Persons Act, S. 15 (1) (3) provides thus "Where no remand home is conveniently situated a child or young person ordered to be detained in a custody may in the discretion of the officer or the court, as the case may be, be detained in an approved institution or in a prison provided that if a child or young person be detained in a prison he shall not be allowed to associate with adult prisoners.

16. This is contrary to the Article 37 (3) of the CRC which stipulated that every child should be separated from adult inmates in prisons. See also Okɔli B. Nigeria: The Constitution and Child Rights *op. cit.*

17. In a study by the Nigerian Institute of Advanced Legal Studies 42% of the juvenile inmate said that their arrest involved verbal abuse while 40% reported that their arrest involved the use of threat of physical abuse. See also Ayua, I. A. and Okagbue, I. E., The Rights of the Child in Nigeria, Nigerian Institute of Advanced Legal Studies, Nigeria, 1996 p. 254.

18. Rule 12 of the UN Standard Minimum Rules provides that "In order to best fulfill their functions, police officers who frequently or exclusively deal with juveniles or who are primarily engaged in the prevention of juvenile crime shall be specially instructed and trained. In large cities, special police units should be established for that purpose.

19 Ahire, P. T. "Juvenile Delinquency and the Handling of Young Prisoners in Nigerian Borstal Institutions" in "Nigerian Prisons Service and the Public", Nigerian Prisons Service, Abuja, 1987, Section 12.

20. Ogbonna, C. being field notes and report on the condition of juvenile offenders in Nigeria Prisons.

21. Ayua, I. A. and Okugbue, I. E. The Rights of the Child in Nigeria, Nigerian Institue of Advanced Legal Studies, Nigeria 1966; Alemika, E.E.O. "Professionalism in the Nigerian Prisons Service" in the Nigerian Prisons Service and the Public, Nigerian Prisons Service, Abuja, 1987; Alemika E.E.O. "Policing and Perception of Police in Nigeria" in Police Studies. *International Review of Police Development* Vol. 11 (4), 1988 pp. 161-176; Alemika, E.E.O. "Socio-Economic and Criminological Attributes of Councils in Two Nigerian Prisons" in *Journal of Criminal Justice*, Vol. 16 (3), 1988 pp. 197-207.

22. Ahire, P. T. "Juvenile Delinquency and Handling of Young Prisoners in Nigerian Borstal Service and the Public" ibid. Human Rights Monitor, Administration of Juvenile Justice. The Example of the Borstal Training Institute, Kaduna, 1997.

23. Ahire, P. T. "Juvenile Delinquency and Handling of Young Prisoners in Nigerian Borstal Service and the Public" *ibid.*

24. For instance sections 10, 11 and 12 of the Approved Institutions Regulations in Nigeria provided for the education, vocational training and religious training of inmates. Of particular note is section 10 which states that "Every inmate shall receive education according to his age and development and such education shall be at least the equivalent of that which he would receive in his own special circumstances, were he attending school in the usual way of education".

25. Nigerian Law Reform Commission, Report and Draft Bill for Reform of Prisons in Nigeria, Section 2, Lagos, 1983.

26. Child Rights Act, Section 207 provides that specifically trained police officers deal exclusively with prevention, apprehension and investigation of alleged child offenders and use their discretionary powers to divert children from the formal justice system to community based programmes whenever possible.

27. Ahire, P. T. "Juvenile Delinquency and the Handling of Young Prisoners in Nigerian Borstal Institutions" *op. cit.*

28. Alemika E.E.O. "Policing and Perception of Police in Nigeria" in Police Studies: *International Review of Police Development*, Vol. 11 (4) 1988 pp. 161-176; Alemika, E.E.O., "Socio-Economic and Criminological Attributes of Convicts in Two Nigerian Prisons" in *Journal of Criminal Justice*, Vol. 16 (3) 1988, pp. 197-207; Alemika E. I. "Penal Crisis and

Prison Management in Nigeria" in *Lawyer's Bi-Annual,* Vol. 1 (2), 1994 pp. 62–80.

29. The principle advocates that the growing minds and bodies of children should have first call on society's capacities, and that children should be able to depend upon that commitment in good times and in bad. Whether a child survives or not, whether a child goes to school, should not have to depend on whether interest rates rise or fall, or whether commodity prices go up or down, or whether a political party is in power or whether the economy has been well managed, or whether a country is at war or not, nor on any other trough or crest in the endless undulation of political and economic life in the modern nation state.

Role of Judiciary to Institutionalise Human Rights in India

MAHAVIR SINGH KALON*

INTRODUCTION

We can trace the roots for the protection of the rights of man in the Babylonian laws. Babylonian King Hammurabi had issued a set of laws to his people which is called Hammurabi's codes, established fair wages, offered protection of property and required charges to be proved at trial. Assyrian laws, Hittiti laws and the Dharm of the Vedic period in India[1] also devised different sets of standards by which obligations of one was provided to another. Jurisprudence of Lao-Tze and Confucius in China also protected human rights. A few Greek and Roman philosophers recognized the idea of natural rights. Plato was one of the earliest writers to advocate a universal standard of ethical conduct. The Roman jurist Ulpian stated that according to law of nature, all men are equal and by the same law all are born free. Aristotle wrote in politics that justice, virtue, and rights change in accordance with different kinds of constitutions and circumstances. Cicero, a Roman statesman laid down the foundations of natural law and human rights in his work. He believed that there should be universal human rights laws that would transcend customary and civil laws. Thomas Aquinas, rooted natural law in a divine law which was revealed to man in part discoverable by man through his God-given right reason.[2]

The Magna Carta or the Great Charter of the Liberties of England granted by King John of England to the English barons

---

* *Senior Lecturer, Faculty of Law, University of Delhi, Law Centre-II, ARSD College, Delhi.*

on June 15, 1215 was in response to the heavy taxation burden created by the third crusade and the ransom of Richard I, captured by the holy Emperor Henry VI. The English barons protested the heavy taxes and were unwilling to let King John rule again without some concessions in their rights. The Carta set forth the principle that the power of the King was not absolute. The Carta was strengthened in 1628 by the Petition of Rights and in 1689 by the Bill of Rights, to form the platform for parliamentary superiority over the Crown and to give documentary authority for the rule of laws in England.

The concept of fundamental rights of man was stated in the declarations and constitutional instruments of many States. For instance, the Declaration of Independence of the Thirteen United States of America in 1776, the Constitution of the United States of 1787 with amendments in 1789, 1865, 1869 and 1919 specified a number of rights of man. The French Declaration of the Rights of Man and the Citizen of 1789 stipulated that men are born and remain free and equal in rights the aim of all political association is the conservation of the natural and inalienable rights of man.

In the classical period which was influenced by the theory of State sovereignty, international law was solely concerned with States. A vision based on the hypothesis that only States create rules of International Law, and as such, rules are valid fro them alone. Thus, no place was left for the individuals, and therefore, they had no legal significance from the International Law point of view. Individuals were related to one State through the bond of citizenship or nationality, and this stood in relation to other States in the role of aliens. If an injury was caused to an individual it was the state alone which owed the responsibility under International Law to another State. Even in those cases where individuals enjoyed certain rights and duties in conformity with, or according to International Law such as the rights enjoyed while on foreign territory by Heads of State, diplomatic enjoys and even private citizens[3]. Rights in question were enjoyed by the individuals concerned not as rights in International Law but as rights derived from national law.[4]

A paradigm shift in the position of the individuals after the Second World War has been one of the most remarkable developments in contemporary International Law. The Charter of the United Nations by using the words "Peoples of the United Nations' in the Preamble has given a place of importance to individuals. However, this alone did not change the position of the individuals in the domain of International Law. They are regarded as the real subjects and beneficiaries of International Law by virtue of having rights and duties flowing directly from International Law.[5] While a few rules are directly concerned with regulating the position and activities of individuals, a few others, indirectly affect them.[6] That is, rules may also be applicable to certain inter-relationship of individuals themselves, where such inter-relationship involve matters of international concern. However, as long as the international community is composed of States, it is only through the exercise of their will alone rights and duties are conferred to them. They may agree to confer particular rights on individuals which will be enforceable under International Law, independently of municipal law.

The term human rights is a new formulation of the classic phrase "the rights of man". Its first use seems to have been made by Franklin Roosevelt in his famous message to Congress in January 1941 calling for a world founded on four essential freedoms. These he listed as freedom of speech, freedom of religion, freedom from want and freedom from fear. In the course of his four freedom message, the President declared: "Freedom means the supremacy of human rights everywhere. Our support goes to those who struggle to gain these rights or keep them.: The phrase human rights was used again in the Atlantic Charter and the same formula was repeated shortly thereafter in the Declaration of the United Nations signed on First January, 1942. Then came the Dumbarton Oaks' proposals on the basis of which the San Francisco Conference prepared and opened the Charter of the United Nations. The Charter referred to human rights in its Preamble and in six different articles and this concern of the United Nations in the promotion and encouragement of respect for human rights and fundamental freedoms was translated in the Universal Declaration of Human Rights adopted by the General Assembly on 10th December, 1948[7].

The Universal Declaration was the first of the series of documents intended to constitute an International Bill of Rights and it was followed by two important Covenants transforming the principles enunciated in the University Declaration into treaty provisions establishing legal obligations on the part of each ratifying country. One was the International Covenant on Civil and Political Rights and its Optional Protocol and the other was the International Covenants were adopted by the General Assembly on 16th December 1966 and the International Covenant of Economic, Socia and Cultural Rights came into effect on 3rd January 1974 and the International Covenant on Civil and Political Rights entered into force on 23rd March 1976. India, has ratified both these Internationa Covenants with certain reservations[8].

The majority of legal scholars and philosophers agree that every human being is entitled to some basic rights. Thus, there is universal acceptance of human rights in principle in domestic and international plane. Human rights is a generic term and it embraces civil rights, civil liberties and social, economic and cultural rights. It is, therefore, difficult to give a precise definition of the term human rights. However, it can be said that the rights that all people have by virtue of their being human are human rights. These are the rights in which no one can be deprived without a grave affront to justice.[9] It is so because they may affect the human dignity. Thus, the idea of human rights is bound up with the idea of human dignity. Justice J.S. Verma, the then Chief Justice of India, has rightly stated that human dignity is the quintessence of human rights[10]. All those rights which are essential for the protection and maintenance of dignity of individuals and create conditions in which every human being can develop his personality to the fullest extent may be termed human rights. However, dignity has never been precisely defined on the basis of consensus, but it accords roughly with justice and good society.[11]

The Universal Declaration enumerates the basic postulates and principles of human rights in a most comprehensive manner. It dealt not only with civil and political rights, but with social and economic rights as well[12].

CIVIL AND POLITICAL RIGHTS

Articles 2 to 21 deal with those civil and political rights which have been generally recognized throughout the world. These are as follows:

(i) Right to life, liberty and security of persons–Article 3.

(ii) Freedom from slavery or servitude–Article 4.

(iii) Prohibition against torture, inhuman or degrading treatment or punishment–Article 5.

(iv) Recognition as a person before the law-Article 6.

(v) Equality before the law and equal protection of the law without any discrimination–Article 7.

(vi) Effective remedy before the national tribunals–Article 8.

(vii) Freedom from arbitrary arrest, detention or exile–Article 9.

(viii) Right to a fair and public hearing by an independent and impartial tribunal– Article 10.

(ix) Presumption of innocence until proved guilty in a public trial with all guarantees necessary for defence in criminal cases– Article 11, Para 1.

(x) Freedom from ex-post facto laws– Article 11, Para 2.

(xi) Right to privacy, family, home and correspondence–Article 12.

(xii) Right to freedom of movement and residence within the borders of a State– Article 13, Para 1.

(xiii) Right to leave any country, including his own and to return to his country– Article 13, Para 2.

(xiv) Right to seek and to enjoy in other countries asylum from persecution– Article 14, Para 1.

(xv) Right to a nationality– Article 15.

(xvi) Right to marry and to found a family– Article 16.

(xvii) Right to own property– Article 17.

(xviii) Right to freedom of thought, conscience and religion - Article 18.

(xix) Right to freedom of opinion and expression– Article 19.

(xx) Right to freedom of peaceful assembly and association–Article 20.

(xxi) Right to participate in the government of his country Article 21.

ECONOMIC AND SOCIAL RIGHTS

Articles 22 to 27 of the Declaration deal with economic and social rights which are as follows:

(i) Right to social security- Article 22.

(ii) Right to work and free choice of employment- Article 23.

(iii) Right to rest and leisure- Article 24.

(iv) Right to a standard of living adequate for the health of himself and of his family- Article 25.

(v) Right to education- Article 26.

(vi) Right to participate in cultural life- Article 27.

(vii) Right to good social and international order- Article 28.

The Declaration of Human Rights in 1948 inspired the leaderships of all the countries for securing basic rights to their people. In India, after securing freedom from British Raj, Gandhiji and Nehru spearheaded to institutionalize the basic rights for humanity in India. Gandhiji assured "I shall work for an India in which the poorest shall feel that it is their country in whose making they have an effective voice, an India in which there shall be no high class or low class of people; an India in which all communities shall live in perfect harmony. This is the India of my dream[13].

Pursuant to Ghandian humanism and Nehru's scientific temper, the new Constitution enacted and adopted in 1950 contributed in ushering a new legal and constitutional philosophy embodying ideals of liberty, equality and human dignity. The Preamble of the Constitution together with Fundamental Rights and Directive Principles constitute the *Bhagwadgita* of Indian sociological jurisprudence. Its core principles make the people of India the ultimate sovereign, the country socialist, democratic and republican in character in order to secure to all its citizens justice-social, economic and political. Such is the constitutional rubric of Indian social system which act like Sermon on the Mounty to legislature, executive and judiciary. Likewise the Fundamental Rights in the Constitution constitute the *magna carta* of individual liberty and human rights and the Directive Principles, the social character of economic justice and it is paramount that courts ought to synthesise these twin goals in a spirit of mutual accommodation and co-existence to subserve the social ends free from coercion and exploitation necessary for founding an egalitarian society in India. This is what Granville Austin also characterize as the 'conscience of the Constitution. He remarks,[14] 'The Indian Constitution is first and foremost a social document. The majority of its provisions are either directly aimed at furthering the goals of social revolution or attempt to foster this revolution by establishing the conditions necessary for its achievement. Yet despite the permeation of the entire constitution by aim of national renascence, the core commitment to the social revolution lies in Parts III and IV in the Fundamental Rights and Directive Principles of State Policy.

The pattern of social legislation in India since independence has been in accordance with the constitutional mandate. In fact, ninety per cent of social legislation enacted by the Parliament has been concerning human rights of Indians be it laws concerning agrarian reforms, abolition of zamindari system, ceilings on landholdings, regulation and control of labour problems, laws concerning labour welfare, safety, health wages, bonus, gratuity, social insurance and social security, protection of migrant workers, women and child labour, contract labour, bonded labour, equal remuneration for equal work, laws concerning social and family relations of Hindus in particular regarding marriage, divorce, dowry, succession, adoption, guardianship, reforms in social status of Harijans, Girijans by protecting their civil rights, abolition of untouchability, suppression of immoral traffic in women and girls, prohibition laws, laws concerning bail, detention, arrest, control of population explosion by way of medical termination of pregnancy, punishment of tax evasion, trafficking narcotic drugs, protection of environment pollution, etc. Law, therefore, has been extensively used as a tool of effective social change and for eradicating social and economic evils.

ENGLISH LEGAL SYSTEM REJECTED

The British legal system developed the principle that 'justice is blind' or judges ought to live in 'Ivory tower' meaning thereby they are required to interpret law logically and statistically unmindful and unconcern of social consequences or effects of their judgement on society. The Indian judges like M.C. Chagla, P.B. Gajendragadkar, Krishan Iyer, P.N. Bhagwati, D.A. Desai, Chinnappa Reddy have rejected the Anglo-Saxon jurisprudence being anti-people, draconian, cancerous and smuggled system which is utterly alien to the genius of the country. Krishna Iyer, J. scoffed[15] at the notion that principles of justice, equity and good conscience are to be equated with English common law during the reign of Queen Victoria.

FREEDOM OF PRESS FOR SAFEGUARDING THE FOURTH PILLAR OF DEMOCRACY

The freedom of the press, implicit in the right of the freedom and expression, is essential for political liberty and proper functioning of democracy. The American Press Commission has said, "Freedom of the press is essential to political liberty. When man cannot freely convey their thoughts to one another, no freedom is secured, where freedom of expression exists the beginning of a free society and means for every retention of liberty are already present. Free expression is therefore, unique among liberties"[16]. The Indian Press Commission has also expressed a similar view. It says that "Democracy can thrive not only under the vigilant eye of its Legislature, but also under the care and guidance of public opinion and the press is par excellence, the vehicle through which opinion can become articulate." Lord Mansfied has defined "The Liberty of the press" as: "it consists in printing without any licence subject to the consequences of law". The Supreme Court of India in case of *Indian Express Newspapers* v. *Union of India*[17] recognizing the utility of freedom of press observed:

"The expression "freedom of the press" has not been used in Article 19 but it is comprehended within Article 19 (1)(a). The expression means freedom from interference from authority which would have the effect of interference with the content and circulation of newspapers. There cannot be any interference with that freedom in the name of public interest. The purpose of the press is to advance the public interest by publishing facts and opinions without which a democratic electorate cannot make responsible judgements. Freedom of the Press is the heart of social and political intercourse. It is the primary duty of the courts to uphold the freedom of the press and invalidate all laws or administrative actions which interfere with it contrary to the constitutional mandate.[18]

In case of *Romesh Thapper* v. *State of Madras*[19], a law banning entry and circulation of journal in a State was held invalid. The

Court said that there can be, no doubt, that freedom of speech and expression includes freedom of propagation of ideas, and that freedom is ensured by the freedom of circulation. The case of *Sakal Papers Ltd. V. Union of India*[20] the Court struck down the Daily Newspapers (Price and Control Order 1960, rejecting the State's argument as it cut circulation by a price rise or publication or dissemination of news, ideas and knowledge by restricting column space. In case of *Express Newspaper (P) Ltd.* v. *Union of India*[21] the petitioners challenged the constitutional validity of a notice of re-entry upon the forfeiture of lease and of threatened demolition of the Express Buildings on the ground that it was violative of Articles 14, 19 (1)(a) and (g). By an agreement of lease the petitioner was allotted certain plots for construction of its press building by the Government of India. The Lt. Governor of Delhi alleged that the new Express Building was constructed in contravention of municipal corporation laws and served a notice for demolition. The Court held that the impugned notices constituted direct and immediate threat to the freedom of the press and were thus violative of Article 19(1)(a) and Article 14 and invalid.

"The basic principle in a democracy is that the people are supreme[22]. It follows that all authorities–whether judges, legislators, Ministers, bureaucrats–are servants of the people. Once this concept of popular sovereignty is kept firmly in mind, it becomes obvious that the people of India are the masters and all authorities including courts are their servants. Surely, the master has the right to criticize the servant if the servant does not act or behave properly. It would logically follow that in a democracy the people have the right to criticize judges. Why then should there be a Contempt of Court Act, which to some extent prevents people from criticizing judges or doing other things that are regarded as contempt o f court?

RIGHT TO PRIVACY

In the case of *District Registrar & Collector* v. *Canara Bank*,[23] the Supreme Court defined privacy as "the state of being free from intrusion or disturbance in one's private life or affairs". In case of *Govind* v. *State of Madhya Pradesh*[24], it was held that the right to personal liberty, and the right to move freely and speech could be described as contributing to the right to privacy. However, the right was not absolute and would always be subjected to reasonable restrictions. The right would necessarily have to go through a process of case by case development. In case of *Malak Singh* v. *State of Punjab*[25], the question related to as to when surveillance of a person would be infringement of his "right to privacy". In this case, the name of the petitioner was included in the surveillance register by the police under Section 23 of the Punjab Police Act, he not being given opportunity of being heard. Since, he was not so heard, inclusion of his name in that register had infringed his right to privacy under Article 21. The Supreme Court held that so long as surveillance was for the purpose of prevention of crimes and confined to the limits prescribed Rule 23 (7) of the Punjab Police Act, a person could not complain against the inclusion of his name in the surveillance register and in these mattes, the Court held that the rule of natural justice was not attracted. The scope of right to privacy which was held to be implicit in the right to life and personal liberty guaranteed under Article 21 were explained in the case of *R. Rajagopal* v. *State of Tamil Nadu*[26]. The Court held that the right to privacy meant a right to be let alone. The Court observed:

> "A citizen has a right to safeguard the privacy of his own, his family marriage, procreation, motherhood, child bearing and education among other matters. None can publish anything concerning the above matters without his consent-whether truthful or otherwise and whether laudatory or critical. If he does so, he would be violating the right to privacy of the person concerned and would be liable in an action for damages."

The Supreme Court, in case of *State of Maharashtra* v. *Amdhulkar Narain*,[27] held that even a woman of easy virtue was entitled to the right to privacy under Article 21 and that no one could assail her privacy as and when he liked. Interpreting the basic structure theory, the Supreme Court in case of *People's Union for Civil Liberties* v. *Union of India*[28], held that "democracy based on adult franchise is part of basic structure of the Constitution." And ruled that "once a person becomes a candidate to acquire police office", declaration about his criminal antecedents as also about his assets and liabilities would not affect his right of privacy.

TELEPHONE TAPPING–AN ATTACK ON PRIVACY

Section 5(2) of the Indian Telegraph Act, 1885, empowers the Central Government or the State Government or any specially authorized officers, to intercept messages if satisfied that it is necessary or expedient so to do in the interest of the sovereignty and integrity of India, the security of the State, friendly relation with foreign States, public order, or for preventing incitement to the commission of an offence. It can be done in the event of the occurrence of a public emergency or in the interest of public safety for reasons to be recorded in writing. In case of *People's Union for Civil Liberties* v. *Union of India*,[29] laid down certain procedural safeguards to be observed before resorting to telephone tapping under Section 5(2) of the Act. The telephonic interaction, the Court held, was a part of modern man's life and an important aspect of a man's private life. Therefore, the Court ruled that telephone tapping would attract Article 21, unless it was permitted under the procedure established by law.

NO RIGHT TO HAVE AS MANY CHILDREN AS ONE CHOOSES TO HAVE

The problem of population explosion is a national and global issue. It provides justification for priority in policy oriented legislations wherever needed.[30] The Supreme Court in this upheld the validity of Section 175(1)(q) of the *Haryana Panchayati Raj Act, 1994*, which disqualified a person with more than two living children from holding office in Panchayati Raj Institutions. The provision was held not violative of the right to life and liberty, howsoever expanded the meanings of the right might be.

RIGHT OF A MAJOR TO LIVE WITH ANYBODY

Our country is a secular and free democratic country and so, any person who has attained majority, has the right to live freely with any one. The Allahabad High Court in *Jyoti* v. *State of Uttar Pradesh*[31], ruled that a person, he or she, who has attained 18 years of age, being major according to Section 3 of the Indian Majority Act, 1875, was deemed to understand his/her welfare and hence he/she could go wherever he/she liked and live with anybody. One could not be restrained from doing so, even by the parents. Individual liberty under Article 21, the Court held, had the highest place in our Constitution.

RIGHT TO PRIVACY AND DISCLOSURE OF DREADFUL DISEASES

The controversy was raised by a patient with regard to disclosure of the facts about his HIV positive. In the land mark decision of

Mr. X. v. *Hospital Z*[32], the Supreme Court held that the right to privacy was not absolute and might be lawfully restricted for the prevention of crime, disorder or protection of health or morals or protection of rights and freedom of others. Later on, the Supreme Court in case of *Mr. X* v. *Hospital Z*[33] held that the observations by the Court as to what rights and obligations arise in such context as to right to privacy or confidentiality or whether such persons are entitled to be married or not or in the event such persons marry they would commit an offence under law or whether such right is suspended during the period of illness, were unnecessary, when concerned. Since, the Court had rested their decision on the facts of the case, those observations were held to be uncalled for. The Court, therefore, partly overruled the decision in *Mr. X* v. *Hospital Z*, and confined it to that "it was open to the hospital or the doctor concerned to reveal such information to persons related to the girl whom he intended to marry and she had a right a right to know about the HIV positive status of the appellant". Now it is a settled fact that the right to privacy is not treated as absolute and is subject to such action as may be lawfully taken for the prevention of crime or disorder or protection of health or morals or protection of rights and freedom of others. If there is a conflict between fundamental rights of two parties, that right which advances public morality would prevail.[34] In case of *Mr. X.* v. *Hospital Z*[35] the controversy before Delhi High Court related to the application of the husband seeking DNA test of the slides of tubular gestation of his wife whose tubular pregnancy was terminated, which was preserved in the hospital. Asserting that foetus of the wife, discharged from the body, could not be treated as a part of the mother, it being a unique organism, which had been preserved in the Hospital she could not claim that it should not be put to any test. The Court therefore, held that in divorce proceedings in which adultery was one of the grounds, application by the husband for DNA test could not amount to compelling the wife to submit to any test as right to privacy has become a part of public document.

ARREST OF A JUDGEMENT-DEBTOR

In *Jolly George Varghese* v. *Bank of Cochin*[36] the appellants were the judgement-debtors, against whom warrant for arrest and detention in the civil prison were issued for the non-payment of an amount due to the respondent Bank, which had ripened into a degree and had not yet been discharged. The warrant was issued under Section 51 and Order XXI, Rule 37 of the C.P.C., 1908, in execution of the degree for the repayment of a debt. The then Justice Krishna Iyer speaking for the Court held such arrest and detention being inhuman, going by the standards of Article 11 of the International Convention on Civil and Political Rights and Article 21 of the Constitution.

RIGHT AGAINST ILLEGAL DETENTION

The Supreme Court in *Joginder Kumar* v. *State of U.P.* discouraging illegal detention of the people by the police, laid down the following guidelines governing arrest of a person during investigation:

(1) An arrested person being held in custody is entitled, if he so requests to have one friend, relative or other person, who is known to him or likely to take an interest n his welfare, told as far as is practicable that he has been arrested and where he is being detained.

(2) The Police Officer shall inform the arrested person when he is brought to the police station of this right.

(3) An entry shall be required to be made in the diary as to who was informed of the arrest.

The Court held that these protections from police power must be held to flow from Articles 21 and 22(1) and enforced strictly.

RIGHT TO GO ABROAD

The Supreme Court in case of *Satwant Singh Sawhney* v. *Assistant Passport Officer, New Delhi*[37] held that right to travel abroad was included within the expression personal liberty within the meaning of Article 21. The Apex Court set at rest the controversy in case of *Maneka Gandhi* v. *Union of India*, in which the passport of the petitioner was impounded under Section 10(3)(c) of the Passport Act, 1967, which empowered the Government to do so in the interest of the general public. The Government explained that since the presence of the petitioner before a Commissioner of Inquiry, in connection with various complaints against her, was necessary, the passport was impounded to ensure such presence and to restrict her leaving the country. Delivering the majority judgement, the then Justice Bhagwati upheld the constitutionality of Section 10(3)(c) of the Passport Act, 1967, as not violative of Articles 14, 19(1)(a) or (g) or Article 21. However, the Court laid down the principles of law in respect of the scope of the rights conferred by Articles 14 and 21. The Court further held that Article 21 required a procedure established by law for depriving him of his right The procedure contemplated in Article 21 could not be arbitrary, unfair or unreasonable. If a law depriving a person of personal liberty and prescribing a procedure for that purpose within the meaning of Article 21 had to stand the test of one or more of the rights conferred by Article 19 which may be applicable in a given situation *ex hypothesi* it must also be liable to tested with reference to Article 19.

RIGHT TO FREE LEGAL AID-RIGHT TO APPEAL

The Supreme Court in case of *M.H.Hoskot* v. *State of Maharashtra*[38], the held that right to free legal aid at the cost of the State to an accused, who could not afford legal services for reasons of poverty, indigence or incommunicado situation, was part of fair, just and reasonable procedure implicit in Article 21. Free legal aid to the indigent has been declared to be "a State's duty and not government Charity". Further in case of *Suk Das* v. *Union Territory of Arunachal Pradesh*[39], the Supreme Court held that the conviction reached without so informing the accused and inquiring form him whether he wanted a lawyer to be provided to him at State's cost and the accused remaining unrepresented by a lawyer in the trial, the conviction would clearly be in violation of the fundamental right under Article 21. Such a trial must be held to be vitiated on account of a fatal constitutional infirmity.

COMMON LAW DUTY OF TAKING REASONABLE CARE

In case of *Bhajan Kaur* v. *Delhi Administration*[40], the Supreme Court held that it is a duty of the State to create a climate where members of the society, belonging to different faiths, caste and creed, live together and to protect their life, liberty, dignity and worth of an individual which should not be jeopardized or endangered. Reiterating the guarantee under Article 21, the Supreme Court in case of *P.A. Narayana* v. *Union of India*[41], held that there was a common law duty of taking reasonable care attached to all carriers including the railways. In this case the Court awarded Rs. 2.00 lacs as compensation to the husband of the deceased who was criminally assaulted and also robbed of her ornaments while traveling in a train between Bandra and Andheri railway station while the train was in motion. On her pulling the alarm chain neither the guard nor the motorman stopped the train and she ultimately succumbed to the injuries in the compartment.

RIGHT TO SPEEDY TRIAL

In case of *Hussainara Khatoon (No. 1)* v. *Home Secretary, State of Bihar*[42], the Supreme Court held that Article 21 requires that a person can be deprived of his liberty only in accordance with procedure established by law which should be a just, fair and reasonable procedure. A procedure cannot be reasonable, fair or just unless it ensures a speedy trial for determination of the guilt of the person deprived of his liberty. Reiterating the above approval, the Apex Court in case of *Pratap* Singh v. *State of Jharkhand*[43], held that the right to speedy trial is part of fundamental right to life and personal liberty. A Constitution Bench of five learned judges of the Apex Court in case of *A. R. Antulay* v. *R. S. Nayak*[44] dealt with the question of the right to speedy trial and laid down certain guidelines which may be summarized as follows:

(1) Fair, just and reasonable procedure implicit in Article 21 creates a right in the accused to be tried speedily.

(2) Right to speedy trial flowing from Article 21 encompasses all the stages, namely the stage of investigation, inquiry, appeal, revision and re-trial.

(3) The concerns underlying the right to speedy trial from the point of view of the accused are:

(a) The period of remand and pre-conviction detention should be as short as possible. In other words, the accused should not be subjected to unnecessary or long incarceration prior to the conviction;

(b) The worry, anxiety, expense and disturbance to his vocation and peace, resulting from an unduly prolonged investigation, inquiry or trial should be minimum; and

(c) Undue delay may well result in impairment of the ability of the accused to defend himself, whether on account of death, disappearance or non-availability of witnesses or otherwise.

(4) Where the right to speedy trial is alleged to have been infringed, the first question to be put and answered is who is responsible for the delay? Proceedings taken by either party in good faith, to vindicate their rights and interest, as perceived by them, cannot be treated as delaying tactics nor can the time taken in pursuing such proceedings be counted towards delay.

(5) If delay, all circumstances to be put on record. Each and every delay does not necessarily prejudice the accused. But inordinately long delay may be taken as presumptive proof of prejudice. An accused's plea of denial of speedy trial cannot be defeated by saying that the accused did at no time demand a speedy trial. Ultimately, the Court has to balance and weigh the several relevant factors. Where the Court comes to the conclusion that right to speedy trial of an accused has been infringed, the charges or the conviction, as the case may be, shall be quashed. It is neither advisable nor practicable to fix any time limit for trial of offences. An objection based on denial of right to speedy trial and for relief on that count, should be first addressed to the High Court.

The Supreme Court, in *Hussainara Khatoon (VII)* v. *Home Secretary, Bihar*[45]holding that orders for the enforcement of the guidelines given in earlier cases[46], could not be issued, made a request to the Chief Justices of the High Courts to undertake a review of such cases in their States and give appropriate directions where needed to ensure proper and effective implementation of the guidelines. In case of *Anil Rai* v. *State of Bihar*[47] held that while justice delayed is justice, justice withheld is even worse than that. The Court took a serious note of delay in delivery of judgements and observed that any inordinate, unexplained and negligent delay in pronouncing the judgement by the High Court, infringed the right under Article 21 of the Constitution. Such a delay actually negatived the right of appeal conferred upon the parties. Such a course was stated to be contrary to the maximum "*Actus Curiae Neminem Gravabit*" that an act of the Court shall prejudice none.

RIGHT TO FAIR TRIAL

Free and fair trial has been said to be the *sine qua non* of Article 21. It is said that justice should not be done but it should be seen to have been done. "If the criminal trial is not free and fair and not free from bias, the judicial fairness and the criminal justice system would be at stake, shaking the confidence of the public in the system and woe would be the rule of law." Broadening the dimension of fair trial, the Apex Court in *Zahira Habibulla H. Sheikh* v. *State of Gujarat*[48], commonly known as *Best Bakery Case*, said that a trial which is primarily aimed at ascertaining truth, has to be fair to all concerned. Not only the accused be fairly dealt with, but also the victims or their family members and relatives. Denial of a fair trial is as much injustice to the accused as is to the victim and the society. Further the Court held that there could be no analytical, all comprehensive or exhaustive definition of the concept of a fair trial. It would have to be determined in seemingly infinite variety of actual situations with the ultimate object in mind, viz., whether something that was done or said either before or at the trial deprived the quality of fairness to a degree where a miscarriage of justice had resulted. The Apex Court emphasized that a fair trial would obviously mean a trial before an impartial judge, a fair prosecutor and atmosphere of judicial clam, that in which bias or prejudice for or against the accused, the witnesses or the cause which was being tried, was eliminated. Where, the witnesses got threatened or were forced to give false evidence, or where material witnesses were not heard, fair trial would be said to have been denied. The State, the Court asserted, thus had a definite role to play in protecting the witnesses, to start with, atleast in sensitive cases involving those in power, having political patronage, could wield muscle and money power, to avert trial getting tainted and derailed and truth becoming a casualty.

RIGHT TO BAIL AND NO RIGHT TO ANTICIPATORY BAIL

In case of *Babu Singh* v. *State of U.P.*, the Supreme Court held that refusal to grant bail to an accused person without reasonable grounds would amount to deprivation of his personal liberty under Article 21. In this case, six appellants were acquitted by the Sessions Judge in a murder case. In appeal by the State, the High Court convicted them and sentenced them to life imprisonment. The appellants applied for bail during pendency of their appeal before the Supreme Court. The appellants were the entire male members of their family and all of them were in jail. For that reasons, their defence was likely to be jeopardized. During appeal before the High Court, the State did not press for their custody. For the period of five years, there was nothing to indicate that there had been any conduct on their part suggestive of disturbing the peace of the locality, threatening any one in the village or otherwise thwarting the life of the community or the course of justice. Keeping in view the above circumstances, the Supreme Court held that the appellants eligible to be enlarged on bail but they were to observe two conditions, viz. that they would not enter Bharaiyam village which was alleged to be the hot bed of clan clashes and secondly, they would report once every week at the Tandiawan Police Station. In case of *State of M.P.* v. *Ram Kishna Balothia*[49], the Supreme Court upheld that impugned Section 438 of Cr.P.C., 1974 and held that it did not violate Article 21. The Court held that anticipatory bail was not an essential part of right to life enshrined in Article 21.

RIGHT TO WRITE A BOOK

The petitioner, in case of *State of Maharashtra* v. *Prabhakar Panduranga*[50], was detained under the Preventive Detention Act, 1950. During his detention in jail, he wrote a book on science and sought permission from the Government to send the manuscript of the book to his wife for publication. The Government refused permission. The Court held the refusal as an infringement of his personal liberty as the restriction was not authorized under the Prevent Detention Act, 1950. The Court laid down that the right to personal liberty under Article 21, included the right to write a book and get it published. When a *detenu* exercises this right, its denial without the authority of law, would violate Article 21.

RIGHT AGAINST BAR FETTERS

The Supreme Court in case of *Sunil Batra* v. *Delhi Administration*[51] laid down that the treatment of a human being which offended human dignity, imposed avoidable torture and reduced the man to the level of a beast, would certainly be arbitrary and could be question under Articles 21 and 14. So, putting bar fetters for an unusually long period without due regard for the safety of the prisoner and the security of the prison would certainly be not justified.[52] Expressing their resentment on keeping the under trial prisoners in bar fetters, the Supreme Court, in case of *Harbans Singh* v. *State of Uttar Pradesh,* the Supreme Court observed, "We fail to understand why proper security arrangements cannot be made in jail to guard the under-trials. Armed guards can be posted to guard them if security reasons so demand but it seems inhuman to keep them in fetters while they are awaiting trial which is delayed, notwithstanding this Court's order to expedite them.

RIGHT AGAINST INHUMAN TREATMENT

For upholding the basic rights of humanity with a view to safeguard the rights of the prisoners and persons in police lock-up, particularly of women and children, the Supreme Court in a number of cases has taken a serious note of the inhuman treatment meted to the prisoners and has issued appropriate directions to prison and police authorities[53] the incidents of torture, assault, injury and deaths in police custody have been said to be the worst form of human rights violation.[54] The Supreme Court, in *Sheela Barse* v. *State of Maharashtra,* took a serious note of violence committed on women prisoners confined in the police lock up in the city of Bombay. The Court emphasized on the importance of legal assistance to a poor or indigent accused who was arrested and put in jeopardy of his life or personal liberty. Emphasizing the need for setting up a machinery for providing legal assistance to prisoners in jails, the Court directed the I.G. of Prisons, Maharashtra to issue a circular to all Superintendents of Police in the State requiring them to provide facilities and information to the Legal Aid Committees, so as to render legal assistance to the under-trial prisoners. In another case[55], the Supreme Court held that torture by police struck a blow at the rule of law. Custodial violence has been held to be a calculated assault on human dignity, perhaps one of the worst crimes in a civilized society governed by Rule of Law. Any form of torture or cruel inhuman or degrading treatment would fall within the inhibition of Article 21.

RIGHT AGAINST DELAYED EXECUTION

The Apex Court, in case of *T.V. Vatheeswaran* v. *State of Tamil Nadu*[56], held that prolonged detention to await the execution of a sentence of death is unjust, unfair and unreasonable, violative of Article 21. In this case, the Court held that delay exceeding two years in the execution of a sentence of death should be considered sufficient to entitle the person under sentence of death to invoke Article 21 and demand the quashing of the sentence of death. Procedure established by law, did not end with the pronouncement of sentence but it included the carrying out of sentence. The Court ruled that prolonged delay in executing a sentence of death would make the punishment inhuman and degrading. It would be cruel and would have dehumanizing effects.

RIGHT TO EDUCATION

It is a fact that education is a basic human right. For the success of democratic system of government, education is one of the basic elements. An educated citizen has to choose the representatives who form the government. Education gives a person human dignity who develops himself as well as contributes to the development of his country. The framers of the Constitution realizing the importance of education have imposed a duty on the State under Article 45 as one of the directive policy of State to provide free and compulsory education to all children until they complete the age of 14 year within 10 years from the commencement of the Constitution. The Supreme Court also in case of *Unnikrishnan*[57] declared that the right to education for the children of the age of 6 to 14 is a fundamental right. Even after this, there was no improvement. To fill up the gap between the literate and illiterate, 86th Constitutional Amendment Act, 2002 has added a new Article 21A after Article 21 and has made education for all children of the age of 6 to 14 a fundamental right. It provides that "*the State shall provide free and compulsory education to all children of the age of 6 to 14 years in such manner as the State may, by law, determine*".

FREEDOM OF RELIGION

For maintaining the belief of the people of India in their respective religions there is sufficient provision in our Constitution. Judiciary has also played a role of catalyst in setting the fabric of the secularism in India. Article 26 of the Constitution says that subject to public order, morality and health every religious denomination of any section of it shall have the following rights:

(a) to establish and maintain institutions for religious and charitable purposes,

(b) to manage its own affairs in matters of religion,

(c) to own and acquire moveable and immovable property,

(d) to administer such property in accordance with law.

In *Bira Kishore Dev* v. *State of Orissa*[58], the Shri Jagannath Temple Act took the management of secular activities of temple from the Raja of Puri and vested it in Committee constituted under the Act. The Court held the Act valid as it did not affect the religious aspect.

The Supreme Court of India, in case of *Gulam Abbas* v. *State of UP*[59], held that the direction given by the Supreme Court for shifting a property connected with religion to avoid clashes between two religious communities or sects does not affect religious rights being in the interest of public order. In that case the facts were that there had been a long standing dispute between the Shias and Sunnis of Mohalla Doshipura, Varansi, regarding performance of religious rites by members of Shia sect on certain plots and properties situated in the Mohalla. To find a permanent solution to the problem, the Supreme Court appointed a committee of 7 persons and the committee recommended the shifting of two graves of Sunnis so as to separate the places of worship of Shias and Sunnis.

The Supreme Court of India, in case of *Bramchari Sidheswar Shai* v. *State of West Bengal*[60], popularly known as the Ramkrishna Mission case, held that the followers of Ramkrishna, who are collection of individuals, and who adhere to a system of beliefs as conducive to their spiritual well being, who have organized themselves collectively and who have an organization of definite name as Ramkrishna Math or Mission can be regarded as a religious denomination within Hindu religion as they satisfy the tests regarding a religious denomination and would, therefore, be entitled to claim the fundamental rights conferred on them under Article 26 of the Constitution.

The petitioner, Atheist Society of India, in case of *Atheist Society of India* v. *Government of Andhra Pradesh*[61], prayed for issuing a writ of mandamus directing the State Government to prohibit breaking of coconuts, performing of poojas, chanting of mantras or sutras of different religions at State functions. The Andhra Pradesh High

Court rejected their prayer and held that these activities have been a part of the Indian tradition and are meant to invoke the blessings of Almighty for the success of the project undertaken.

In case of *Javed* v. *Haryana*[62], the Supreme Court held that Section 175 (11) (q) of the Haryana Panchayati Raj Act, 1994 which disqualifies persons having more than two children from contesting election for the post of Sarpanch and Panch is Panchayat does not violate Article 25 of the Constitution.

RIGHT OF MINORITIES TO ESTABLISH AND MANAGE EDUCATIONAL INSTITUTIONS

The Supreme Court of India has laid down, through interpretation, to establish that minorities have also their right to manage their educational institutions in the following leading cases:

In case of *D.A.V. College, Bhatinda* v. *State of Punjab*[63], the University declared that Punjabi would be the sole medium of instruction in the affiliated colleges. The Court held that the right of the minority to establish and administer educational institution of their choice includes the right to have a choice of medium of instruction.

In case of *St. Xaviers College* v. *State of Gujarat*[64], a 7 Judges Bench of the Supreme Court had an occasion to examine the extent and scope of Article 30(1). In this case, the validity of Sections 33A, 40, 41, 51A and 52A of the Gujarat University Act, 1949 was challenged whereby every College was under the management of government body which included amongst its members, a representative of the University nominated by the Vice-Chancellor and representatives of teachers, non-teaching staff and students of the College. The Court held that these provisions abridged the right of the minority to administer the educational institution of their choice and hence did not apply to minority institutions.

The case of *St. Stephen's College* v. *University of Delhi*[65], wherein the validity of admission programme and the preference given to Christian students by the College was challenged as violative of Delhi University circulars for admission to B.A. and B.Com. courses. The University issued another circular to all Colleges stating that admission to B.A. courses be based on the merit of percentage of marks secured by students in the qualifying examination. The College filed a writ petition before the Supreme Court. The Supreme Court by majority of 4 to 1 held that the College was not bound to follow the University circulars as it would deprive the College of their minority character. But in case of *Unni Krishnan*[66], the Court had prescribed the fee to be charged by private unaided and aided recognized and affiliated educational institutions conducting professional courses such as engineering, medical etc. but such fee could not exceed the maximum limit fixed by the State. It held that commercialization of education was not permissible. The Court held that the decision in *Unni Krishnan*, scheme relating to the grant of admission and the fixing of the fee was not correct and to that extent are overruled.

The leading cases, T.M.A. Pai[67], *Islamic Academy of Education* v. *State of Karnataka*[68], P.A. Inamdar *v.* State of Maharashtra[69]. Supreme Court of India has settled the dust regarding management, fee structure and admissions to the private colleges.

PROTECTION OF ENVIRONMENT

Judiciary has played a significant role in protecting the environment of India by giving a number of leading judgements. A few of them are given below:

In case of *Rural Litigation and Entitlement Kendra* v. *State of UP*[70], the Court ordered the closure of certain lime stone quarries on the ground that there were serious deficiencies regarding the safety and hazards in them. In case of *Shriram Food and Fertilizer case*[71], the Supreme Court directed the Company to take all necessary safety measures before reopening the plant which manufactures hazardous and lethal chemicals and gases posing danger to health and life of the workmen and surrounding peoples. In case of *M.C. Mehta* v. *Union of India*[72], the Supreme Court ordered the closure of tanneries at Jajmau near Kanpur, polluting the Ganga. In case of *M.C. Mehta*(2) v. *Union of India*[73], the petitioner brought a PIL against water pollution requiring the Court to issue appropriate directions for the prevention of Ganga water pollution. The Court ordered to make adequate provisions for the treatment of trade effluent flowing out of the factories. In case of *M.C. Mehta* v. *Union of India*[74] (Pollution of Taj Mahal) the petitioner field a public interest litigation in the Court drawing the attention towards the degradation of the Taj Mahal due to the atmospheric pollution caused by a number of foundries. The Court ordered the closure of the surrounding foundries.

PROTECTION OF WOMEN

In case of *Apparel Export Promotion Council* v. *A.K. Chopra*[75], the Supreme Court took a serious note of the incidents of sexual harassment of women at work places. Such an incident, the Court said, resulted in violation of the Fundamental Right to Gender Equality and the Right to life and liberty-two most precious fundamental rights. In case of *State of Punjab* v. *Ramdev Singh*[76], the Supreme Court said apart from being a dehumanizing act, was an unlawful intrusion on the right of privacy and sanctity of a female.

DIRECTIVE PRINCIPLES AS A END OF FUNDAMENTAL RIGHTS

Today we are living in an era of a Welfare State which has to promote the prosperity the prosperity and well being of the people. The Directive Principles lay down certain economic and social policies to be pursued by the various Governments in India; they impose certain obligation on the State to take positive action in certain directions in order to promote the welfare of the people and achieve economic democracy. The Directive Principles are the ideals which the Union and State Governments must keep in mind while they formulate policy or pass a law. They lay down certain social, economic and political principles, suitable to peculiar conditions prevailing in India. Dr. B.R. Ambedkar aptly describes the objectives of a Welfare State. He said:

> ".... Our Constitution lays down what is called Parliamentary democracy. By Parliamentary democracy we mean "one man, one vote". We also mean that every Government shall be on the anvil, both in its daily affairs and also at the end of a certain period when the voters and the electorate will be given an opportunity to assess the work done by the Government..".

The first step was taken to provide supremacy for Directive Principles in the form of Article 31C which was added to the Constitution by the 25th Amendment Act, 1971. The effect of the insertion of Articles 31C was to provide supremacy for Directive

Principles contained in Articles 39(b) and 39(c) over Fundamental Rights contained in Articles 14, 19 and 31. It enhanced the utility of the Directive Principles. In case of *Randhir Singh* v. *Union of India*[77], it was held that equal pay for equal work has not been secured as a fundamental right but is deductible from Articles 14, 16 and 39(d). In case of *Olga Tellis* v. *Bombay Municipal Corporation*[78], the Supreme Court held that right to livelihood was part of the right to life guaranteed by Article 21.

In *re Kerala Education Bill*[79], the Supreme Court held that though the Directive Principles cannot override the fundamental rights, nevertheless, in determining the scope and ambit of the fundamental rights, the Court should not entirely ignore the directive principles, but should adopt the principle of harmonious construction and should attempt to give effect to both as much as possible. It has been held that both Fundamental Rights and Directive Principles aim at the same goal of bringing about a social revolution and the establishment of a Welfare State. The opinion so expressed was reiterated and followed with approval in *Minerva Mills Ltd.* v. *Union of India*[80]. The Court observed that the Constitution was founded on the bed-rock of balance between Part III and IV. To give absolute primacy to one over the other was to disturb the harmony of the Constitution which, was as essential feature of the basic structure of the Constitution.

CONCLUSION

The protection and promotion of human rights are clearly important functions of the state. While fundamental rights are generally couched in the language of negative rights against the state, the state apparatus ought to function in an active manner that protects the rights and freedoms of its people. In fact, the important wings of government–the legislature, the executive and the judiciary–function with a view to ensure the rights and freedoms of people. There is a need for India to consider accepting the jurisdiction of certain important committees under the international human rights system. This is not only because its own record in protecting and promotion human rights will come under international scrutiny, but also for India to continue to play a leadership role in persuading other developing countries to consider accepting the jurisdiction of these committees[81].

NOTES

1. See Laws Promulgated in the reigns of Urkagnia of Lagash (3260 B.C), Sargon of Akkad (2300 B.C.) and Hammurabi of Babylon (1750 B.C).
2. See Henle, S. J., 'A Catholic view of Human Rights : A Thomistic Reflection in Alan S. Rosenbaum, 'The Philosophy of Human Rights, International Perspectives (1980).
3. Aggarwal, H.O., Human Rights, Central Law Publications, Allahabad, p. 1.
4. Oppenheim, '*International Law*', Vol. I, Ninth Edition (1992), p. 847.
5. The Nuremberg Tribunal.
6. Oppenheim, *International Law*, p. 846.
7. P. N. Bhagwati, Foreword to Human Rights, Central Law Publications, Allahabad.
8. *Ibid.*
9. Maurice Craston quoted in L.J. Macfarlane, 'The Theory and Practice of Human Rights (1985) p. 7.
10. 'The New Universe of Human Rights', p. 3.
11. David P. Forsythe, 'The Internationalization of Human Rights, p. 1.
12. Aggarwal, H.O., Human Rights, Central Law Publications, p. 38.
13. Dhyani, S.N., Fundamentals of Jurisprudence, An Indian Approach, Central Law Agency, Allahabad, p. 328.
14. The Indian Constitution-Corner Stone of a Nationa, p. 50 (1966).
15. *Rattan Lal* v. *Vardesh Chander*, A.I.R. 1976, SC 588.
16. *Brij Bhusan* v. *State of delhi*, AIR 1950 SC 129.
17. (1985) 1 SCC 641.
18. Harjai Singh, AIR 1997 SC 73.
19. AIR 1950 SC 124.
20. AIR 1962 SC 305.
21. (1986) 1 SCC 133.
22. Markundey Katju, Justice, Supreme Court of India, *The Hindu*, January 22, 2007.
23. 2005 (1) SCC 496,
24. AIR 1975 SC 1378.
25. AIR 1981 SC 760.
26. AIR 1995 SC 264.

27. AIR, 1991, SC, 207.
28. AIR, 2003, SC, 2363.
29. AIR, 1997, SC, 568.
30. *Javed* v. *State of Haryana* AIR 2003 SC 3057.
31. AIR 2004 All 45.
32. AIR 1995, SC, 495.
33. AIR 2003 SC, 664.
34. *Sharda* v. *Dharampal* AIR 2003 SC 3450.
35. AIR 2002 Delhi 217.
36. AIR 1980 SC 470.
37. AIR 1967 SC 1836.
38. AIR 1978 SC 1548 *Sheela Barse* v. *State of Maharashtra*, AIR 1983 SC 378.
39. AIR 1986 SC 991.
40. AIR 1985 SC 231.
41. AIR 1998 SC 1659.
42. AIR 1979 SC 1360
43. 2005(3) SCC 551
44. AIR 1992 SC 1701.
45. (1995) SCC 326; *Upadhyaya* v. *State of Andhra Pradesh*, AIR 2000 SC 1756.
46. *A. R. Antulay* v. *R. S. Nayak*, AIR 1992 SC 1701; *Kartar Singh* v. *State of Punjab* (1994) 3 SCC, 569.
47. AIR 2001 SC 3173.
48. AIR 2004 SC 3114.
49. AIR 1995 SC 1198.
50. AIR 1966 SC 424.
51. AIR 1978 SC 1675.
52. AIR 1978 SC 1675.
53. *Rama Murthy* v. *State of Karnataka*, AIR 1997 SC 1739; *Khedat Mazdoor Chetna Sangath* v. *State of Madhya Pradesh*, AIR 1995 SC 31.
54. *Justice A.S. Anand*, "Third degree methods, Criminal Act", The Tribune, 11.12.2000.
55. *D. K. Basu* v. *State of West Bengal*, AIR 1997 SC 610.

56. AIR 1983 SC 361.
57. (1993) 1 SCC 645.
58. AIR 1964 SC 1501.
59. (1984) 1 SCC 81.
60. (1995) 4 SCC 646.
61. AIR 1992 AP 310.
62. AIR 2003 SC 3057.
63. AIR 1971 SC 1731.
64. AIR 1974 SC 1389.
65. (1992) 1 SCC 558.
66. (1993) 1 SCC 645.
67. AIR 2003 SC 355.
68. AIR 2003 SC 3724.
69. AIR 2005 SC 3236.
70. (1985) 2 SCC 431.
71. *M.C. Mehta* v. *Union of India* , (1986) 2 SCC 176.
72. (1987) 4 SCC 463.
73. (1995) 3 SCC 212.
74. AIR (1997) SC 735.
75. AIR 1999 SC 1988.
76. AIR 2004 SC 1290.
77. AIR 1982 SC 879.
78. AIR 1986 Sc 180.
79. AIR 1958 SC 956.
80. AIR 1980 SC 1789.
81. C. Raj Kumar, *The Hindu,* June 19, 2006.

Capital Punishment: International and National Perspectives

PRAKASH CHANDRA SHUKLA*

INTRODUCTION

At the dawn of the 21st Century, the debate over the capital punishment has acquired renewed vigour. It is considered by most civilized nations as a cruel and inhuman punishment but for others it has always been an effective punishment for murderers and dangerous offenders and has both deterrent and preventive effects. For some people the death penalty is ruled out entirely as something absolutely evil which, like torture, should never be used however many lives it might save and for others the death penalty is something which morality actually demands, a uniquely appropriate means of retribution or "reprobation" for the worst of crimes, even if its use adds nothing to the protection of human life[1].

The term '*capital*' begins from Latin '*Capitalis*' means '*regarding the head*'. Capital punishment is the execution of a person by the state as punishment for a crime[2]. In other words, it is the practice of deliberately putting to death an offender as a measure of social policy imposed by the governing authority.

The controversy over capital punishment is not new. Its roots lie deep in human history but after emergence of democratic order in most of the civilized states and particularly after the advent of

* *(HRDE) (Gold Medalist) Banaras Hindu University, Varansai; Lecturer, Department of Law, North Eastern Hill University, Shillong, Meghalaya (India).*

United Nations this controversy gained wave. Now in 21st century when new types of crimes have come; human rights awareness has increased; society is pretending to be more human oriented; stereotype ideologies are withering away; women rights defenders are asserting claims, etc; the controversy over capital punishment has also renewed vigor.

In this background, this article aims to discuss the historical background of capital punishment; controversy between abolitionist and retentionist; and international, national and other human rights instruments on capital punishment. Further, this article intends to discuss Indian approach on capital punishment.

HISTORICAL BACKGROUND OF CAPITAL PUNISHMENT

Capital punishment[3] was vogue throughout the ages in many countries in every part of the world for grave breaches. We can trace it in Hammurabi Codes; Twelve Tables; Customary laws of German tribes; Torah (Jewish law), Draco's law in Ancient Greece (621 B.C); Solon law etc. But during Tang Dynasty of China, death penalty was abolished for a brief period (747-759 A.D)[4]. The earliest German Imperial Criminal Code, the Constitution Criminalis Carolina of 1532, was based on a system of capital and corporal punishment.[5] In India, Mahabharata contains references about the offender being punished with the sentence of amputation by bits which was called Vadhadand. Similary, Kautilya Arthastra, provides death sentence for rape of women in custody[6] but plethora of ancient Indian texts indicates that death sentence was discouraged[7].

The pioneer religions of the world denounce capital punishment but prescribe it in exceptional circumstances. For example, Fifth Commandment of Christians contains "Thou Shall not Kill". Jescheck said, "*... no man is at liberty to take the life of another on the ground of imposing punishment*"[8] but Bible says that: "*Whoever sheds the bold of man, by man shall his blood be shed.*[9]" Chapter 10 of the Dhammapada of Buddhists contains "*Do not kill or cause to kill*". Similarly, Judaism pleaded for abolition of capital punishment[10]. According to Imam Ali, the fourth Khalifa after Prophet Muhammed, instructed the governor of Egypt to rule with mercy and tolerance towards all his subjects: "*Let the dearest of your treasuries be the treasury of righteous action. Infuse your heart with mercy,* *love and kindness for your subjects. Be not in the face of them a voracious animal, counting them as easy prey, for they are of two kinds: either they are your brothers in religion or your equals in creation".*[11]

On the basis of the above discussion it may be submitted that capital punishment was rooted in the soil of the human civilization bit efforts were always being made to curtail it for exceptional circumstances.

RETENTIONISTS VS. ABOLITIONISTS: A CONTROVERSY OVER CAPITAL PUNISHMENT

Death penalty has been the subject of an age- old debate between Abolitionists and Retentionists, although recently the controversy has come in sharp focus. Both the groups are deeply anchored in their antagonistic views. Both firmly and sincerely believe in the righteousness of their respective stands, with overtones of sentiment and emotion. Both the camps can claim among them eminent thinkers, penologists, sociologists, jurists, judges, legislators, administrators and law enforcement officials[12].

ARGUMENTS IN FAVOUR OF CAPITAL PUNISHMENT

The justification advanced in support of capital punishment is that it has both retributive and deterrent effects. It respects public sentiments; it removes burden of exchequer and releases state from the duty of maintenance and discipline inside the jail. It also incapacitates the criminal[13]. In this connection argument given by Eruest van Den Hagg is worth quoted where he says:

> *"...it is lawful to forfeit the life of a person who takes away another's life. The motives for the death penalty may indeed include vengeance. Legal vengeance solidifies social solidarity against law-breakers and probably is the only alternative to the disruptive private revenge of those who feel harmed.*[14]"

J. J. Rouseau, one of the great social contract theorists advocates for the death penalty to the person who breaks social contract in following words:

> *"...every rogue who criminously attacks social rights becomes, by his wrong, a rebel and a traitor to his fatherland. By contravening its laws, he ceases to be one of its citizens: he even wages war against it. In such circumstances, the state and he cannot both be saved: one or other must perish. In killing the criminal, we destroy not so much a citizen as an*

enemy. The trial and judgments are proofs that he has broken the social contract, and so is no longer a member of the state.[15]"

Supporting the same argument, Sir Henry Maine observed, '*punishment evolved form social necessity....The notion that the threat of punishment by the State will restrain the potential criminal is one of the most commonly accepted justification for it*'[16]. Similarly, Montesquieu in *L'Esprit des Lois* regarded the death penalty as repugnant, but necessary-"*remedy of a sick society*"[17]. Kant and Hegel had supported death penalty as '*societal revenge against the wrongdoer*'[18] and in this connection observation of Immanuel Kant in his '*Philosophy of law*' is noteworthy:

"*It is better that one man should die than that whole people should perish for if justice and righteousness perish, human life could no longer have any value in the world*"[19].

John Stuart Mill had made a very strong speech in the House of Commons advocating the use of the death penalty when it was applied to the most heinous cases[20].

The former Prime Minister of England Lloyd George had emphatically supported capital punishment in following words:

"*The first function of capital punishment is to give emphatic expression to society's peculiar abhorrence of murder.... It is important that murder should be regarded with peculiar horror.... I believe that capital punishment does, in the present state of society, both express and sustain the sense of moral revulsion for murder*[21]."

Another argument in favour of capital punishment is retribution[22] and deterrence. In this context Report of British Royal Commission is worth while:

'*....Prima facie the penalty of death is likely to have a stronger effect as a deterrent to normal human being than any other form of punishment, and there is some evidence... that this is in fact so...*[23]'

Sir James Fitzjames Stephen favored the retention of capital punishment and perhaps most strongly put forward the value of capital punishment, as an aspect of deterrence in following words:

"*No other punishment deters men so effectually from committing crimes as the punishment of death....In any secondary punishment, however terrible, there is hope; but death is death; its terrors cannot be described more forcibly.*[24]"

J.J. Maclean, the Canadian Parliamentarian justifies, from another angle, the right of the State to award capital punishment for murder:

"If the State has the right and the duty to defend the community against outside aggression, such as in time of war, and within the country, for instance, in case of treason, crimes against the State, etc., and that to the extent of taking the life of the aggressors and guilty parties, if the citizen wants to protect his own life by killing whoever attacks him without any reason, the State can do the same when a criminal attacks and endangers the life of the community by deciding to eliminate summarily another human being....Capital punishment must be retained to prove the sanctity of that most precious thing which is the gift of life; it embodies the revulsion and horror that we feel for the greatest of crimes....For most people, life is priceless and they will do anything and suffer the worst privations to preserve it, even when life itself does not hold many consolations or bright prospects for the future.... As a deterrent, the death penalty is playing its part for which there is no substitute....I suggest that statistics do not prove much, either on one side or the other....There are too many variations, too many changes as regards circumstance, conditions, between one period and the other, to enable us to make worthy comparisons[25]."

Speaking in favour of death penalty Professor Donald Atwell Zoll of Arizona State University states as follows:

"Capital punishment ought not to be abolished solely because it is repulsive, if infinitely less repulsive than the acts which invoke it....If we are to preserve a humane society we will have to retain sufficient strength of character of will to do the unpleasant in order that tranquility and civility may rule comprehensively. It seems very likely that Capital punishment is a ...necessary, if limited, factor in that maintenance of social tranquility and ought to be retained on this ground. To do otherwise is to indulge in the luxury of permitting a sense of false delicacy to reign over the necessity of social survival[26]."

Taking into consideration the views of scholars and jurists mentioned above it may be submitted that the focal arguments in favour of capital punishment are incapacitation of the criminal; less burden on state exchequer; retribution and deterrence.

ARGUMENTS AGAINST CAPITAL PUNISHMENT

The chief arguments of the Abolitionists are the irreversibility and irrevocability of death penalty; its deterrent effect is not well established; it is cruel, inhuman and degrading punishment[27];

it is not a viable form of crime control; and it is arbitrary in nature[28] etc.

The movement to abolish death penalty[29] started with the humanitarian doctrine evolved by Marchese De Cesare Bonesana Beccaria, Italian publicist. In 1764, Bonesana published the famous little treatise Dei Delitti a dell Pena[30], where he asserted that all capital punishment is wrong in itself and unjust. He maintained that since man was not his own creator, he did not have the right to destroy human life, either individually or collectively. It is the ultimate cruel, inhuman and degrading punishment, and violates the right to life. Its basic value, he affirmed, is its incapacitative effect[31]. He was of the view that capital punishment not only offends against the fundamental ideals of the sanctity of human life but also operates to destroy the very purpose for which it is inflicted and called it absurdity by saying:

> *"Is it not absurd that the law which detect and punish homicide should in order to prevent murder publicly commit murder themselves?[32]"*

In 1808 Romilly made effort for the abolition of the death penalty in many cases but he was not an '*abolitionist*' in the sense of the term today[33].

Thorston Sellin writes that death penalty has failed to be effective even as a measure of social defence and as an instrument of retributive justice. It has never shown to deter crime more effectively than other punishments[34]. In his opinion, retribution seems to be outdated and unworkable and capital punishment is an archaic custom of primitive origin that has disappeared in most civilized countries and is withering away in the rest[35].

Another scholar Arthur Kostler writes, "*capital punishment, while pretending to support, revenge for human life, does in fact tend to destroy it.[36]*"

The great messenger of peace, truth and non-violence Mahatma Gandhi wrote long ago in Harijan:

> God alone can Take Life.
>
> *Because He Alone Gives it[37].*
>
> Quoting from *Shanti Parva* of Mahabharata[38], he wrote in Harijan[39]:
>
> "*Distruction of individuals can never be a virtuous act.*" He also said at one occasion:

"Once a man is killed, the punishment is beyond recall or reparation[40]."

Tolstoy also protests against death sentence[41].

Another argument against capital punishment is its irrevocability. The administration of justice is a human function and human beings are not infallible, an error may occur and if an error does occur in a capital case, it cannot be corrected after the sentence. In this connection observation of Prof. A. L. Goodhart deems fit to be quoted. He observes[42]:

> *"...it would be a terrible thing, if a man has been hanged for a crime which he has not committed. In such a case the law itself would be the murderer..."*

Similar approach was adopted by justices Brennan and Steward in Furman vs. Georgia[43], where they said:

> *'Capital punishment is unique in its severity, finality and its enormity. It is unique in its total irrevocability. It is unique in its rejection and rehabilitation of the convict as a basic purpose of criminal justice and in its absolute renunciation of all that is embodied in our concept of humanity'.*

Stressing upon the infallibility of human beings Marquis De Lafayette says:

> *"I will believe in the death penalty when you will prove to me the infallibility of human beings[44]."*

Andrie Sakharov, in a message to the Stockholm conference on Abolition of Death penalty organized by amnesty International, Dec 10-11, 1977 put the point more bluntly:

> *'I regard the death penalty as a savage and immoral institution which undermines the moral and legal foundations of a society... I reject the notion that the death penalty has any essential deterrent effect on potential offenders. I am convinced that the contrary is true-that savagery begets only savagery...I believe that the death penalty has no moral or practical justification and represents a survival of barbaric customs of revenge.[45]'*

Justice Krishna Iyer while holding that reformation, not retribution, is the sentencing lodestar[46] and death penalty contradicts the very sanctity of life which all human society claims to hold among the highest values. Anguished Iyer J. posed a serious question: can the hanging of the murderer bring the murdered back to life? And pathetically answered, *'The dull cold ear of death'* cannot hear the cries or see the tears of the dying convict[47].

Similar argument was adduced by Bhagwati J. also where he said:

> *"The civilized goal of criminal justice is the reformation of the criminal and death penalty means abandonment of this goal for those who suffer it.[48]"*

Former Prime Minister of Canada Mr. Pierre Trudeaux, while pleading for abolition of death penalty, posed a question as follows[49]:

> *"Are we as a society so lacking in respect for ourselves, so lacking in hope for human betterment, so socially bankrupt that we are ready to accept state vengeance as our penal philosophy?"*

At Delhi Conference on the Abolitions of the Death Penalty, Lok Nayak Jai Prakash Narain said:

> *'To my mind, it is ultimately a question of respect for life and human approach to those who commit grievous hurts to others. Death sentence is no remedy for such crimes. A more humane and constructive remedy is to remove the culprit concerned from the normal milieu and treat him as a mental case. I am sure a large proportion of the murderers could be weaned away from their path and their mental condition sufficiently improved to become useful citizens.[50]'*

Most. Rev.David B.Thomson, Bishop of Charleston S.C. said[51]:

> *"Capital punishment feeds the cycle of violence in society by pandering to a lust for revenge. It brutalizes us, and deadens out sensitiveness to the precious nature of every single human life."*

In the same spirit, Most. Rev. Josepth A. Fiorenza, President, National Conference of Catholic Bishops, 1999 said[52]:

> *'We oppose the death penalty not just for what it does to those guilty of heinous crimes, but for what it does to all of us, it offers the tragic illusion that we can defend life by taking life."*

Condemning capital punishment as one of the mode of punishments, the Austrian member of the Human Rights Committee, Kurt Herendl aptly observes[53]:

> *"Capital punishment is in itself regrettable under any point of view and is obviously not in line with fundamental moral and ethic principles prevailing throughout Europe and other parts of the world."*

Justice Pius Langa said in *The State vs. Makwanyane*[54], *'the constitution, in deference to our humanity and sense of dignity, does not allow us to kill in cold blood in order to deter other from killing. Nor does it allow us to kill criminals simply to gent even with them. We are not to stoop to the level of the criminal'*. It follows that a *'punishment'* the death penalty is a violation of the right to life. *'It is cruel, inhuman and degrading; it is also a severe affront to human dignity'*. Similarly, Justice Yvonne Mokgoro puts forward that *'once the life of a human being is taken in the deliberate and calculated fashion that characterizes the described methods of execution the world over, it constitutes the ultimate cruelty with which any living creature could ever be treated….It is inhuman and degrading to the humanity of the individual, as well as to the humanity of those who carry it out.'*

The abolitionists like David Dressler often argue that death penalty brutalizes human nature and cheapens human like. Thus it vitiates the humanitarian sentiments concerning sacredness of human life[55].

Keeping in view the aforesaid discussion it may be submitted that the main reasons adduced for abolition of capital punishment are: denial of basic right; lack of deterrence; irrevocability; irreversibility; fallibility of human being; prolonged uncertainty; cruel and unusual; uncivilized in theory and unfair and inequitable in practice.

INTERNATIONAL CONCERN FOR ABOLITION OF CAPITAL PUNISHMENT

Article 3 of the Universal Declaration of human Rights, 1948 states that 'every one has right to life....'This article became the source of inspiration for movement against capital punishment in post world war period. In the year, 1959 on November 20, the United Nations General Assembly by Res 1396 (xiv) invited the ECOSOC to initiate study of the question of capital punishment, of the laws and practices relating thereto, and the effects of capital punishment and the abolition thereof on the rate of criminality. Pursuant to this Resolution, the ECOSOC prepared a report with the help of French Jurist Marc Ancel, entitled "*Capital Punishment*". In its third chapter, it contained a cautious statement:

> *'...the deterrent effect of the death penalty is, to say the least, not demonstrated*[56]*.'*

In the meantime in order to continue the effort, an Adhoc Advisory Committee of Experts on the Prevention of Crime and the Treatment of Offenders, 1963 was established.

In order to met out the criticisms of Universal Declaration of Human Rights, 1948 on the grounds of non-binding effects; absence of implementing mechanism etc., the United Nations adopted International Covenant on Civil and Political Rights, 1966. Article 6(1) of the covenant provides, '*every human being has the inherent right to life. This right shall be protected by law. No one shall be arbitrarily deprived of his life.*' Although Article 6(2) of the Covenant permits the imposition of the death penalty for the most serious crimes yet the scope of such crimes should not go beyond international crimes with lethal or other extremely grave consequences[57] but Art.6(5) prohibits death sentence of persons below 18 years and of pregnant women for crimes committed by them. Article 6(6) is the most important article for the purpose of present study as it emphasis on progressive abolition of capital punishment[58].

In order to implement Article 6(6) of the International Covenant on Civil and Political Rights, 1966, the U N General Assembly adopted the second Optional Protocol to the ICCPR in 1989, which aims at abolition of the death penalty[59]. In the meantime, the General Assembly by Res 32/61 of December 8, 1977 reaffirmed[60]:

> ...*the desirability of abolishing capital punishment in all countries.*'

In the year 1997, the Human Rights Committee of the U.N. adopted a resolution which demands for a moratorium on the death penalty and consideration of complete abolition of the death penalty[61]. ECOSOC Resolution 2000/65, adopted on April 26, 2000, urges all retentionist states not only to comply with standard and safeguards in implementing the death penalty but to establish moratoriums on execution with a view to completely abolishing the death penalty[62].

The International Criminal Court does not prescribe death punishment for any of the offences its tries. It reads, 'nothing in this part of the statute affects the application by States of penalties prescribed by their national law.'[63] Is it not an insignificant development since such a large body of countries has overwhelmingly rejected the death penalty as a form of punishment? For those concerned with popular opinions and majoritarian views, the ICC statute cannot be possibly ignored[64].

The Nation States[65] in pursuance to the developments at international level started abolishing death penalty from their respective criminal laws. After coming into force of Protocol No. 6 to the European Convention for Human Rights and Fundamental Freedoms, capital punishment stands abolished in member countries of the Council of Europe[66] and Protocol No. 13 provides total abolition of death penalty in all countries of Europe[67]. Recently United Nation General Assembly in its 62nd session in 2007 called for a universal ban on capital punishment[68]. At present over 102 Nation states are considered as abolitionists including France[69], Germany[70],Gabon[71], South Korea[72], Uzbekistan[73] etc.

On the basis of the aforesaid discussion, it may be submitted that developments at international level and its repercussions and effects at national levels demonstrate an enormous political will to abolish the death penalty worldwide and make the right to life a universally accepted and unconditionally implemented human rights standard. In this connection observation of special Rapporteur on Extra judicial, summary or arbitrary execution, Asma Jehangir[74] is worth quoted:

> *"Human rights can best be respected in a culture of democracy, and no democratic process is sustainable with out the support of an independent legal judicial system. Without these basic ingredients, the right to life cannot be guaranteed."*

CAPITAL PUNISHMENT IN INDIA

Capital punishment has been one of the modes of punishment[75] in Indian society since time immemorial but it was used in a controlled manner in an exceptional circumstances. Moghul rulers were also invoking this mode to eliminate unwanted criminals. They used crudest methods for execution of death sentence. This mode of punishment was also vogue in British period and death penalty became a prescribed form of punishment under Indian penal Code, 1861.

Indian Penal Code, 1860 provides death sentence as alternative punishment for certain specified offences which are as follows:

(i) Waging war against the Government (section 121).

(ii) Abetment of mutiny (section 132).

(iii) Fabrication of false evidence leading to one's conviction for capital offence. (section 194).

(iv) Murder (section 302).

(v) Murder by a convict undergoing a term of life imprisonment (section 303[76]).

(vi) Abetment of suicide of a child or insane person(section 305).

(vii) Attempt to murder by a life convict (section 307).

(viii) Dacoity with murder (section 396).

Prior to the Amendment in section 367(5) of the Code of Criminal Procedure, 1898 in 1955, this section was read as follows:

> *"If the accused is convicted of an offence punishable with death and the court sentences him to any punishment other than death, the court shall in it judgment state the reason why sentence of death was not passed."*

But after this Amendment Act, position reversed and now the courts are required to record reasons for awarding death sentence where death is an alternative punishment. Thus the law relating to death penalty has considerably liberalized.

Being influenced by the debate at international level over the efficacy of capital punishment, Law Commission of India made a study of it in Indian context and submitted its 35th Report in 1967 in which it justified retention of death penalty in following manner:

> *"Having regard...to the conditions in India, to the variety of the social upbringing of its inhabitants, to the disparity in the level of morality and education in the country, to the vastness of its area, to the diversity of its population and to the paramount need for maintain law and order in the country at the present juncture, Indian cannot risk the experiment of abolition of capital punishment.....On a consideration of all the issues involved, the Commission is of the opinion, that capital punishment should be retained in the present state of the Country."*

The Law Commission of India in its 42nd and 48th Reports did not recommend any material change in the offences which are at present punishable with death sentence under Indian Penal Code, 1860. However, it suggested that children below age of 18 should not be sentenced to death.

Section 354(3) of the new Code of Criminal Procedure, 1973, marks a significant shift in the legislative policy underlying the Code of 1898, according to which both the alternative sentences of death or imprisonment for life provided for murder and for certain other capital offences under the Penal Code, were normal sentences. Section 354(3) of the current Code provides:

> *"When the conviction is for an offence punishable with death or, in the alternative, with imprisonment for life or imprisonment for a term of years, the judgment shall state the reasons for the sentence awarded, and, in the case of sentence of death, the special reasons for such sentence."*

It means court must record '*special reasons*' justifying the award of death sentence and state as to why an alternative sentence would not meet the ends of justice in that particular case but in this context provision as laid down in section 235(2) of the Code of Criminal Procedure, 1973 is noteworthy, which casts a statutory duty upon the court to hear the accused on the point of sentence i.e. called pre-sentencing hearing.

CONSTITUTIONAL VALIDITY OF CAPITAL PUNISHMENT IN INDIA

The constitutional validity of death sentence has been raised before the Supreme Court at various occasions in contravention of Articles 14, 19 and 21.An initial challenge to the constitutionality of death sentence was made in Jagmohan vs. State of U.P[77] on following grounds[78]:

(i) Firstly, the death sentence puts an end to all rights guaranteed under clause (a) to (g) of sub-clause (1) of Article 19 and, therefore, the law with regard to capital sentence is unreasonable and not in the interest of the general public.

(ii) Secondly, the discretion vested in the judges to impose capital punishment is not based on any standards or policy required by the Legislature for imposing capital punishment in preference to imprisonment for life and thus constituted an abdication by the legislature of its essential function attracting the vice of excessive delegation.

(iii) Thirdly, the uncontrolled and unguided discretion in judges to impose capital punishment or imprisonment for life is hit by Article 14 of the Constitution, because two persons found guilty of murder on similar facts are liable to be treated differently-one forfeiting his life and the other suffering merely a sentence of life imprisonment.

(iv) Lastly, the provisions of the law do not provide a procedure for trial of factors and circumstances crucial for taking the choice between the capital penalty and imprisonment for life. The trial under the Criminal Procedure Code is limited to the question of guilt. In the absence of any procedure stabled by law in the matter of sentence, the protection given by Article 21 of the Constitution was violated and hence for that reason also the sentence of death is unconstitutional.

The five judges bench negated all the aforesaid questions and held that, capital punishment was neither unreasonable nor opposed to public interest[79]; the discretion in the matter of sentence is liable to be corrected by superior courts and the exercise of judicial discretion of well-recognized principle is the safest possible safeguards for the accused[80]; the death sentence imposed after trial in accordance with the procedure established by law cannot be said to be unconstitutional under Article 21[81].

Again the constitutional validity of death sentence was challenged on the grounds of discretionary power vested in courts to award death sentence; criteria and considerations for the award of death sentence and relevance of death sentence in changed circumstances and the rope of access was Article 136 of the Constitution of India in *Rajendra Prasad vs. State of U.P*[82] together with *Kunjukunju Janardhanan vs.State of Kerala*[83]. The court held that death penalty is constitutionalised by reading into section 354(3), CrPC, those 'special reasons' which validate the sentence as reasonably necessitous and non-arbitrary, as just in the special societal circumstances[84]. The only correct approach is to read into section 302, IPC and section 354(3), CrPC, the human rights and humane trends in the Constitution[85]. If we go only by the nature of the crime we get derailed by subjective paroxysm. "*Special reasons*' must vindicate the sentence and so must be related to why the murderer must be hanged and why life imprisonment will not suffice. The punishment is on the person though for the offence[86]. The death sentence should be imposed only if other wise public interest, social defence and public order would be smashed irretrievably[87]. If a man is a murderer, so hardened, so bloodthirsty, that within the prison and without, he makes no bones about killing others or carries on a prosperous business in cadavers, then he becomes a candidate for death sentence[88]. The extreme penalty can be invoked only in extreme situations.

Again the constitutionality of the death penalty for murder was challenged on additional arguments based on subsequent events and changes in law and because of inherent differences in the views of expressed by the honourable Supreme Court judges in *Jagmohan and Rajendra Prasad*, the Supreme Court took up the matter in *Bachan Singh vs. State of Punjab*[89]. The principal questions that fall to be considered in this case are[90]:

(i) Whether death penalty provided for the offence of murder in Section302, Penal Code is unconstitutional?

(ii) If the answer to the foregoing question be in the negative, whether the sentencing procedure provided in section 354(3) of the Code of Criminal Procedure, 1973 is unconstitutional on the ground that it invests the court with unguided and untrammeled discretion and allows death sentence to be arbitrarily or freakishly imposed on a person found guilty of murder or any other capital offence punishable under the Indian Penal Code with death or, in the alternative, with imprisonment for life?

Subsequent to the judgment of Supreme Court in Jagmohan, three developments took place which influenced the judgment of Bachan Singh in one or another way. These developments were: enactment of new Code of Criminal Procedure, 1973 and its section 354(3); the decision in Maneka Gandhi vs. Union of India which required that every law of punitive detention both in its procedural and substantive aspects must pass the test of reasonableness on a collective reading of articles 14, 19 and 21; and India's accession to the International Covenant on Civil and Political Rights, 1966[91].

The court affirmed the decision in Jagmohan and overruled Rajendra Prasad in so far as it sought to restrict the imposition of death penalty only to cases where the security of the state and society, public order and the interest of the general public were threatened. The court rejected the second limb of the challenge to the validity of section 354(3) of the CrPC, on the ground that it permitted imposition of death penalty in an arbitrary and whimsical manner[92]. The court also recorded the possible aggravating and mitigating factors on the suggestion of amicus curiae Dr. Y. S. Chitale, Senior Advocate, though it was not inclined to lay down standards or norms for guiding the exercise of judicial discretion[93].

The concluding remarks in the majority marked the real shift in the judicial attitude towards sentencing. It also reflected the changing perceptions of the judiciary influenced as it was by major strides in human rights jurisprudence[94]. The majority remarked[95]:

> "....*A real and abiding concern for the dignity of human life postulates resistance to taking a life through law's instrumentality. That ought not to be done save in the rarest of rare cases when the alternative option is unquestionably foreclosed.*"

But dissenting opinion of Bhagwati, J[96] is also remarkable for academic purpose and has jurisprudential value. He is of the view that section 302 of the Indian Penal Code in so far as it provides for imposition of death penalty as an alternative to life sentence is ultra vires and void as being violative of Articles 14 and 21 of the Constitution since it does not provided any legislative guidelines as to when life should be permitted to extinguished by imposition of death sentence.

In Machhi Singh vs. State of Punjab[97], the Supreme Court emphasized that death penalty need not be inflicted except in the 'gravest of cases of extreme culpability', and that '*life imprisonment is the rule and death sentence is an exception.*' The court further said that death sentence is to be imposed only when '*life imprisonment appears to be an altogether inadequate punishment having regard to relevant circumstances of crime...*'In addition to these, the court formulated certain broad guidelines for determining the '*rarest of the rare cases*' in which murderers should be awarded death sentence instead of life imprisonment. Before deciding whether nature of offence falls in the category of "*rarest of rare cases*", the judges must ask themselves two questions[98]:

(i) Whether there is something uncommon about the crime which renders a life imprisonment sentence inadequate and calls for a death sentence?

(ii) Whether the circumstances of the crime are such that there is no alternative but to impose the death sentence even after according maximum weightage to the mitigating circumstances which speak in favour of the offender?

Thus, the judges must draw up a balance sheet of aggravating and mitigating circumstances before the option is exercised[99].

APPLICATION OF RAREST OF THE RARE CASES RULE

Although Supreme Court had made reference of mitigating and aggravating factors in computing the death sentence way back in Ediga Anamma case[100] but these factors became more considerable after Bachan Singh, and worked as a weighing machine in application of 'rarest of the rare.'

It is neither necessary nor is it possible to make a catalogue of the special reasons which must justify the passing of the death sentence in a given case. Yet, the following special reasons have been considered by the apex court as reasonable justifications for the imposition of death sentence[101]. For example, murder of teenagers[102], series of gruesome brutal murders[103], deliberate and cold blooded murder of wife by husband[104], bride burning[105], attempt to rape and murder of his Bhabhi and niece[106], murder of collector by throwing bombs[107], causing death of a young girl after dragging her into house for committing criminal assault[108], rape and murder of a girl of five years by a married man[109], rape and murder of minor girls[110],rape of 18 years girl followed by heinous and brutal death[111], killing of step brother and his whole family including three tiny tots of 45 days, two and half years and four years by a woman along with her husband[112] etc.

Similarly, the court considered sudden impulse of provocation[113]; uncontrollable hatred arising out of sex indulgence[114]; family feud or land dispute[115] etc as extenuating circumstances justifying leniency[116] and commutation[117] of death sentence to that of imprisonment for life but the studies shows that commutation of death sentence is not done on any set pattern of sentencing[118].

DISPARITY IN SENTENCING

The application of the 'rarest of the rare cases' rule to a given situation has proved to be not an easy task and the sentencing disparity in awarding the capital punishment has been observed in a number of cases. In many cases death sentence was not awarded in which murder was pre-mediated and well calculated with extreme cruelty and brutality or the victims were innocent and had done no harm to the culprits[119]. The reason may be various such as the application of the *'rarest of the rare case'* rule is facts based, not principle based[120]. In words of Justice Eswara Prasad, *'the disparity in awarding death sentence is due to the fetters imposed by the Supreme Court in Bachan Singh'*[121].

Although, this disparity in sentencing does not demand for the abolition of the *'rarest of the rare cases'* rule yet provides a basis for a reconsideration of the issue of retention of capital punishment in this country. It also belies the Apex Court's hope that after the introduction of the *'rarest of rare cases'* rule the elements of arbitrariness and the possibility of error will considerably minimized[122]. This is evident from the decisions of Supreme Court in *State of Maharstra vs Damu Gopi Nath Shinde*[123]; *Sushil Murmu vs State of Jharkhand*[124]; *Gayasuddin Khan vs. State of Bihar*[125]; *Kishori vs. State (NCT) of Delhi*[126]; *State vs. Paltan Mallan and Ors*[127]; *Holiram Bardoloi vs State*[128] etc. where it commuted the death sentence to life imprisonment or held it improper.

In addition to the foregoing discussions, there are certain special legislations which contain specific provision for death penalty. For example, Narcotics Drugs and Psychotropic Substances Act, 1985[129]; The Scheduled Castes and Scheduled Tribes (Prevention of Atrocities) Act, 1989[130]; The Commission of Sate (Prevention) Act, 1987[131]; The Terrorist and Disruptive Activities(Prevention) Act, 1987[132]; The National Security Guards Act, 1966, Indo-Tibetan Border Police Act, 1992; infallibility of human agencies; hanging of innocent person[133]; there is no automatic right of appeal to the Supreme Court in cases where death sentences awarded by a trial court get confirmed by the High Court. It is only where there is a reversal of acquittal by the trial court and awarding of life sentence or death sentence or a sentence of ten years or more by the High Court that the CrPC and the Constitution provide for an automatic right of appeal. The only remedy is to file a Special Leave Petition within sixty days of the receipt of the certified copy of the order; uncertainty of the mercy jurisdiction[134] etc provide necessary and sufficient cause for the abolition of death sentence in India[135].

While international human rights instruments have restricted and in some cases even banned capital punishment, its application is still not against customary international law. Much more debate continues as to whether it constitutes an appropriate punishment, at least to the most heinous crimes. In recent years, the debate has been further fuelled by the threat of global terrorism[136]. This hydra-headed monster threatens the existence of civilized society as such. This global threat has been made the ground for legislating or applying severe penal codes to punish those who indulge in terrorist acts and to deter others from joining such organizations. Thus, in contemporary scenario death penalty seems to have formed newer and firmer justification.

Similarly, women organizations and other social activists groups are demanding death penalty for the crimes against women[137], particularly for rape, which undermines the dignity of the women. Rape is considered worst crime than murder. Similar kind of demand is for a crime which contains rape and murder both.

Another area for consideration in the context of death penalty is the new and modern crimes and criminals such as cyber crimes, public welfare criminals, and criminals filled with religious fanaticism, caste prejudices etc who are beyond the therapeutic treatment because these new class of criminals are more dangerous than the traditional capital offences. Use of scientific and technological gadgets in doing crimes which shows no direct involvement must also be keep in mind while analyzing the relevance of capital punishment in India and world. Publication of private scenes through various means, prepared by using secret cameras in toilets and bedrooms of hotels and resorts which defames the person/persons in wider horizon must also be taken into consideration because character and reputation play vital role in Indian society.

Nevertheless, abolitionists continue to fight their battle against capital punishment unabated. There believe in the sacredness of life and death penalty is an abomination and their argument is remarkable that if murder by an individual or a group of individuals is undesirable how could it be rationally permitted and juridically justified when committed by the state or the body politic[138].

CONCLUSION

Capital punishment is the deliberate taking of life by State as a means of social regulation. It based on ancient *'lex talionis'* or law of retaliation against violator. Gradually, State became the executor of collective retribution and justified on the ground of deterrence but instances are also for opposition of death penalty. This controversy over death penalty is continuing and battle is still not concluded. Views and thoughts are being exchanged in favour and against of it. The main arguments in favour of death penalty are: incapacitation of the criminals; less burden on State in terms of cost; retribution and deterrence whereas opponents of death penalty are adducing arguments like: denial of basic rights; possibility of error; irrevocability of death sentence; punishment to innocent persons; lack of deterrence; prolonged uncertainty etc.

The development of modern human rights law and changing outlook of societies and bent the movement towards abolition of death penalty but again the controversy gained wave because of certain acts like terrorism, insurgency; crime against women etc. The position is also not clear because of lack of political will and in most of the cases we see politics over capital punishment, for example *Afzal Guru Case* (convicted in Parliament attack case). We rarely hear about execution of death penalty to the criminals having beckoning of politicians, economic storehouses etc and thus death penalty has become punishment for poor and destitute.

Thus, we see that emerging human rights jurisprudence casts a shadow of doubt on the legitimacy of the death penalty and provides a new perspective for addressing of the controversies on the death row phenomenon and more or less inhuman method of execution. The death penalty constitutes a violation of the right to personal integrity and human dignity.

In a country like India where death penalty has become a 'cruel lottery' because of discretion lying in judiciary with inadequate safeguards against it; political manoeuvability in cases of clemency, the issue of death penalty requires an objective and dispassionate scrutiny by the highest judiciary in the light of international human rights instruments keeping in view the contemporary needs and conditions of country.

When more than 112 nations are abolitionists and have followed that death penalty is a violation of the right to life and personal liberty. It is cruel, inhuman and degrading and is also a severe affront to human dignity, why the same cannot be understood by India which has been an abode of ancient civilization in the world and, whose constitution pays no less respect to human dignity, justice, rule of law and human rights etc than those so called abolitionists. Should *'kill the killer'* policy continue in the name of retribution and deterrence in a civilized, humane and compassionate society like India? If yes, then capital punishment would destroy humanity as Gandhiji had once said:

> *"....an eye for an eye would make the whole world blind."*

Therefore, India should take effective steps in progressive abolition of death penalty in the country in line of international instruments. For this India should sign or ratify Second Optional Protocol to the International Covenant on Civil and Political Rights, 1989 and make suitable amendments in criminal and other special legislations abolishing death penalty which is negation of the values of human life. In this connection the observation of then Chief Justice of India, Y.K. Sabharwal is noteworthy:

> *"We should not have the death penalty and that we can have a life sentence for entire life. This is because it is difficult for any one toward something that cannot be restored.... In the whole Europe, it is not there. In many of the States in the U.S. it is not there....It is a socio-political question and ultimately whether it is to be continued or not is a decision to be taken by the Indian Parliament.*[139]*"*

Justice Malimath Committee[140] recommends that in respect of offences for which death is a punishment, the sentence for 'imprisonment for life without commutation or remission' be prescribed as an alternative sentences, but this recommendation is not altogether refusing death penalty as one of punishment. Therefore, it is submitted that sentencing policy in India requires urgent review.

In short, it may be submitted that while dealing with the issues like capital punishment one preposition should always be kept in mind that death penalty is negation of the sanctity of *'right to life'* and can a person or State be allowed to take a thing which he/it cannot give, return or replace.

NOTES

1. Herbert L. A. Hart, 'Murder and the Principles of Punishment: England and the United States', *Northwestern University Law Review*, vol. 52, 1957-58, quoted in Rajendra Prasad V. State of U. P. (1979) 3 SCC 646 at 705
2. *http://en.wikipedia.org/wiki/capital punishment.*

3. See Mona Lynch, 'Capital Punishment' in Herbert M. Kritzer (ed) *Legal Systems of the World: A Political, Social and Cultural Encyclopedia,* Vol. I, Pentagon Press, 2005, pp. 267-269.
4. *http;//en.wikipedia.org/wiki/capital punishment*
5. Jurgen Meyer, 'Germany: Country without Capital Punishment', in K.D. Gaur, *Criminal Law and Criminology,* Deep and Deep Publications, New Delhi, 2003, pp 417-430, at 418;For corporal Punishment see Lauren Dundes, 'Corporal Punishment', in Herbert M. Kritzer (ed) *Legal Systems of the World: A Political, Social and Cultural Encyclopedia,* Vol. I, Pentagon Press, 2005, p. 362.
6. Rama Jois, *Seeds of Modern Public Law in Ancient Indian Jurisprudence* Eastern Book Company, Lucknow, 1990, p. 93.
7. Kautilya Arthastra, "Capital sentence should be imposed for offence of rape committed against a woman arrested by an officer of the state", p. 256. *Ibid,* p. 194. For discussion on feasibility of death sentence on the basis of ancient texts, see *Ibid,* pp. 93-95.
8. For religious and ethical arguments see Jurgen Meyer, 'Germany: Country without Capital Punishment', in K.D. Gaur, *Criminal Law and Criminology,* Deep and Deep Publications, New Delhi, 2003, pp 421-422.
9. Genesis 9:6, *http:// www.bbc.co.uk/religion.* For Biblical reasons for the abolition of death penalty, see Hanks, Gardener C, Capital Punishment and the Bible, Herald press, 2002.
10. Supra 2.
11. Mahanthagowda Basavanna Biradara, ' Abolition of Death Sentence', *Nyaya Deep,* 2007, pp. 70-79, at 78-79.
12. Sarkaria, J., in Bachan Singh Vs. State of Punjab (1980) 2 SCC p. 712.
13. Isaac Ehrlich stresses another purpose of capital punishment, namely, incapacitation of the offender, which, in fact, is another aspect of its deterrent effect. To quote his words:

    "There is an additional point worth stressing. Even if punishment by execution or imprisonment does not have any deterrent effect, surely it must exert some incapacitative effect on punished offenders by reducing or eliminating the possibility of recidivism on their part." (1980) 2 SCC at 717. For intensive studies of the deterrent effect of capital punishment see generally Isaac Ehrlich, ' The Deterrent Effect of Capital punishment: A Question of Life and Death', *American Economic Review* 65 (1975) pp. 397-417;Issac Ehrlich,' Capital punishment and Deterrence: Some Further Thoughts and Additional Evidence', *Journal of Political Economy,* (85) 1977, pp. 74-88; Baldus,

David C, and James W.L. Cole, 'Statistical evidence on the deterrent effect of Capital punishment: A Comparison of the work of Thorsten Sellin and Isaac Ehrlich on the deterrent effect of Capital punishment', *Yale Law Journal*,(85), 1975, pp. 170-186.

14. The Voice (USA) June 4, 1979 quoted in Bachan Singh Vs. State of Punjab, (1980) 2 SCC at p. 722. See also, S.K. Kumbhaj, 'Death Penalty: Indian Penological Retrospect: A Review' in K.D. Gaur (ed) *Criminal Law and Criminology*, Deep and Deep Publications, 2003, pp 438-447 at 443.

15. J. J. Rouseau, *The Social Contract*,1762, *http://www.wesleylowe.com/cp.html*

16. (1979) 3 SCC at 691.

17. *Ibid.*

18. Supra 5 at 420.

19. (1979) 3 SCC at 691.

20. ([1]*Parliamentary Debates* 3rd Series, Vol. 191, 1047-1048) *Ibid.* For John Stuart Mill, 'Speech in favour of Capital punishment' in British Parliament on April 21, 1868 in opposition to a bill banning capital punishment, see *http://ethics.sandiego.edu.*

21. Thorsten Sellin (ed) *Capital Punishment,* 1967, quoted in Bachan Singh vs. State of Punjab, (1980) 2 SCC at 722.

22. Lord Justice Denning, appearing before the British Royal Commission on Capital Punishment, 1949-55, stated his view on retribution as one of the function as under:

    "Punishment is the way in which society expresses its denunciation of wrongdoing; and, in order to maintain respect for law, it essential that the punishment inflicted for grave crimes should adequately reflect the revulsion felt by the great majority of citizens for them. It is a mistake to consider the objects of punishment as being deterrent or reformative or preventive and nothing else....The truth is that some crimes are so outrageous that society insists on adequate punishment, because the wrongdoer deserves it, irrespective of whether it is a deterrent or not". Para 103, (1980) 2 SCC, p. 720.

23. Para 100, (1980) 2 SCC, p. 720.

24. Rajendra Prasad vs. State of U. P., (1979) 3SCC 646-714 at pp. 691-692

25. Thorsten Sellin, *Capital punishment,* p. 84, quoted in (1980) 2 SCC p. 723.

26. *http://www.wesleylowe.com/cp.html*

27. For more Comprehensive study see W. A. Schabas, *The Death Penalty as Cruel Treatment and Torture: Capital punishment challenged in the World's Courts, Boston,* 1996.
28. See generally, B. Nakell *et al, The Arbitrariness of the Death Penalty,* Philadelphia, 1987.
29. For more detail see generally, Heline Theodore, *Capital Punishment: Historical Trends Toward its Abolishment,* New Age Press, 1965; Galliher, John F.,Gregary Ray, and Brent Cook, 'Aboliton and reinstatement of Capital punishment during the progressive era and early 20th century', *Journal of Criminal Law and Criminoloy,* 83 (3), 1993, pp. 538-576.
30. Bonesana Beccaria, *An Essay on Crime and Punishment:* Academic Reprints, Stanford, California, 1953.
31. Rajendra Prasad vs. State of U.P. (1979) 3 SCC at 692-693.
32. See Sumer Singh Chauhan, 'Aboliton of Capital Punishment in India', *Indian Journal of Legal Studies,* Vol. I, 1978.
33. Rajendra Prasad vs. State of U.P. (1979) 3 SCC at 694.
34. N.V. Paranjape, *Studies in Jurisprudence and Legal Theory,* CLA, Allahabad, 2004, p. 168.
35. Bachan Singh vs. State of Punjab (1980) 2 SCC at 716.
36. See Arthur Kostler, *Reflections on Hanging,* Macmillan, New York, 1957.
37. Rajendra Prasad vs. State of U.P. (1979) 3 SCC at 662.
38. Bachan Singh vs. State of Punjab (1980) 3 SCC 24-131 at 41 (in dissenting opinion of Bhagwati J).
39. Rajendra Prasad vs. State of U.P. (1979) 3 SCC at 673.
40. Bachan Singh vs. State of Punjab (1980) 3 SCC 24-131 at 62(in dissenting opinion of Bhagwati J).
41. I Cannot Be Silent, *Mainstream,* October 14, 1978, p. 17.
42. See Sumer Singh Chauhan, 'Aboliton of Capital Punishment in India', *Indian Journal of Legal Studies,* Vol. I, 1978.
43. (1971) 402 US 183. For more on capital punishment in United States see generally, Daniel Suleiman, 'The Capital Punishment Exception: A Case For Constitutionalizing The Substantive Criminal Law', *Columbia Law Review,* Vol. 104, 2004 pp. 426-457; Jo Ann Brenn Gurnsey, *Should We Have Capital Punishment?,* Lerner Publication Company, Minnesota, 1993; H. Herbert H, *Against Capital Punishment: the anti-death penalty movement in America,* 1972-1994,Oxford University Press, 1996; Hugo Adam Bedau, *The Death Penalty in America,* Oxford University press, New York, 1982; Barry, Rupert V, 'Furman to Gregg:

The Judicial and Legislative History', *Howard Law Journal*, 1979, 22, pp. 53-117; Filler Louis, 'Movements to abolish the death penalty in the United States', *Annals of the American Academy of Political and Social Science*, 284, (November), 1952, pp. 124-136;Kristi Prinzo, 'The United States-'capital' of the World: An Analysis of why the United States Practices Capital Punishment while the International Trend is Towards Its Abolition', *Brooklyn Journal of International Law*, 24, 1999, pp. 855-889.

44. Mahanthagowda Basavanna Biradara, ' Abolition of Death Sentence', *Nyaya Deep*, 2007, pp. 70-79, at 78.
45. Rajendra Prasad vs. State of U.P. (1979) 3 SCC at 672.
46. *Ibid*, at 678.
47. *Ibid*, at 674.
48. Bachan Singh vs. State of Punjab (1980) 3 SCC 24-131 at 80 (in dissenting opinion of Bhagwati J).
49. *Ibid.*, at 84.
50. Rajendra Prasad vs. State of U.P. (1979) 3 SCC at 672.
51. *www.buzzle.com*
52. *Ibid.*
53. B. C. Nirmal and Prakash C.Shukla, 'Sentencing Policies And Practices in India: Need for Reform, *Soochow Law Journal*, Vol. IV, No. 1, 2007, pp. 1-71 at 29.
54. 1995, South African Supreme Court, *Ibid*, pp. 29-30.
55. David Dressler, *Readings in Criminology and Penology*, p. 486, referred in N.V. Paranjape, *Studies in Jurisprudence and Legal Theory*, CLA, Allahabad, 2004, p. 168.
56. Bachan Singh vs. State of Punjab (1980) 3 SCC 24-131 at 48-49(in dissenting opinion of Bhagwati J).
57. The U.N.Safeguards Guaranteeing Protection of the Rights of those Facing the Death Penalty (1984), UNGAOR 39/118 of 14 December, 1984, U.N. Human Rights Commission has passed resolution on the abolition of capital punishment. See Resolutions 1997/12, 1998/8.
58. 'Nothing in this article shall be invoked to delay or to prevent the abolition of capital punishment by any State Party to the present Covenant'.
59. According to current thinking on the subject, 'abolition of death penalty contributes to enhancement of human dignity and progressive development of human rights' and further 'all measures of abolition

of death penalty should be considered as progress in the enjoyment of the right to life.' See Preambular Paragraph of the Second Protocol to the ICCPR, 1989. The 1990 Protocol to the American Convention on Human Rights to Abolish the Death Penalty also provides for the abolition of the death penalty. See also B.C. Nirmal and Prakash C. Shukla, 'Sentencing policies and practices in India: Need for Reform', *Soochow Law Journal*, Vol. IV, No. 1, 2007, pp. 1-71 at 38-39.

60. Bachan Singh vs. State of Punjab (1980) 3 SCC 24-131 at 49 (in dissenting opinion of Bhagwati J).

61. Hans-Jorg Albrecht, 'The Death Penalty: International and Human Rights Perspectives on the Future of Capital Punishment' in K. I.Vibhute (ed) *Criminal Justice*, EBC, Lucknow, 2004, pp. 257-271 at 262. For more detail see Toni Fine, 'Moratorium 2000: An International Dialogue toward a Ban on Capital punishment', *Columbia Human Rights Law Review*, 30:2000, pp. 421-438. See also, Roger Hood, *The Death Penalty: A Worldwide Perspective*, Clarendon Press, 1996.

62. *Ibid* at 258.

63. Article 80 of Statute of International Criminal Court, 1998.

64. S. Muralidhar, 'Hang Them Now, Hang Them Not: Indian's Travails with the Death Penalty', *Journal of Indian Law Institute*, Vol. 40,1998, pp 141-173 at 170. For detail study on jurisdiction etc of ICC see, B.C. Nirmal, 'Jurisdiction of the International Criminal Court,' *ISIL Year Book of International Humanitarian And Refugee Law*, Vol. III, pp. 116-134; B.C.Nirmal, 'Crimes Within the Jurisdiction of The International Criminal Court And The Indian Response,' *ISIL Year Book of International Humanitarian And Refugee Law*, Vol. VI, pp. 106-125.

65. On dialogue among nations concerning death penalty see Report of the Secretary-General, Crime prevention and Criminal Justice: Capital punishment and Implementation of the Safeguards Guaranteeing Protection of the Rights of Those Facing the Death Penalty, E/2000/3; 31 March, 2000.

66. The EU Declaration on the Abolition of the Death Penalty, 18th June, 1997. See B. C.Nirmal and Prakash C. Shukla, supra 59 p. 39.

67. Hans-Jorg Albrecht, 'The Death Penalty: International and Human Rights Perspectives on the Future of Capital Punishment' in K. I.Vibhute (ed) *Criminal Justice*, EBC, Lucknow, 2004, pp. 257-271 at 261.

68. *http://en.wikipedia.org*

69. Statute for the Abolition of the Death Penalty, 1981; France ratified Protocol 13 on February 1, 2008.

70. Supra.

71. Abolished capital punishment on September 14, 2007.

72. December 31, 2007.

73. January 1, 2008.

74. *www.un.org/pubs/chronicle*

75. For discussion over theories of Punishment see, Thom Brooks, 'Rethiking Punishment', *International Journal of Jurisprudence and Philosophy of Law*, 2007,1(1-2) pp 26-33; For critical inquiry of modes of punishment in India see, B. C. Nirmal and Prakash C. Shukal, Supra 59 at 16-64; For right to compensation of victims see, Arun Kumar Singh, 'Human Right And Crime Victim's Right to Compensation,' *International Journal of Jurisprudence and Philosophy of Law*, 2007, 1(1-2) pp. 89-100. See Dilip S. Dahanukar vs. Kotak Mahindra co. Ltd. (2007) 6 SCC 528.

76. In Mithu vs. State of Punjab (1983) 2 SCC 277 section 303 of Indian Penal Code, which prescribed death as the minimum punishment for murder by a person under sentence of imprisonment for life was declared unconstitutional because of being violative of Articles 14 and 21 of the Constitution. For detail see D.P. Mohanty, 'Constitutionality of Section of Indian Penal Code,' in K.D.Gaur, supra 5 at 448-455.

77. (1973) 1 SCC 20-36.

78. *Ibid,* at 24.

79. *Ibid,* para 12.

80. *Ibid,* paras 24 and 26.

81. Ibid, paras 28 and 29.

82. (1979) 3 SCC 647-714(Special leave from judgment of Allahabad High court in Criminal Appeal 501 of 1974).

83. 1979) 3 SCC 647-714(Special leave from the judgment of the Kerala High court in Criminal Appeal 213 of 1977).

84. *Ibid,* para 64.

85. *Ibid,* para 46.

86. *Ibid,* para 45.

87. *Ibid,* paras 50,59-60.

88. *Ibid,* para 61.

89. (1980) 2 SCC 684-752.

90. *Ibid* at 695.

91. *Ibid* at 694.
92. S. Muralidhar, 'Hang Them Now, Hang Them Not: India's Travails with the Death Penalty', *Journal of Indian Law Institute*, Vol. 40,1998, pp. 143-173, at 146.
93. (1980) 2 SCC at 740-750.
94. S. Muralidhar, supra 64 at 147.
95. Bachan Singh at 751.
96. *Ibid* at 751. For detail see Bachan Singh vs. State of Punjab, (1982) 3SCC 24-131.
97. AIR 1983 SC 947 or (1983) 3SCC 470.
98. (1983) 3 SCC at 489.
99. *Ibid*. See also Munawar Harun Shah vs. State of Maharashtra, AIR 1983 SC 585.
100. AIR 1974 SC 799.
101. For detail discussion on 'Rarest of the Rare cases and its application' see B. C.Nirmal and Prakash C.Shukla, Supra 59 at 16-22.
102. Chopra Children Murder case, AIR 1981 SC 1572.
103. Joshi-Abhyankar Murder Case, AIR 1983 SC 585.
104. A. S. Joshi vs. State of Maharashtra, (1994) 6 SCC 201.
105. Kailash Kaur case, 1987 Cri.L.J. 850.
106. Jay Kumar vs. State of M.P. (1999) 5 SCC 1.
107. Param Hans Yadav (1987) 2 SCC 197.
108. Nathu Garam, AIR, 1979 SC 716; T.V.Vatheeswaran vs. State of Tamil Nadu (1983) 2 SCC 68.
109. Shankarlal Gyarsilal Dixit Vs. State of Maharshtra (1981) 2 SCC 35.
110. Dhananjoy Chatterjee vs State of West Bengal (1994) 2 SCC 220.
111. Shivu and Another vs. Registrar General High Court of Karnataka and Another, (2007) 4 SCC 713.
112. Ram Singh vs. Sonia and Others, (2007) 3 SCC 1.
113. Dalbir Singh vs. S.O.Punjab, AIR 1979 SC.
114. Ediga Anamma vs. S.O.AP, AIR 1974 SC 799.
115. Chawla vs. S.O.Haryana, AIR 1974 SC.
116. Sushil Murmu vs, State of Jharkhand 2004 cri.L.J. 658 SC; Sahadeo and Ors vs. State of U.P. 2004 Cri.L.J. 2876 SC; Mohd. Gayasuddin Khan vs. State of Bihar 2004 Cri.L.J. 295 SC.

117. State of Tamil Nadu vs. Suresh (1998) 2 SCC 372; State of U.P vs. Bhoora (1998)1 SCC 128; Nirmal Singh vs. State of Haryana (1999) 3 SCC 670.

118. See B.C.Nirmal and Prakash C.Shukla supra 59 at 20-22; See also S. Muralidhar supra 64 pp. 149-154.

119. *Ibid,* at 20.

120. Panchi vs. State of UP (1998) 7 SCC 171.

121. See J. Eswara Prasad, 'Death Sentence as Effective Deterrent', 46 *Journal of Indian Law Institute*, 2004, pp. 443-448 at 446.

122. B.C. Nirmal and Prakash C. Shukla supra 59 at 20.

123. 2000 Cri. L.J. 2925.

124. 2004 Cri.L.J. 658.

125. 2004 Cri.L.J. 395.

126. 2000 Cri.L.J. 756.

127. 2005 Cri.L.J. 918.

128. 2005 Cri.L.J. 2174.

129. Section 31A prescribed a mandatory death sentence for certain offences committed by a previous offender under the Act.

130. Section 3 (2)(i) prescribes a mandatory death sentence,' if an innocent member of a scheduled or scheduled tribe be convicted and executed in consequence of such false or fabricated evidence, the person who gives or fabricates such false evidence shall be punished with death.'

131. This Act prescribed death penalty to the persons who abets, directly or indirectly, the commission of Sati.

132. Although repealed one but it can take rebirth with new name etc as its origin and demise depend upon the outlook of Governments. This Act was providing death penalty as an alternative punishment for the commission of a terrorist act.

133. In India hanging is the prescribed mode for death sentence under Section 354(5) CrPC, 1973. It was found constitutionally valid by Supreme Court in Deena vs. Union of India (1983) 4 SCC 645. For study on mode of execution of death sentence in India see, Arun Kumar Singh, 'Execution of Death Sentence in India: A Need To Be More Humane', *National Law News*, Jan-April, 2008, pp. 34-36.

134. The power of the executive to grant clemency is vested in both the President and the Governor under Articles 72 and 161 of our Constitution respectively. The Constitution is silent on the manner of exercise of this power but it seems that like other powers of president,

it is expected to be exercised on the advice of the cabinet. This power is not a purely legal matter and involves several ethical and social implications. Unfortunately, a few misconceptions prevail on the subject, because of the failure to appreciate several important sociological aspects. Explaining the necessity of executive clemency in the hands of highest office, the U.S. Supreme Court held in Grossman case (1925) 267 US, 87:69 Law Ed. 527:

"The administration of justice by the courts is not always wise or certainly considerate of circumstances which may properly mitigate guilt. To afford a remedy, it has always been through essential in popular Governments, as well as in monarchies to vest in some authority other than the court, power to ameliorate or avoid particular judgments....Our Constitution confers this discretion on the highest office in the nation in confidence that he will not abuse it." See P. M. Bakshi, *The Constitution of India,* Universal Publishing House, Sixth Edition, 2005, pp. 101-102. For Mercy Jurisdiction and commutation of sentence see B.C. Nirmal and Prakash C. Shukla supra 59, pp. 53-61.

But the scope of executive clemency in the Constitution of India is vulnerable for political manoeuvability. For detail see Mahendra P.Singh, 'Capital Punishment: A Political Compromise', *The Banaras Law Journal,* Vol. 17, 1981, pp. 93-101.

135. For detail discussion see S. Muralidhar supra 64 pp157-164

136. For terrorism, human rights and counter-terrorism legislations in India and abroad and world's attitude towards after September 2001, see, B.C. Nirmal, 'Counter-Terrorism Legislations *vis-à-vis* Human Rights: A Comparative Study,' *Indian Law Institute Golden Jubilee* (1956-2006) 2007, pp. 246-261.

137. For violence against women and international and national human rights jurisprudence see, B.C. Nirmal, 'Taking Violence Against Women Seriously: International And Domestic Human Rights Jurisprudence', in Bimal N.Patel (ed)*India and International Law,* Volume 2, pp. 413-453, Koninklijke Brill NV, The Netherlands.

138. Mahendra P. Singh, 'Capital Punishment: A Political Compromise', *The Banaras Law Journal,* Vol. 17, 1981, 92-101 at 92. See also, R.V. Rao, 'Certain Live Thoughts on Death Penalty: An Indian Perspective,' in K.D. Gaur, Supra 5 pp. 431-437.

139. *The Hindu,* October 21, 2005, p. 11

140. Report on Reforms of Criminal Justice System In India, 2003, p. 288.